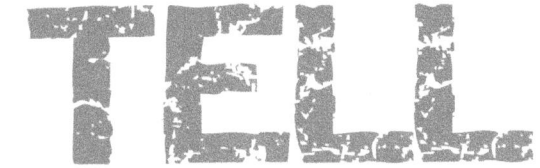

FINDING HOME AFTER FAMILY BETRAYAL

KATHY ISAAC

DON'T TELL
Copyright © 2021 by Kathy Isaac

All rights reserved. Neither this publication nor any part of this publication may be reproduced or transmitted in any form or by any means, electronic or mechanical, including photocopying, recording or any information storage and retrieval system, without permission in writing from the author.

Unless otherwise indicated, all scripture quotations are taken from the Holy Bible, New Living Translation, copyright ©1996, 2004, 2015 by Tyndale House Foundation. Used by permission of Tyndale House Publishers, a Division of Tyndale House Ministries, Carol Stream, Illinois 60188. All rights reserved. Scripture quotations marked (TLB) are taken from The Living Bible copyright © 1971. Used by permission of Tyndale House Publishers, a Division of Tyndale House Ministries, Carol Stream, Illinois 60188. All rights reserved. Scripture quotations marked (TPT) are from The Passion Translation®. Copyright © 2017, 2018 by Passion & Fire Ministries, Inc. Used by permission. All rights reserved. Scripture quotations marked (MSG) are taken from THE MESSAGE, copyright © 1993, 2002, 2018 by Eugene H. Peterson. Used by permission of NavPress. All rights reserved. Represented by Tyndale House Publishers, a Division of Tyndale House Ministries. Scripture quoted by permission. Quotations designated (NET) are from the NET Bible® copyright ©1996, 2019 by Biblical Studies Press, L.L.C. http://netbible.com All rights reserved. Scripture quotations marked (ICB) taken from the International Children's Bible®. Copyright © 1986, 1988, 1999 by Thomas Nelson. Used by permission. All rights reserved. Scripture quotations marked (NKJV) from the New King James Version®. Copyright © 1982 by Thomas Nelson. Used by permission. All rights reserved. Scripture quotations marked (NCV) from the New Century Version®. Copyright © 2005 by Thomas Nelson. Used by permission. All rights reserved. Scripture quotations marked (Voice) taken from The Voice™. Copyright © 2012 by Ecclesia Bible Society. Used by permission. All rights reserved. Scripture quotations marked (NIV) are taken from the Holy Bible, New International Version®, NIV®. Copyright © 1973, 1978, 1984, 2011 by Biblica, Inc.® Used by permission of Zondervan. All rights reserved worldwide. www.zondervan.com The "NIV" and "New International Version" are trademarks registered in the United States Patent and Trademark Office by Biblica, Inc.® Scripture quotations marked (ERV) taken from the HOLY BIBLE: EASY-TO-READ VERSION © 2001 by World Bible Translation Center, Inc. and used by permission. Scripture quotations marked (CEV) are from the Contemporary English Version Copyright © 1991, 1992, 1995 by American Bible Society, Used by Permission. Scripture quotations marked (ESV) are from the ESV® Bible (The Holy Bible, English Standard Version®), copyright © 2001 by Crossway, a publishing ministry of Good News Publishers. Used by permission. All rights reserved. Scripture quotations marked (GW) are taken from GOD'S WORD, Copyright © 1995 by God's Word to the Nations Bible Society. All rights reserved. Used by permission. Scripture quotations marked (NLV) are taken from the New Life Version, copyright © 1969 and 2003. Used by permission of Barbour Publishing, Inc., Uhrichsville, Ohio 44683. All rights reserved.

The author has tried to recreate events, locales and conversations from the memories of some individuals who were part of the story. In order to maintain their anonymity in some instances she has changed the names of individuals and places, she may have changed some identifying characteristics and details such as physical properties, occupations and places of residence.

ISBN (Softcover): 978-1-4866-2077-7
ISBN (Hardcover): 978-1-4866-2079-1
eBook ISBN: 978-1-4866-2078-4

Word Alive Press
119 De Baets Street Winnipeg, MB R2J 3R9
www.wordalivepress.ca

Cataloguing in Publication information can be obtained from Library and Archives Canada.

ADVANCED PRAISE FOR *DON'T TELL*

"Joanie Brusseau's life story is nothing short of an amazing account of God's love and faithfulness. Her younger years were fraught with tragedy and misery as her earthly family let her down time after time. But then her wonderful Heavenly Parent stepped in with immense healing! Her post salvation days are more exciting in goodness than her pre-salvation were in sadness! He supplied deep friendships and fascinating adventures. To Him be the Glory!"

—**Toni Schirico Horras**
Area Co-ordinator at Safe Families for Children Greater Chicago Area

"Kathy Isaac captured me and brought me into the life of Joanie. It is a story of heartbreak, hope and healing as she finds her way home. This is such an emotional read. I wonder how many more Joanie's we may sit beside? Grab a kleenex "

—**Bonnie Gallant**
Co-founder of Agora Network Ministries
Co-author of *The Beautiful Strokes of God*

"What sets *Don't Tell* apart from many others is the way it draws you in. You know you're going to hear what you don't want to, but like a magnet pulling you too close for comfort, author Kathy Isaac pulls back the curtain to reveal the hidden mystery. Family betrayal, the horror of incest and emotional agony far too reminiscent of the evening news keeps you reading while looking for a thread of hope. One wonders—is their hope for Joanie—will she ever recover from her downward spiral?

As the narrative unfolds something inside the reader seems to call out; 'this can't be true.' Tell me it's only a story. Isaac unravels the plot like a driver swerving down a mountain road - causing your heart to pound and your mind to race. Why? Because Joanie's life becomes a mirror of too many stories that perhaps have been hidden deep in your own soul or that of a friend.

Don't Tell is more than a story—it's a true story! And as that story unfolds it seems to only get darker until one thinks the last flicker of hope will be snuffed out. But the power of *Don't Tell* comes alive with the redemptive rescue of a woman. A woman who is on the precipice and experiences the miracle of Divine intervention.

Read it, enjoy it and soak in it because *Don't Tell* is a 'must read.' It's the book you will be telling your friends to read this year."

—**Dr. Mike Sherbino**
Mike Sherbino Ministries

"Author Kathy Isaac is a tremendously gifted story teller. In *Don't Tell*, Isaac reveals the dark and brutal story of paternal sexual abuse a little girl from Chicago lived in real-time, but was sworn *never* to tell! You will have an eye witness account of the miraculous difference Jesus made in driving out the darkness and despair and utterly transforming young Joanie Brusseau by lavishing her with redemption, hope, healing, purpose and a place of belonging in the family of God."

—**Neil Boron**
Program Director/Host, WDCX Radio

"Roughly 20 years ago Joanie Brusseau eagerly and enjoyably entered the Judson Baptist Church (Oak Park, IL) family where I served as pastor (1994-2007). Reading Joanie's gripping story—*Don't Tell: Finding Home After Family Betrayal*—helped me to see that JBC was just the next in a series of steps in Joanie's amazing journey. Her life and testimony are a tribute to how God powerfully uses people (knowingly and unknowingly) as His instruments of healing where injury and pain have been self-inflicted or weaponized by others.

Joanie's "need-to-be-told" story needs a wide reading. It can be a be a beacon of light and life to those who have been abused, traumatized and left to live with such horrors. Furthermore, while Joanie's experiences are foreign to many, Joanie's invitation into her story has the potential to birth compassion and empathy for those in our families, communities and churches who feel the weight of betrayal and abuse. My prayer is that the Lord will use Joanie's story to help us reexamine our attitudes and actions toward hurting people and to open our hearts, lives, homes and churches for the healing of the broken."

—**Arthur Jackson**
PastorServe, Assistant Regional Director, Mid-west
Author at *Our Daily Bread*

To Joanie and all children who have known the devastation of this world's broken love. There is hope. His name is Jesus.

CONTENTS

A Message from Joanie — ix
Acknowledgements — xi
Foreword — xiii

PART ONE: BROKEN

Chapter One: The Valley of Darkness — 3
Chapter Two: The Secret — 10
Chapter Three: Honor Your Father? — 15
Chapter Four: Hey Mom, I'm Pregnant — 22
Chapter Five: Brian — 28
Chapter Six: Starting Over — 33
Chapter Seven: Best Friends — 38
Chapter Eight: An Insignificant Fault — 44
Chapter Nine: Cinderella — 53
Chapter Ten: The Felony — 60
Chapter Eleven: Exposed — 67
Chapter Twelve: Blessed Are… — 75
Chapter Thirteen: Nowhere to Lay My Head — 82
Chapter Fourteen: War and Death — 92

PART TWO: REDEEMED

Chapter Fiveteen: Daddy — 103
Chapter Sixteen: Transformation — 111

PART THREE: RESTORED

Chapter Seventeen: Testing God — 121
Chapter Eighteen: A New Perspective — 128
Chapter Nineteen: Don't Block the Blessing — 136
Chapter Twenty: My Heart's Desire — 144
Chapter Twenty-One: The Clashes — 151
Chapter Twenty-Two: Black and White — 158
Chapter Twenty-Three: Growing In His Grace — 164
Chapter Twenty-Four: Blessed to Be A Blessing — 173
Chapter Twenty-Five: Be Stil My Heart — 181
Chapter Twenty-SIx: Do You Know Jesus? — 188
Chapter Twenty-Seven: Irungu — 194
Chapter Twenty-Eight: Amazing Grace — 200

Afterword — 207
About the Author — 211

A MESSAGE FROM JOANIE

IF YOU ARE DISCOURAGED, WANT TO GIVE UP ON LIFE, OR NEED TO HAVE YOUR FAITH reaffirmed, this book is for you. My story will show you the strength and faithfulness of God to the broken individual I was. Rescued from a dark pit, I was renewed when I began to look to Him for direction. He turned my whole life around, and He can do the same for you.

ACKNOWLEDGEMENTS

THIS COMPELLING STORY COULD NEVER JUMP OFF THE PAGE IF IT HAD NEVER MADE it onto the page, and it wouldn't have made it to the page without the help of some generous people.

Annette Walker, for the endless hours of listening to and recording Joanie's stories, and sharing those recordings with me… thank you.

Richard and Marjorie Beck Gibson (Dick and Gram), for adding color to Joanie's sketchy memory… thank you.

Dr. Grant Mullen, and his book *Emotionally Free*, for defining the medical context to Joanie's emotional state in the story… thank you.

My husband Gary, for yelling down the hall, pushing for the next, yet unwritten chapter… thank you.

My manuscript pre-readers, for your "brutally honest" review of the first draft… thank you.

Joanie, for bravely reliving your darkest days to share the light of Jesus… thank you so very much.

FOREWORD

WHEREVER YOU ARE, WHENEVER YOU ARE, WHATEVER IS HAPPENING AROUND YOU as you read these words, I'd like to encourage you on a risky and precious journey. The drama of this woman's extraordinary life is about to intrigue you. Though raw, and not without many sorrows, her tale will suspend your disbelief and compel you towards deeper understanding of the ultimate meaning and purpose in the human experience. As an eyewitness to much of it, I certify that this story is true, and that Joanie and the people and events she recounts are absolutely real.

You also are living a story. We are often blind to the drama, decisions, and changes which forge us. History is a telling of the lives of people who live much like us. We read novels and watch movies to learn how to live. As you hear this memoir from Joanie's own telling, you will be drawn to love her. I know her well and can tell you that she is a dear and beautiful woman, both inside and out. You will also grieve with her, both in the damning devices thrust upon her as well as in those of her own making. But before the story is finished, you will learn with her a great secret about life.

Do not fear this journey, for it is bringing something very good! Though many times Joanie found herself feeling alienated and alone, she was never alone. If you are looking for strength to endure through pain, this story is especially for you. You are not alone.

Even if your life is very different from Joanie's experience, you will benefit from her hard-bought wisdom. Waiting at the end is the dessert of life: forgiveness and unconditional love. Most people would never guess that a person so hurt and broken could become so strong, happy, and loved. Even the pain and filth of memory can be cleaned away, and in their place will be found beauty and a purpose for good. This is Joanie's story. I hope it will become yours, too.

I am praying for you. Blessings on your journey.

—Pastor James Roland
Littlefield Abbey
November 6, 2020

PART ONE
BROKEN

CHAPTER ONE
THE VALLEY OF DARKNESS

Lord, even when your path takes me through the valley of deepest darkness… You remain close to me…
(Psalm 23:4, TPT)

I'VE KNOWN OPULENCE, AND NEED. I'VE KNOWN EXUBERANCE, AND AGONY. SOMETIMES I've even known myself. But now, I only wish to know death.

"Hey, can I make some copies?" I call out, interrupting the social workers standing by the watercooler, thoroughly engaged in their Y2K Labor Day weekend plans. "I have some important papers, and I need to make copies."

They're supposed to verify any copies residents make, but they're usually too busy to actually check. I've brought along some medical forms, just in case.

The tall one looks over and waves me on. "Sure. Go ahead, sweetie." Just as quickly, she turns back to the engaging watercooler conversation.

I hit the print button, smiling wryly as my suicide note prints fifteen copies. Pretty ironic, isn't it? Copying my suicide note in the office, right in front of the people who are supposed to help me during the year the world is supposed to end? But there is no help for me. I'm far beyond help.

As the printer finishes, I gather my copies, wave a thanks to the ladies in the corner, and go back to my room. I've been living in Chicago's SRO housing for years now. These single-room occupancy units are small furnished rooms aimed at providing affordable housing for the homeless or other dregs of society. Like me.

I live on the third floor, in a tiny ten-by-ten-foot room. Pretty convenient, actually. I can cook, get a glass of ice water out of my fridge, and read, all from the comfort of my own bed. Not that I actually ever do cook, but I could if I were so inclined.

I hop up on the bed, grab the book beside me, and open it up. *Right to Die*, by Jack Kevorkian. It's not a big book, only about one hundred twenty pages. I lick my finger as I turn the pages, easily leafing through to find the checklist I'm looking for.

Let's see. You have to write that you know what you're doing, that you're of sound mind. Yeah… like you're of sound mind when you decide to kill yourself! You also have to date the suicide note, and say that you don't want to be revived. Check, check, and check. Everything's in order.

After years of living in utter turmoil, fighting some entity deep inside me, I feel a quiet hush in my life at having made this decision to end my life. Finalizing the plans seems to settle me somehow, like my inner demons have surrendered and there's nothing more for them to fight for. They've won.

Or have they? I feel a calming presence over me. Tranquility surrounds me. I feel strangely protected, but I'm really not sure from what.

The phone rings. I lean over and pick it up.

"Hello? Dick?" I say. "This weekend? A ticket at the Greyhound station?"

My blood begins to boil. I pause, a warmth spreading through my veins to my fingers and toes, up to my flushing face.

Why would you do that? I think. *You're really infringing on my plans.*

Richard Gibson was my supervisor back when I worked at a plastics manufacturer in Chicago. He married Marj, the love of his life, while we were all working together. How can I describe Marj? Marj is like Aunt Bee from Mayberry. She's the sweetest lady you'd ever want to meet.

Together, I call them Dick and Gram. They're about ten to fifteen years older than me and living in Ohio now. I consider them like my parents. They took me in when I had nowhere to go.

Evidently, Dick has bought me a bus ticket to go out and visit them. Any other time, I'd be thrilled to visit, but this is my weekend to die! I've made painstaking efforts to plan this out. I intended to do it over the Labor Day weekend so that by the time the staff find me, I'll already be dead-dead. My fear is that somebody will find me and revive me, but not quite soon enough, leaving me brain-dead, a vegetable. That just can't happen.

I've carefully selected the date. On Monday, the office at the Major Jenkins apartments is closed. The social workers who would normally check up on me after not hearing from a resident for a while will be gone for Labor Day. There will only be one security guy on the schedule, to open the door, and I know him; he never leaves his office. If I do it Saturday morning, I could be dead by Saturday night. Then there's all day Sunday and Monday before anyone actually comes looking for me on Tuesday. It'll be plenty of time.

I really have thought this out, with forethought, intention, and a sound mind, just like the book says. I've made copies and everything.

"Do you have plans?" Dick asks.

"Yeah, I do," I say, the words escaping from my mouth.

"Well, whatever you have planned, you can just do it another time. We really want to see you. There's a ticket with your name on it waiting for you at the bus terminal for Friday. Marj and I will pick you up on this side."

He's always so happy. His voice suggests a great big silly grin and eyes dancing behind his glasses.

"Well, it's there," he adds. "Use it, don't use it, whatever. You've got a couple of days to think about it, but we really hope you come. Gram's making apple pie."

He knows that's my favorite.

Dick and Gram were missionaries in Belgium. They can't afford this ticket, especially since I'm not going to use it.

I'm livid. I could just scream! But I keep thinking about the money. They've gone to all this trouble… what could it hurt? I'm still going to kill myself, just not this weekend.

I decide to put my suicide off. I slump back into my pillow. I suppose two days of being dead-dead is as good as three.

The "L" train in downtown Chicago is busy this Friday afternoon. Summer's winding down and there's an energy in the air brought on by the sultry saxophone drifting over from the jazz festival in the distance as I walk to the Greyhound station. Everybody's so happy, yet I can't muster a grin. I collapse into a seat in the bus terminal and pull my hoodie over my face. I have no joy. I just don't want to live. It's all very inconvenient, this trip to Dick and Gram's.

"Cleveland, calling Cleveland," the conductor calls out in a booming voice.

I rouse slowly, my red, swollen eyes peeking out and blinking from the light. I pull the ticket from my pocket. Findley, Ohio. Oh joy, can't wait.

I get on the bus and sprawl out, praying that nobody will sit beside me.

About eight hours later, we're finally approaching my destination. It's been a long ride, and I'm exhausted.

Dick and Gram are waving and laughing just outside the window. A smile slips across my lips. Just seeing them lifts my spirits. The fresh aroma of Gram's rose-scented lotion wafts through my nostrils, and I hold onto her just a bit longer than is generally acceptable.

Beaming, Dick grabs my suitcase, places it in the trunk of the car, and we're on our way. A second wind rushes over me, I chat frantically all the way to their place, a tiny little gingerbread house in the middle of the woods.

I'm led to the guest room. It's warm and homey, and though I've not visited here before, it's filled with familiar things. I run my fingers across the books on the shelf by the closet: Hemingway, Austen, Tolkien, Lewis. The bookcase is new, but the books are well-known. I'd read a good chunk of these books when I last stayed with them.

I love books. I love reading curled up under a blanket on a comfy chair with a glass of wine. Okay, a bottle of wine.

A gust of lavender fills the room as I open the closet. The potpourri sachet falls off the hanger as I hang up my jacket.

The smells drifting in from the kitchen are too sweet to ignore… homemade bread and apple pie. They cook! A whole meal—meat, vegetables, and dessert. Comfort food, like a snuggly quilt on a cold winter day.

My lungs fill with the sweet and yeasty aroma. Almost floating through the house, my nose leads me straight into the kitchen.

It's still a warm summer evening, so we enjoy the meal outside. What a treat. We eat, we talk, we eat some more. I sit back in my chair, puff out my cheeks, and contentedly rub my full belly. I'm so full. Everything is good.

I hear a laugh. Was that me? Am I laughing? Oh, I am… I'm belly laughing! As we reminisce, I lean back into the lawn chair and stretch my feet, the cool grass tickling my toes. Things are always better with Dick and Gram.

After dinner, Gram gets up to do dishes. I stand up to help.

"Oh no," she says. "We have a dishwasher now. You stay out here and catch up with Dick."

I don't want to stay alone with Dick. I want to go in and do the dishes with Gram. But she insists, lifting her chin toward the yard. "Go on, go with Dick. I've got this."

I hang my head, quietly turn, and obediently walk out to the back lawn with Dick. Lowering myself onto the bright green grass, I stretch out and take in a deep breath of the country air. Oh, it smells so fresh and earthy out here.

Through the pink and lavender hues of twilight, the stars begin to emerge. We sit silently for about a half-hour, watching the sky as the stars begin to twinkle.

"It's really dark here," I say. "Look at all those stars. There must be a million of them. It's so amazing, so beautiful."

I've never seen a sky so big and bright, ever. It just doesn't get this dark in Chicago.

Dick looks up, nodding. "It sure is. Psalm 19 says the heavens declare the glory of God. The sky above proclaims His handiwork. Isn't it wonderful how God loves us so much that He created a universe with the perfect conditions for us to exist? And then He sent his only Son so we could be in perfect relationship with Him."

That's it. He's started talking about Jesus. I guess I knew he would. It always comes up.

Suddenly, I remember the events of the past week, months, years. My head whirls and I feel woozy and nauseous. I wrap my hands around my spinning head. All my secrets… it's just too much.

I start crying. "I just can't think about Jesus, or look at Jesus. I just can't!"

"Why?"

"You don't understand. You're just not like me," I stammer. "There are things I've done that just can't be forgiven."

He comes closer and places his hand on my shoulder. "Joanie, I feel like that every day."

Sure! I look at him and see a guy who's got it all together. He and Gram are missionaries, for gosh sakes. What could he have done in comparison to me?

Evidently, I'm not wearing my quiet face as I incredulously gawk at him.

"You don't think I wake up every day, go to His throne, and apologize?" he asks. "You don't think I put my sins down in front of Him and know He's going to help me go on?"

It's the first time I've ever thought about Jesus sitting on a throne. I let that thought simmer for a while.

"No," I say. "No, I don't see that at all. I don't see how you can do anything so wrong you need to go before Jesus's throne."

He chuckles a bit behind his warm smile. "Well, I do, because I'm human. There's stuff in me I need to be forgiven for."

I want examples. I want to know I'm not alone, that even Dick could have faults.

He starts talking about Gram, and about the lust in his mind. "When I see a beautiful woman," he says, "my mind strays, and it isn't holy."

Oh my gosh! Head cocked, my eyes widen. My jaw drops as the words almost slip out. He's telling me about stuff he's *thinking* of, but he has no idea the things I've actually *done*. I want him to get it. He has no clue about my reality. In my head, I scream back, *You have no idea how bad people can be in the real world! The people in the hood... I know I'm white, but whites just don't get it. I live there! You've never lived there. You just don't get it!*

But the words stay inside me.

His head tilts inquisitively. "What do you think you could do that would make Him not forgive you?"

"I've broken every commandment," I spit out. "I've been through nine years of Catholic school. I know them by heart."

"So have I," he quietly reflects.

"No, you haven't." I pause. "You've never killed someone."

"And you have?" His voice cracks.

I feel his eyes fixed on me. I can't look up, but I quietly mutter under my breath. "Yes, I just did." I gulp. "I killed somebody I'd never met before."

Suddenly I realize what I've said: Joanie Brusseau has killed someone.

With a look of terror, I plead, "Please don't tell Gram."

Right on cue, Gram walks out. "Are you done?"

I wait for Dick to answer.

"No," he whispers, holding up his finger. "We need a minute yet."

She smiles and returns to the house to find some knitting to do. Dick turns his attention back to me, trying not to look shocked. He's comparing his sin to mine, like they're both bad. We talk well into the evening.

"It's all sin," he says. "As long as we repent and turn away from that sin, God is there to forgive us."

I don't quite believe it, but a yawn escapes. I'm tired. I thank him for the talk and head back inside. It's been a long, exhausting day.

Was it only this morning when I folded up my suicide letters, placed them in a clear plastic bag, and hid them in the freezer? It's been a crushing week.

I walk into my room and notice a small light flickering in the corner. The light on the night table illuminates the book atop the delicate pink and white doily, its glowing gold letters radiating the words *HOLY BIBLE*. Gram always places a Bible next to the bed, and today it seems to reach out to me.

Turning my head, I crawl into bed, snuggle under the blue comforter, and switch out the light. I'm drained. Today has given me too much to think about.

I don't even remember my head hitting the pillow.

I stay for a week, laughing and resting. It's so good to rest. My bus leaves at about 4:00 on Sunday afternoon. Dick once again grabs my suitcase, storing it under the bus, as Gram hands me a brown paper bag; she's made sandwiches for the ride home, with homemade bread. She then gives me a big hug, longer than is generally acceptable, and we say our goodbyes.

Dick comes over with a gift of his own. "I know you love to read a good adventure. Get through the first chapter and you'll be hooked."

He smiles and hands me a book. He knows me so well.

Tears well up in my eyes. I won't be seeing them again. I've gotten through this week all right, but next weekend's my weekend to die.

On the bus I take my seat next to a stately looking woman wearing a jeweled cross necklace. My eyes are drawn to the cross. The only thing I like better than books is jewelry, and it's a stunning piece. She and I look at each other and nod a courteous hello.

I turn over the book. Hmm, *Left Behind*. That's what I feel like. I snuggle in and begin to read.

At the beginning of the second chapter, I turn to the woman and ask, "Are you a Christian?"

"Yes." I've noticed her looking over as I read.

"Do you know this book, *Left Behind*?" I lift the worn book.

"I've heard of it, but haven't read it," she offers, curiously inspecting the book.

"It says here that to become a Christian, I just have to pray this prayer…"

She smiles. "That's right. It's easy to do, but to keep it isn't as easy. It takes a bit more work."

"But I don't believe homosexuals are going to be condemned, and I don't believe a man is over a woman!" I retort. "And apparently, if you can't believe one part of the Bible… well, you just can't take bits and pieces."

"You're right, ah…" She raises her eyebrows, searching for my name.

"Joanie." I lean in, more interested in her response than her name.

"Joanie… good. All scripture is inspired and useful for teaching." Carefully planning her next words, she pauses. Then she says something that really makes sense, and it's something I've never heard from Christians before. "But Joanie, God is going to meet you right where you are. You don't have to believe a man is over a woman. You don't have to believe God condemns homosexuals. Truth is, we all need God, and all He wants you to do is trust Him, right here, right now. He's going to meet you right where you are." Her eyes are bright and full of hope. A glimmer of light dances around her. "Right now, to be His child, you don't have to believe that other stuff. All you need to know is that He is who He says He is. He's your Father and He loves you."

With that, she begins sharing the Gospel.

"Joanie, you and I and everyone else on this bus and in this world have done wrong. We have sinned. We are sinners. God is perfectly good. No wrong, no mistake, no sin can come into His presence, and that's why we can't have a relationship with Him. The sin needs to be paid for, wiped out, and we can't do it because we aren't perfect. Only Jesus can pay for it. He is God and He is perfect. So God the Father sent His Son Jesus to come to earth as a man and pay the price for our sin so we could come to God without our sin."

She checks to see if I'm still engaged. I am.

"He is who He says He is," she continues. "It's as simple as that. Admit you're a sinner, thank Him for dying on the cross for your sins, and ask Him for help, through Holy Spirit, to turn away from sin."

"But I killed somebody," I protest. "I killed somebody."

With a little flinch, she asks, "Are you going to kill somebody again?"

My head retreats in shock. What is she thinking? "No!"

"That's all He's asking you to do. To not do what you've done. Those sins you know aren't good for you or others, just don't do them again."

Wow. Sounds way too easy.

"He wants to be your Father, Joanie… your Daddy." Her tear-filled eyes glisten as she reaches for my hands. A warmth overcomes me, from my fingertips to deep inside my soul.

He wants to be my father?

…my…

…Father.

CHAPTER TWO
THE SECRET

For all that is secret will eventually be brought into the open, and everything that is concealed will be brought to light and made known to all.
(Luke 8:17)

I FEEL HIS FULL WEIGHT ON ME. I CAN'T BREATHE. HE HASN'T SHAVED AND HIS WHISKERS are rubbing up against my face. His feet hang over the end of the bed. I want to scream, but his hand is covering my mouth. I struggle to get out from under him, but he's too big. I'm too little. I can't move.

He whispers in my ear, "Keep quiet, it will be over soon."

How can this be happening? Why would he do this?

• • •

It wasn't the first time I had sex. It was the 70s and I was a freshman. I'd had my first romance already. Earlier that same year, actually.

Since I'd just turned fourteen years old, some would call it rape, of course, but if you'd asked me, I'd have simply said it was sex. I would have said that I loved him, that I hadn't known how to do it and he'd helped me.

I stayed with him once for three days over a long weekend, playing house while his wife was gone. I felt so seductive, so adult. He was my best friend's husband. I babysat their kids.

Is it strange that my best friend was an adult? I didn't think so. I was really mature for my age. I mean, I didn't know if anybody at home had ever really been concerned that I was gone. I was a grown up, right?

When I got home from school one day after this, Dad beat me. He threw three punches and called me a whore. How'd he find out? I hadn't told him.

As for my best friend, the wife… well, she found out. I ran into her at the drug store. She grabbed me by the arm, pulled me around a corner, and looked me straight in the eyes. She was so mad that she grit her teeth. Her spit moistened my face, even landing in my gaping mouth. She told me never to come back or she would tell my mother. I didn't want Mom to know. She loved me so much. She didn't get mad when I forgot to do the laundry, or when I stayed out late, or when I was a problem.

You see, Mom is wonderful. She's the most beautiful thing I've ever seen, like Jackie Kennedy Onassis. She glides through a room like a swan on the lake, a radiant smile on her face, her dress always neat and tidy and flowing around her. Her short, dark, bouncy hair is always just so. She has it done at the salon every week. She makes her beautiful home and is a generous hostess to Dad's many friends. She works so hard to please him.

Everybody loves Mom. No, she didn't need to know about this. I was already such a problem.

I never went back. I still miss my friend.

Mom had worked at a hardware store ever since we'd moved to Glen Ellyn, a suburb of Chicago. When Dad was jobless, she had to take on extra work. So when I was about ten, Mom worked two jobs and Dad stayed home to watch me—and he'd drink. My sister Marie had moved out already. Ann was gone, too. And Rose? Well, she worked at a drycleaners during high school and didn't get home until after dinner. Mom would leave early in the morning and not get home until 11:15 p.m.

As the youngest sibling, I was basically home alone. I began losing myself. Sometimes a dark, heavy blanket of numbness covered me. I couldn't seem to feel anything. I didn't even know I was alive. I started cutting and burning myself to see if I could feel anything.

Mom wasn't one for affectionate talk, but if I had a burn or otherwise hurt myself, she mothered me. She let me crawl up on her lap and she'd bandage the wound, hold me, and gently rock me to and fro. The burns were so worth it because it felt so good when she tended to me.

I was such a problem. I tried burning in hidden places, so people couldn't see. Even so I couldn't see.

Dad? Well, Dad tried. He was tall and strong and of French-Canadian descent, with short dark hair. When things were good and he was working, he was my hero and a lot of fun. When I was younger and Mom left early for work, he would make breakfast: eggs with ketchup, and hamburgers or hotdogs. And he'd laugh. Boy, could he laugh! The room would shake with his booming voice.

But when he didn't have work, we needed to keep our distance. It was hard for him to find regular work. When I was six, he moved us from Connecticut to Illinois for a job.

It was especially hard for me to leave Aunt Ninna in Connecticut. She was my grandmother's sister and had no children. Mom had lived with her for a while when she was young, so we were like her grandchildren. My real grandparents had died before I was born. We always had such a great time with Aunt Ninna. Even after we moved out to Glen Ellyn, we'd still visit her sometimes. She made the best cream potatoes and chicken, and there was always ice water in her fridge. I've always loved ice water! She also had thin-sliced bread with ham and mustard. She had those shiny cut-glass lamps that glow… shiny things have always caught my eye.

But there was a smell in her apartment, an old musty smell. It made sense; she had to be like a hundred.

She always said, "You better pray to God, because I think He's forgotten about me." But how bad would it have been if God had forgotten about her and she lived forever?

Before we moved, we saw her every week for Sunday dinner and then watched Ed Sullivan on the old RCA television. We always had to put foil on our TV's antenna at home to get it to work, but not hers. I loved it when Topo Gigio was on the show. We also watched Lassie on Channel 2. If we were really good, one of us would get to stay overnight.

Oh, and then there was crazy Aunt Jean. Well, she was different, but I don't think she was crazy. I haven't seen Aunt Jean since we left Connecticut.

Christmas was a time for alcoholics to drink, and Dad took advantage, but never before Father Parnisari's midnight mass.

When I was younger, we'd wait for Mom to get home from work and put on our best clothes. Dad would drive. Then we'd walk up to the front door of St. James the Apostle Church together, hand in hand. I was so little, and the front step was so big. To make it, I had to take a big step, clutching on to my parents' hands, making sure not to let my mittens slip off.

Father Parnisari would meet us at the door. He'd get right down on his knees and look me straight in the eye. He'd ask if I'd seen baby Jesus out on the front lawn. Of course I had. There was always a big bright star over the creche, shining down so bright on the baby Jesus that you couldn't miss it. The baby was cute. I liked babies, but I liked the animals better. Anyway, Father Parnisari would tell me he'd listen for me when we sang Silent Night during the service. I promised I would sing loud.

"How loud?" he'd ask.

"This loud!"

Then he'd ask again, a little bit louder, "How loud?"

"THIS LOUD!"

He'd smile, then pull out a candy cane from his long sleeves, tap my nose with the end of it, and place it in my little cupped hands.

Father Parnisari was Dad's good friend. I'd say his best friend, so Dad didn't want to disappoint. Dad drank on Christmas Eve day, but he was never drunk for mass. He'd drink mostly when he got home.

Christmas was wonderful. It was about the only time we actually sat down and ate together at the table. We had so much fun, opening presents and staying up until three or four in the morning. Dad was the drinker. He drank beer, wine from the boxes, and gin. He drank whatever was around, but he didn't like to drink alone. Mom drank Drambuie, so every Christmas he bought her a big bottle; half of it would be gone before we turned in for the night. After a long day, Mom would get tired and stumble around a bit.

But if Dad hadn't been working, there wouldn't be any money, and there wouldn't be any Christmas. On our first Christmas Eve in Glen Ellyn, Mom worked late closing up at the hardware store while Dad was out with his friends.

Rose and I were home watching *It's a Wonderful Life* for the hundredth time on our good ol' Zenith color TV. I always loved the part in the movie where the little girl says, "Every time a bell rings, an angel gets its wings." I was seven and I still believed in angels then.

Rose was slouched over on the orange couch, painting her nails. I lay on the carpet on the floor with my hands cupped around my chin, knees bent and feet swaying in the air. The tree was already trimmed and standing by the front window, baubles and tinsel hanging from its branches, a gleaming star on top. Snow fell outside, those big heavy flakes that are great for building snowmen. It was a picture perfect day, except there were no presents under the tree.

At about 8:00, the doorbell rang. Rose kicked me and told me to go get the door. The show had just started and I didn't want to get up, so I whined and told her to. We argued back and forth for what seemed like forever, but really it must have only been a few minutes. As always, I lost.

Still glued to the TV, I walked over to the front entrance, opened the door, looked out, and gasped. Tears welled up in my eyes and started rolling down my cheeks. I choked; I just couldn't believe it. It was a winter wonderland! I've still never seen anything like it in all the years since. There were about ten long steps from our door down to the driveway, and each step was covered with the whitest snow.

And there were presents! Presents everywhere! Lots of presents, and a turkey, and pies! Everything you'd need for a Christmas dinner.

Shrieking, I ran outside, looking down the street. But I never saw anyone.

By this time, Rose had come to the door to see what all the commotion was about. We grabbed each other, jumping up and down, screaming in delight at the top of our lungs.

That was a very special Christmas. So bright! Magical! I wonder, who would have done that? It must have been someone from church. Mom had a lot of friends there.

It didn't really matter. What mattered was that we had presents for Christmas. I got a beautiful warm winter coat with fur and a purse with one of those old-fashioned openings that had two balls that clasped together. The purse had two dollars in it—two brand-new dollar bills. I still have them. I don't think I'll ever spend them.

I was in the second grade then, and I often got invited to spend the night with my very best friend, Mary Ellen Shanley, even on school nights. Mary Ellen and I would huddle together and sleep under the pink comforter in her queen-sized white canopy bed. Mrs. Shanley would cook dinner for us, and when Mr. Shanley would come home from work we'd sit around the table as a family to eat. It was really cool, because we were doing it like those TV people did. We'd watch television together and eat Charles Chips, the chips that got delivered.

I slept so peacefully there. Mrs. Shanley would arrange with my mom for me to stay for one night, but sometimes I even got to stay another. She'd wash my clothes and give me a bath, too. It was wonderful.

Sometimes Mrs. Shanley looked at me in a certain way, like… well, I'm sure she didn't know what was going on, but it sometimes seemed like she knew there was something wrong at home.

We moved after that and I don't get to see them anymore. I miss Mary Ellen's family. They brought light to the dark corners of my life. Since then, the world has gotten darker.

Pitch dark.

•••

I'm in my bed, gasping under the weight of my father. I can't breathe. I smell the beer and gin on his breath. My cheek is raw from the scratching of his bristles. It's been snowing outside and he's cold to the touch. He must have just come in from a late night with the boys.

I hear the dog, Brandy, frantically whining and clawing the carpet outside my bedroom door as the headboard rhythmically hits the wall.

I try calling out—"Brandy… come on, boy, open the door… bark… wake somebody up"—but I have no voice. I can't make a sound.

I want to die.

No, I just don't want to be.

And then… I'm not.

CHAPTER THREE
HONOR YOUR FATHER?

You have taken notice, for you always see one who inflicts pain and suffering. The unfortunate victim entrusts his cause to you; you deliver the fatherless.
(Psalm 10:14, NET)

MY EYES BEGIN TO FLUTTER. IT'S MORNING. THE SUN'S SHINING THROUGH THE CLOSED curtain. I try to move, but it's painful. What's happened? I'm groggy. My mouth is dry. I lick my lips. They're cracked and sore, and I raise my hand to touch them. My cheeks sting, like rug burn. My hair's stuck to my face. My hands… my hands smell awful. My breath is putrid: alcohol? I shiver, I'm cold, and my eyelet covers are on the floor. The sheets gathered at my feet are damp and smell. Oh, my thighs, they're so sore.

My heart starts racing and I gasp for breath.

Suddenly, I remember! I sit up straight in bed, scrambling for my clothes. I look next to me, my eyes darting frantically around the room.

He's gone… I'm alone.

My mind rushes back to last night, my head spinning. How can this be? This wasn't like the last time, with my friend's husband. It wasn't gentle. He wasn't kind. Was it really him? Did this really happen?

I get up out of bed, put on my nightie, and rip the sheets off the bed, throwing them in a pile on the floor. I need a shower.

I quietly open the door.

Brandy's sleeping outside my door. "Good boy, Brandy," I say, patting his head before stepping over him.

It's quiet in the hall. I walk toward the bathroom. Good, it's empty. I turn on the hot water in the shower. Standing at the sink, I look up and wonder, *Who is this reflection in the mirror and what have you done with Joanie?* The ghostly image is strangely familiar. Fingers explore the face in pursuit of validation. The long, brown hair is stringy, bouffanty, and disheveled; lips cracked, shattered like a broken porcelain doll; cheeks chaffed and reddened. A hand runs down the cheek and neck, pulling away the hair to expose bite marks and bruising on the neck. But the eyes! The blue eyes are heavy, hollow and empty. Red lines crackle the whites like a fault line of an erupted volcano; they're encircled and blackened by smudged mascara.

I look deep into the reflection through the now foggy mirror, seeing nothing behind those eyes.

I throw open the shower curtain and get in, beseeching the water to rush over me, but I'm not getting clean. I scrub my face, my stomach, my legs. I scrub hard, over and over.

I need to get clean.

I need to burn.

I need to burn.

I get out of the shower and light a cigarette. There's always a pack on the counter. I blow on it a bit while watching the embers glow a brighter red. Lowering the cigarette to my arm, I press it against the skin; I watch it slowly sear and melt, a thin line of smoke releasing a charcoal-like aroma.

Relief.

I breathe.

I can feel.

I dress. Am I smelling eggs and hotdogs? I follow the savory scent to the bottom of the stairs. Dad's in the kitchen, pots and pans clanging.

"Hey Pookie, I'm making breakfast. It's your favorite, hot dogs 'n eggs." He points to the fridge. "Get the ketchup out of the fridge and pull up a chair."

My feet can't move. I just keep looking at him. Maybe I'm dreaming. Maybe I was dreaming last night. What's real? I'm not really sure.

"What's up? Cat got your tongue?" His gaze penetrates me as a wry smile cracks his face, his teeth gleaming in the sunlight.

"Uh, no… Sure, I'll have eggs," I stammer, walking into the kitchen. "Yeah, hotdogs smell good."

I must have been dreaming. Wow, what a nightmare.

"So, you going out with Danny tonight? It's almost Valentine's, you know. Got any special plans?"

Danny's my boyfriend. He's a senior, I'm a freshman. I really like him and I think he really likes me. He's attentive and takes care of me. I didn't even know Dad knew about him.

"Um, no… no. Well, I don't know." I swallow hard. "I think we'll just hang out or maybe go to the Valentine's dance at his school. He might take me to the senior dance, if that's okay. How 'bout you and Mom? You guys going out or anything?"

I'm unsure of what I'm even suggesting. He would never let me go to a dance at another school, and he and Mom rarely go out together. Dad's usually out with his friends.

"Na, I think we'll both just stay at home. Guess it's time to turn over a new leaf."

A slow smile weaves across his face as he winks. Perplexed, I respond with a reflexive smile. What new leaf?

After breakfast, I rush off to school and contemplate the crazy night. What a nightmare. And how weird was breakfast?

Days go by. Life seems to be back to normal, whatever that is, but I don't sleep well; it's 3:00 and I'm staring at the ceiling. Lights from a passing car shine through the window and reflect across my wall. It must be Mr. White, our neighbor. He works the night shift and sometimes comes home at odd hours. Aside from the car, it's quiet… eerily quiet.

The old wooden floorboards creak in the hallway and I wonder who's going to the bathroom. Brandy's paws click on the linoleum flooring. The latch clicks as the bathroom door is closed. You could hear a pin drop.

The hall floor creaks again, stopping at my bedroom door. There's breathing outside. I gasp and hold my breath. The chills down my spine spike the hairs on my arms, and the pounding in my chest—*duh-dun, duh-dun*—quickens but won't be silenced. I count down the seconds as I close my eyes and lay motionless in the dark, waiting.

The door opens. It's my father… it wasn't a dream. His weight descends on me as the smell of alcohol once again wafts through the room. His breath warms my ear and his lips touch my face.

"If you tell anybody, you'll lose your family," he whispers. His lips smack. "You don't want to lose your family, do you?"

"No," I whimper, barely able to breathe under his crushing weight. Inside I'm screaming, *Get off, go away! I'm Joanie! I'm your daughter!* But I'm voiceless and nothing escapes from my mouth.

I drift, and then I'm gone.

I'm just … not.

Life goes on. With every nocturnal visit, in a low whisper, he reminds me to keep the secret. The secret is safe with me. I don't want to lose my family, ever. I'll do anything to keep my family. Anything. I'll fight to keep my family… I'll be quiet to keep my family.

School's going well. I try to keep busy so I don't have to spend much time at home. Dad's been sober for a while now and has a job working from 3:00 to 11:00. Mom is back to only working one job and is home by 5:30—but if I don't have to see them, it's a good thing.

I've started working at the Seven Dwarfs Restaurant. It's not far, so I ride my bike there after school. The restaurant looks like a Disney movie set. A huge mural of the dwarfs' house in the forest is painted on the wall, and one of Snow White in a beautiful pink dress, carrying a bowl of food as she dances over to a table of dwarfs. Happy is at the piano, banging away at the keys while the animals prance around the room; of course, the wicked queen is in the window dressed in green as the old lady holding up a shiny red, luscious apple. There's the prince and the castle. The whole place is filled with murals that tell the story of family conflict, secrets, death, and finding a new family. It's the story of my life, but I don't have another family to go to.

The restaurant's pretty big, with great comfort food, but lately the smells just turn my stomach. I work at the ice cream fountain counter, making incredible fountain creations. That's where I ran into Mary Ellen Shanley the other day. I haven't seen her for so long. We lost contact after my family moved a few years ago. But we pick up right where we left off, like no time has passed at all. She has a great group of new friends, and somehow they include me in their fun, laughing and joking around, and they want to keep hanging out with me.

The dark shadows over me fade and things are good. Mary Ellen's brought a glimmer of light back into my world.

One morning, my churning stomach wakes me up. I'm groggy and nauseous and the sheets are wet. Slowly sitting up, I put my cold clammy feet down on the carpet and feel the plushness between my toes. I'm lightheaded and woozy, but with a deep breath I stand up.

Feeling like a drunken soldier, I grab the back of the chair by my desk, swaying back and forth. I dry-heave at the smell of burned toast drifting up from downstairs. Crap.

It seems like I've had this stomach flu for a month and I want to stay home, but I have a math test today, and it would be such a pain to take it another time, seeing as it's my first year of high school and school's almost out.

With a shiver, I skip breakfast and rush out the door, making several pitstops on the way to the bus stop. Like Hansel and Gretel's cookie crumbs, you could follow the trail and find me, though it's not nearly as poetic with vomit.

The math test is pretty simple, but I'm sick to my stomach and run out to the washroom twice. I wish I could shake this flu. It's June. It isn't flu season, is it? This is crazy.

"Joanie, can I have a word?" Sister Mary Frances asks as I'm leaving the class.

"Yes, Sister?"

She approaches me and mercifully places her hand on my shoulder, her gentle green eyes and disarming smile putting me at ease. "Joanie," she asks quietly, "how are you feeling? I've noticed you haven't seemed well for a while now."

"I have the stomach flu." I'm glad she doesn't rebuke me for having left the class during the test. "I can't seem to shake it."

"Take a seat, Joanie."

I glance to the corner she's indicated and sit in the chair, away from the view of the door. The nun pulls up another chair and faces me, knee to knee, her clasped hands trembling ever so slightly. She takes a slow, deep breath; her eyes are intent but distant, prayerful, looking off to the side in search of some divine revelation.

With a soft-spoken voice, she asks, "So Joanie, do you think there's a chance you may be… pregnant?"

"Pregnant? No! Of course not!" The chair falls to the floor behind me as I quickly stand to my feet. What is she thinking?

"Have you had your period?" she continues, reaching out for my shoulder again, unwilling to let me go.

"Yeah, I've had my period." I pull my shoulder back. I've had my period for a while. What does she think I am, a child? Why is she asking this? And what does it have to do with my flu?

"Have you had it recently?" she persists as she picks up my chair. "When was the last time you had it?"

I slink back down into the wooden chair. "Well, I get it… I mean, I've had it," I stammer looking out into the distance. "Come to think of it, I guess it's been a while. But what does it matter? Pregnant? You must be joking. I can't be pregnant."

My head spins as I try to remember. When was the last time I had it? Had it come last month? Maybe it was a few months back. Christmas? No, I must have had it since then. It's June!

"Perhaps you should go see your family doctor and get checked out," she suggests, quickly scribbling something on a notepad. "Here's a note so you can go home for the day."

"Yeah, sure," I scoff, but who's she kidding? I can't do that. My family would know.

I snatch the note from her hand and leave the room. My wide eyes gloss over. Looking straight ahead, I see nothing but fog as I teeter back and forth in the hall, droopy shoulders, arms hanging loose, dragging my jaw behind me.

I walk right into my friend Jane's locker.

An unusual look of concern crosses Jane's face. "Are you all right?"

"Yeah, I think so," I mutter, but I'm not. Nothing is all right.

My mind is racing. I don't know how I got here, but I'm at my front door now. Sister Mary Frances must be crazy. I'm not pregnant. This is another one of those nightmares. I just need to go inside and rest, that's all.

• • •

It's been months and rest isn't doing it for me. My head constantly flops at work, as I fade in and out of consciousness, no matter how much sleep I get. I'm not active and the weight is piling on. This morning, I spent fifteen minutes trying to pull up my jeans, jumping up and down, straining to pull up the zipper, one notch at a time. I just can't get into my jeans.

Long-faced, I pull on track pants and trudge downstairs, demoralized as I sit down and drag out the phone book. It must weigh ten pounds. Why do they make them so heavy? I flip over to the Yellow Pages and look up Planned Parenthood. There it is. I scribble the address on the back of an envelope, get my jacket, and make my way to the bus stop to wait.

The teeming rain soaks through me, darkening the hair that clings tightly to my face. Black circles form under my soulful eyes as remorseful tears flow off my quivering chin.

I flop down in a seat on the empty southbound bus and lift my head. With hawkish eyes, I inspect the cabin around me, relaxing when I confirm that I don't know anyone. As I pull a tissue from my pocket to wipe my face, I watch the world outside pass by, unaware and unaffected by my personal struggle.

I recall having seen the Planned Parenthood building while driving around in this neighborhood, but I never took much notice of it. I certainly never thought I'd ever be going there.

A nurse waiting at the door escorts me in. After answering a few general questions, I'm directed to sit in the waiting room until someone calls me. I sit, shoulders hunched, hands resting in my lap as my foot shakes uncontrollably.

When my name is called, I'm led into an examination room. Why is it they make medical facilities look so stark and white? It's really not a friendly looking place. I would paint it blue and put up posters. Some flowers would be nice.

The doctor pats her hand on the examination table and I obediently move towards it. The paper cover crunches under me as I hop up onto the table. She reaches around me for the blood pressure cuff and places it around my upper arm.

"I hear you haven't been feeling well," she begins as the cuff inflates.

I tell her about the flu symptoms I've had for months now. She writes down the BP results and removes the cuff. Unfazed, she takes my temperature, then holds my wrist and looks down at her watch. It's a nice watch, a silver Lucerne. Though it's sleek, the numbers are large enough to read easily, and I can tell the hands glow in the dark. Very cool.

She releases my wrist and writes some more. Tapping the pen on the paper, she licks her lips, then looks up and takes a deep breath.

"When was your last period?" she asks, her voice suspicious.

"I'm not sure," I maintain, having already answered this question earlier for the lady at the desk.

Reaching to the counter, she picks up a cardboard package and hands it to me while directing me to the washroom down the hall. It's a pregnancy kit, and I'm supposed to bring it out to her when I'm finished.

Quietly I stroll down the hall, the cardboard moistening in my shaking hands.

After completing the task, I approach her, chin down, my sad eyes focused on her lips as she reviews the results and rests her hand on my shoulder.

"It's okay, Joanie. We can help."

Her lips are moving, but her words fly past me as I stare blankly. There's a ringing in my ear. Her chair rolls back as she stands up, walks over to the counter, and picks up some brochures. They were already laid out when I came back into the room.

She knew. How did she know? How did I not notice? How did it not even occur to me? I haven't slept with anyone, have I?

My eyes, quick as strobe lights, blink vigorously in an effort to hold back the tears as I walk out, brochures in hand.

I'm pregnant.

CHAPTER FOUR
HEY MOM, I'M PREGNANT

The Lord defends those who suffer.
He protects them in times of trouble.
(Psalm 9:9, ICB)

MY SISTER MARIE HAS A BABY, SO SHE'LL KNOW WHAT TO DO.

I'm unsure how I got here, but I'm standing at her front door ringing the bell, steadying myself against the doorframe with my knees shaking. The door opens.

As if it's evaporated into thin air, blood drains from me and I collapse into my sister's arms. I'm numb.

The baby fusses as we go into the living room and sit on the couch, Marie's worried glances darting back and forth between me and the baby. She's torn between our needs.

"I have to go get him. Will you be all right?" she asks, one hand on my knee.

My body is limp, unable to move. "Sure, I'll be here."

She's back in an instant.

"Do you want to hold him?" She holds little Billy up to me. She knows I love him. Her hopeful eyes are desperate for something to brighten my obviously disheartened spirits.

"I do," I manage. I'm cold and sweating, and my heart's beating a mile a minute.

How do I do this? What do I say? What will she think?

She hands Billy over into my outstretched arms. I lift his little head, kiss his gleaming forehead, and hold him tight. He's so warm, so soft. The rhythm of my heart beats with his as he lays still against my chest. I take in a deep breath of baby smell. I love him so much.

I tell her about being sick and my conversation with Sister Mary Frances, about the clinic and the brochures… oh, the brochures! Abortion. Adoption. Teen mothers… telling your parents, going to school as a mom…

I lean over the baby, and as I pull the cache of brochures out of my purse, the glossy cards slip from my hands and scatter across the floor. She quietly shushes me, touching my hand as she kneels down in front of me to pick them up. I feel a peacefulness in her touch.

"They've given me a few days to decide," I ramble. "Just a few days. Evidently, you can have an abortion up to three months. The test results show I'm about four months along... four months. It's already over. There has to be a doctor giving a reason now, like there's a problem with the baby... or with my life or something. I have the weekend. I don't know! I don't know. What should I do?"

I look at the baby, then helplessly glance back at Marie, who's obviously searching for an answer. She's been quietly listening, thoughtfully reflecting.

Choosing her words carefully, her first words aren't "Who's the father?" That's cool. I'm glad. I don't know the answer to that question anyway. I don't even know how this could have happened. I don't dare ask myself.

"I'm here for you, whichever way you want to go. But with our upbringing," she says, reminding me of our shared Catholicism, "I don't think you want to have an abortion. That's something you'll never... you'll have to live with that for the rest of your life."

She stops. Through her twitching eyes, I see her head is spinning, too. I mean, I'm only in high school.

She anchors her attention to me again. "We're going to have to tell Mom and Dad."

A small smile breaks through my pursed lips and the air that's been pent up in my lungs slowly escapes. Yes, we'll have to tell Mom and Dad.

I won't be on my own.

• • •

But I *am* alone. On that day, it's just Mom, Dad, and me. I don't know where Ann and Rose are, but they aren't home. At the last minute, Marie said she couldn't make it... something about the baby.

Dad has been sober lately, but he's started drinking again. He's been drinking today. There's a bottle of gin next to him. He's slouched back in his chair, his button-down shirt has slipped off his shoulder, exposing his gleaming white undershirt. Mom's next to him on the couch, brushing her fingers over her gingham skirt, then folding her hands in her lap, not a wrinkle in sight.

I stand before them at the coffee table, with knocking knees, lick my dry lips and swallow the lump in my throat. I've come into my own, neither repentant nor demure, having made up my mind. It's too late for an abortion now anyway.

"I'm pregnant," I announce cheekily. "And I'm keeping the baby!"

Dad stumbles as he gets up and starts to yell, his familiar breath against my face. I scream back, teeth exposed, spit flinging, knees shaking.

With a hand on each of our shoulders, my mother softly interjects, and though the tone in the room subsides, we're still talking over each other. Evidently, I'm a minor, and decisions are being made for me. Nobody's asking who the father is. Do they think it's Danny's? Who else, right? But we haven't slept together. I've never spent the night.

"I'll call Father Parnisari in the morning," my father says adamantly as he takes his seat. "You'll go to an unwed mother's home when the time comes. We'll call Catholic Charities, and they'll place the baby. There are people out there who can care for a baby." His eyes narrow dismissively as he flicks his hand. "You certainly aren't capable!"

This is preposterous. Lunging forward, I shout, "This is my baby. It's my decision." My mom holds me back. "I won't put it up for adoption. I'm going to keep this baby! I love this baby. It's the only thing that loves me. You can't make me give it up, I won't… I won't!"

Maniacally, my father rises from his chair, draws back his arm, and swings. His enormous clenched fist makes contact and I careen backward, twisting between the couch and the coffee table. I'm unable to move my feet as I fall back onto the heavy wooden table, the only piece of modern furniture we own. The back of my head strikes a sharp corner as I fall to the floor.

Like Ali against Frazier, I rise up again, nose to nose, and scream into his face. In a frenzy, he swings again. I'm down for the count, arms desperately protecting my head from his repeated punches. Blow after blow lands in my abdomen. He spews horrible names, slurring from drink or rage. He then lifts the television over his head, but Mom grabs his arm before he can hurl it, throwing him off-balance. Her quick thinking saves me as the television crashes to the floor, glass shattering around me. I put my hands down to steady myself, and I feel the sting of glass cutting through my hands.

"I outta kill you, you slut," Dad hollers. He leaps on top of me, pulling my hair with one hand and punching furiously with the other. My body recoils with each stinging blow.

With all her strength, Mom pulls him off me. "Get out! Get out!"

Reeling in pain, I manage to scurry away and run outside, teetering through the doorway. A high, incessant pitch rings in my head as I wrap my hands around it in an effort to stop the internal explosion. A piercing, shrill cry emanates from me and resonates into the neighborhood as I fall to the grass. It's still bright outside and the neighbors must have seen and heard the commotion, but nobody comes to my rescue. Warm blood oozes from my ear and drips between my fingers. I cough and spew blood onto the grass.

Mom's behind me now with the keys and scoots me into the car. Backing out of the driveway, she hands me tissues to wipe off the blood. They're promptly soaked through. She pulls down the visor to hide my face from any onlookers, revealing my reflection in the mirror, but I don't need to look; by the pale expression on her face, I know I'm a mess—bruised, swollen, unrecognizable.

We sit silently. There are no words.

She takes me to the bus station and relays instructions for me to go to Marie's and wait there. I nod compliantly, but I won't do it. I'll go to Danny's instead. He was supportive when I told him last week I was pregnant, and my parents don't know his number or address. I'll be safe there.

Sobbing on the bus, my hand traces my face—my eye, my lip… it's so swollen. Fumbling in my pocket for more tissues, I find only remnants of the already blood-soaked ones. I use them to blot the fresh blood.

"Joanie, what happened?" Danny asks as he opens the door wide.

The words blurt out: "My dad… I told them."

There's a party going on. Danny's brother and a couple of other people are sprawled on the couch, smoking up. They offer me a drag.

"Oh my gosh, are you kidding me?" I snap. "I'm pregnant, and you're offering me that?"

"Oh, right!" the skinny pothead says, coughing. "I'm sorry, I'm sorry."

Danny flashes a smile. "Joanie's not gonna smoke, 'cause Joanie's a good girl."

I flash a bewildered look at him. I'm pregnant. The term 'good girl' doesn't apply to me anymore.

After a restful weekend at Danny's, I return home. Dad's there, asleep in his chair by the coffee table. Looks like he hasn't moved. How could he call me a slut? I'm not a slut. I haven't slept with anybody.

Stealthily, I pass through the house to my room and quietly close the door. I'll keep my distance from him.

In the days to come, Dad's quiet and he doesn't touch me. He's working steadily now and has sobered up again. He works from 3:00 to 11:00, so we don't see each other much. I do my best to steer clear of him.

Mom usually returns from work at 5:30 and she's exhausted. Four or five times a week, she'll come home and announce, "It's not worth it to cook for the two of us. We should go out and eat."

I wonder how we can, since money always seems to be a problem. Maybe since Dad is paying the bills, now that he's working again, she's free to use her pay. I've noticed there's always cash in an envelope tucked in her pocketbook. Either way, she treats me well. I feel special, and we're having such fun times together. We have so much to talk about. I've never felt so wanted.

"I'm so proud of you for having the baby," she whispers, her voice as soft as her touch, as she tenderly wraps her arms around me.

A tear hangs on the end of my lash, I've always longed for affectionate words. They feel so good. She's proud of me.

"Alice, I don't know how you're doing it with Joanie being pregnant," people tell her.

Not missing a beat, she unapologetically counters, "She's my kid! I'm not putting her out. I'm so proud she's giving life to that baby, and not having an abortion."

There are all those positive vibes. She's so supportive. I feel more love from her than I'd ever felt before.

But when I talk about keeping the baby, Mom's demeanor changes. She sits up straight and snaps, "Absolutely not. It will ruin your life." Her chin quivers. She's sad but firm, taking my chin in her hand with steely eyes. "You wouldn't be able to finish school. We've been over this. You won't be able to stay here. We can't keep you and the baby. You would have to move out."

That really sucks. I'm fifteen. Where would I go?

I drop my head and hold my stomach. "I would love you more, little one."

There seems to be loads of money. Bills are getting paid, we're eating out, and I have friends—not from school, though, since I haven't been going. Between Mary Ellen and her friends, there are ten of us. They're my "party pals." We hang out at Mary Ellen's pool and at her parents' clubhouse. We've been having a grand time. They drink beer, but they won't let me drink since it isn't good for the baby. They take such good care of me, and even hold a shower for the baby.

They give me a gift: a fourteen-karat gold heart necklace with an inscription on the back that reads "From Your Party Pals." We huddle in a circle on the carpet and have a big group hug, drenched in joyful tears as they excitedly relay the story. Evidently, when they'd first picked it up, the jeweler had made an error and inscribed it with "From Your Party Pack."

"We're not a pack of wolves!" Susan had told him. "We're pals!"

I admire that boldness in Susan and try to emulate it. She's a strong woman and stands up for herself. She stands up for me, too.

These friends are like family. At Halloween, they call me to come over quickly. They've made me a costume, drawing lines down an orange shirt to make it look like a pumpkin. I'm pretty far along, and perfectly round as we trick or treat from home to home.

While home, I've learned how to knit. I'm knitting a baby blanket with colorful yarn—yellow, blue, and pink. Aunt Ninna would be so pleased. It's just a straight stitch, but I'm proud of my accomplishment. When I'm done, I'll take it to someone who can crochet a scalloped edge around it.

My psychiatrist, Dr. Santucci, says that if I want to, I might like to give something to the baby. I want to give him (or her) something beautiful, something I've made, so he knows I love him.

Dr. Santucci is young for a doctor. She's pretty, about twice my age, with thin lips and a big smile. She's pregnant, too, but I'm due before her.

When I found out I was pregnant, I was overwhelmed and depressed. I hadn't been able to get up out of bed and so I'd ended up at Mercy Hospital for a while. I got special privileges there for being good, so I was allowed to wander the halls alone and even was able to go home one weekend. When I returned to the hospital afterward, I had snuck a razor blade in the insole of my shoe. It's comforting to have one with me.

One morning at the psych hospital, I snuck down the hall and slipped into the chapel. There, before God, Jesus, and the Holy Ghost, I cried out, slashed my wrists, and fell on the altar, blood pooling.

After that, I had to see Dr. Santucci every day.

I've discovered that Dr. Santucci is going to find the baby a home after it's born. I'm defiant, though; it's not going to be placed by Catholic Charities. Still, I trust her to find my baby a good home. She's a shining light that warms my soul in this bleak world.

One day, Mom takes me to a lawyer's office to make sure everything's being handled right. While Mom steps outside the door to smoke, the lawyer leans in and asks me directly who the father is. This is the first time anyone has asked.

"I can't tell you," I say, squirming in my seat.

Leaning further, his knuckles turning white as he grips his desk, his nostrils flare. He keeps asking, again and again. My face warms and tears well up in my blinking eyes as I draw deep into the chair.

I can't. I just can't.

Frustrated, the lawyer stands up and pushes his chair back. The chair screeches along the hardwood floor before smashing against the window ledge behind him. His commanding stature carries him to the door with brisk, heavy steps. He then beckons my mother back in.

Turning, my mother exhales the last drag from her cigarette and delicately perches on the chair off to the right side of the office.

He returns, his eyes fixed on me. Feeling so small and alone, I feel lost in the large leather chair across from him, my crossed feet swinging, unable to touch the floor.

"I don't think Joanie knows how important it is for her to put the father's name on the contract," the lawyer says when my mom joins us. "If we don't have it… well, down the road, the father could give trouble to the adoptive parents because he hasn't relinquished his rights."

My mother cocks a brow. "What do you want from me?" she asks, shrugging her shoulders.

"Joanie won't tell me who the father is."

"Ah," she says, nodding. "She's not saying she won't tell you. She's saying she *can't* tell you, because she doesn't know who it is. There were too many men for her to know."

My mouth drops open. I had slept with too many people to know who the father was? Where has she gotten that from? I haven't said I slept with anyone! I feel like I'm always playing catchup in my head.

There are foggy times. So many foggy times. Maybe I did sleep with too many men…

CHAPTER FIVE
BRIAN

You made all the delicate, inner parts of my body and knit them together in my mother's womb. Thank you for making me so wonderfully complex! It is amazing to think about. Your workmanship is marvelous—and how well I know it.
(Psalm 139:13–14, TLB)

NOW THAT I'VE BEEN DISCHARGED, I SEE DR. SANTUCCI EVERY WEEK AND SHE'S GOING to be there when I have the baby. She promised. I'm not going to go through natural childbirth; I'm going to get a shot. I'll feel nothing. It'll be all good, she has assured me.

Suddenly, it's hard to breathe. I pull my shirt over my pounding head. Every glint of light blinds me as I buckle over, grasping my right abdomen.

I'm rushed to the hospital, and the graphic expressions on the faces of the doctors and nurses who meet me at the door foster a sense of urgency. My blood pressure is sky high. I have toxemia, preeclampsia. Their raucous voices bark orders. The constant movement of the nurses looks chaotic, but it's rhythmic and organized.

I'm wheeled into a room with Mom. Dad is nowhere to be found. Like a metronome, the monitor beeps regularly; the cool plastic of the oxygen mask hugs my face, and with a prick in my arm I'm connected to the IV bag hanging on the post beside the bed. I'm being induced.

The bright lights enhance the starkness of the room. The door slides open; like waves, the low tones of voices outside wash in between the crashing calls over the intercom. The constant sway of the ER characters is nauseating—the doctors' white coats, the police uniforms blue as the ocean, the white caps of the nurses sail by like boats—until my heavy eyes finally close.

When the contractions spike, the doors open again and the room fills with people. The baby is not coming. There's a problem. The doctors are talking. My blood pressure is too high.

I hear one ominous word: "Caesarian."

Through the contraction, I sit up. "No, not until Dr. Santucci comes…" The pain is unbearable. "I talked to her before I left… she's at a meeting… she's on her way… she said she would be here… she promised… you need to wait…"

Another contraction. Exhausted, I lay back.

Breathe, breathe.

"We need to put her under," someone says. Everyone is buzzing around me. "We need to do this now. There are risks to the mother… and the child. We could lose them both if we don't act now!"

"Dr. Santucci…" I say, defiant. "Dr. Santucci, I need her. She said she's coming. She will be here soon. You have to wait." The words slur under my breath.

"Joanie, we need to start now," someone says.

Everyone is trying to convince me: the doctor, the anesthesiologist, the nurse. My mother is in the corner, and the color has drained from her face. She clutches her shaking hands, unable to move.

Desperate, I try to lift my shoulders and remove the mask as firm hands hold me down.

Then, like my white knight, she arrives. Dr. Santucci bursts into the room. "I'm here, Joanie. I'm here."

Immediately every muscle relaxes. Dr. Santucci is here. All will be well. I feel my weight against the operating table… my back, my arms, my shoulders, my head… I can feel the chill of the metal stirrups against my legs.

"You can do it now," I say, succumbing. The mask is placed on my face as I quietly relent.

Dr. Santucci is at my side. She slips my hand in hers and brushes the hair from my face. I feel safe. I hear nothing but her soft voice encouraging me: "You've got this, Joanie. I'm here with you. I'll be here when you wake up."

No longer can I open my heavy eyes. I want to see her face. I take a deep breath. I fade.

• • •

"Joanie… Joanie… can you hear me?" a voice breaks through the fog.

I pull up my eyebrows in a futile attempt to open my eyes, it feels like they've been glued shut. I try again unsuccessfully.

"Joanie… Joanie, you did great."

Finally my eyes open. It's Dr. Santucci. The sun shines in through the window, bathing her face with light. She's glowing. I'm in recovery and she's there with me, just like she said she'd be.

"Once you wake up a bit more, they will move you to a private room," she says, taking my hand. "You don't have to be with the other moms. You can have your friends and family visit you in private. It will be easier for you that way."

As soon as I've recovered, I'm moved to a private room. No one is with me now. I'm alone.

A woman wearing a smart suit enters the room. She looks important… official. She informs me that I'll have to sign the adoption papers seventy-two hours following the birth. There's no reason to wait, though, so I ask for them now. I want to sign them and get it over with. But I can't. Evidently I need to wait and make sure I really want to give the baby up.

I'm underage, though, and like my father said, the decision has been made for me. I don't understand why I need to wait, but I do. She will return in a few days with the papers.

A nurse enters and reads from my chart. "He wasn't a term baby, so he's tiny. He's only a little over four pounds and not fully developed." She looks for a reaction, but I have none. "He has blue baby syndrome. The doctors thought they may have to transport him to a special neonatal hospital. He's been put in an isolette to help him breath and he seems to be doing well." She peers over her glasses. "Would you like to see him?"

"No, I don't think so," I reply dryly.

Where's my family? Where's Dr. Santucci? I feel the rush of my heartbeat in my ears. I'm having trouble breathing and begin wringing my clammy hands. I can't make these decisions myself.

Biting her lower lip, the nurse nods and leaves.

I have lots of visitors, and lots of presents, too! So much powder, the kind with puffs. I enjoy dabbing my body with it. There are also journals, plants… so many gifts.

An elderly bald man saunters in, wire glasses perched on the tip of his nose. He's the jeweler from Wheaton I'd seen a few weeks back. He brings with him a beautiful jewelry case with a card. His voice is a bit gravelly and the sparkle in his eye tells me he's so proud of me. His smile could melt steel.

I stretch out my arms and we embrace before he leaves. He's a kind man. I'm so grateful.

My party pals visit every day. Mom's friends stop by, too. She has a lot of friends. People love my mom. She's effervescent, outgoing, and amicable. Everybody in Glen Ellyn knows her, and she'll talk to anyone on the street. When she shops, I wait for what seems like hours while she chats away. Why, I could go into any store and say, "Put that on Alice's charge," and they'd know who that was and do it for me. Her name and word is good everywhere. She's a good person.

• • •

I hear rumbling and squeaky wheels coming down the hall. A tiny nurse comes into the room pushing a glass box on a cart accompanied by a young man in a suit.

"Here's your little boy," the nurse sings cheerily. "Would you like to hold him?"

"No. No, I don't think so." I bite my lip and strain to look over. What should I do?

Leaving the baby in the corner of the room, the nurse approaches and taps my hand. "We want to make sure you have all the time you need," she reassures me. "I can just leave him here with you for a while, just in case you decide you want to come take a look at him. He's a beautiful baby. You may want to hold him for a bit before he goes to his adoptive parents." She pauses and gestures toward the baby. "You only have a little while with him. You may want to hold him."

The man in the suit swallows hard as he blinks to hold back tears. He turns to blow his nose. I have no idea who he is, but I love that he cares.

The nurse returns to the baby. "This will be your last chance to see him… to hold him." Slowly she moves the cart over to me. She picks up the bundle and holds him on her chest. With his face next to hers, she quietly coos.

"Yes," I finally admit. "Yes, I think I'd like to hold him."

I sit up straight, my heart beating so hard. I really do want to see him, to hold my little baby Brian. A tear rolls down my cheek as I extend my hands. How did she know?

She places him in my arms. He's so light, so little. As the sun sets outside, tranquil red sunlight streams into the room, and the soft hairs of his head shimmer in the reflection. What's this rush of warmth melting my heart and radiating through my body to my fingertips and toes? I close my eyes and kiss his head. My heartbeat slows. I feel a strange contentment, a connection… a presence.

The baby stirs. I open my eyes, but I can't even focus on his face, only the plethora of tubes attached to him. I hadn't noticed them before. I shut my eyes tight, turn my head away, and with trembling hands desperately hand him back to the waiting nurse.

"Wait, I have something for him," I plead. "They told me I could give him something, so he knows I love him. It's right here, beside my bed."

I slowly roll off the bed, pain shooting from my belly, and open up the suitcase sitting on the dresser. The latches snap and I glance over my shoulder to make sure they haven't left. Good, they're still there… waiting patiently.

With a quick sigh, I open the lid. My hand glides over the contents: the handmade blanket, and the poem I wrote entitled "This Child of Mine," handwritten on a piece of carefully folded parchment paper. And then there's a gold jewelry gift box. I carefully remove it. The box creaks a bit, then snaps open. I guardedly remove the contents, holding the tiny bracelet in my fingers. It's so small. A tear rolls down my cheek as my finger skims the engraved name: "Brian Michael." I gently flip it over, and a tear lands on the latch as I read the inscription on the back: "Love Mom… November 16, 1975."

It's perfect.

I had wanted to give my baby a bracelet with its name and birthdate, but I hadn't known if it would be a boy or a girl, or even when it would be born. Heavy-hearted, I'd gone to a jewelry shop in Wheaton and explained my situation to the elderly shop owner, telling him I would name her Jamie Lyn if she was a girl, and Brian Michael if he was a boy.

His eyes had been so kind and gentle as he'd held my hand and told me not to worry. But I had worried.

Slowly I place the items in the nurse's arms. She turns to put them in Brian's cart, and I grab her elbow.

"Please make sure these go with him," I plead. "I don't want him to think his mom doesn't love him. I love him so much."

Tears stream down my face and I'm shaking uncontrollably. She nods and places them in the compartment under Brian's isolette, then turns and walks out of the room with the man in the suit.

I will not see Brian again.

CHAPTER SIX
STARTING OVER

And now, our God, the great and mighty and awesome God, who keeps his covenant of unfailing love, do not let all the hardships we have suffered seem insignificant to you.
(Nehemiah 9:32)

I AM SO TIRED… ALWAYS TIRED. I COULD SLEEP ALL DAY, AGAIN. I TRY LIFTING MY ARM, but it doesn't move. I know I need to get up and go to work. Really, I do.

I haven't made it to school this term at all. Catholic school is not the best place to be if you're pregnant. My party pals have been great, but the kids from school haven't exactly been supportive.

I roll over, my face smushing into the pillow. Maybe I'll go next term.

I'm sad about Brian and wonder if I made the right decision about giving him up. I guess I did… though it wasn't really my decision, was it? My whole day is spent wondering where he is and how he's doing.

The numbers on my clock radio flip over, and I sigh. I trust Dr. Santucci. She'll have found good parents for him, but he was so small and there were all these tubes in him. I quiver as I hold back the tears. The doctors said he was getting better and would be fine. Fine. What does that mean? It's my fault he was born early. I must have done something wrong.

I blind my raw eyelids and a tear escapes, trickling down my cheek and dropping onto the pillow. I'll just stay in bed today. It's winter, after all. Nobody really needs ice cream today anyway.

Wiping my nose on my sheet, I roll over. My feet drop off the edge of the bed.

I sit on the floor and flip through my newest albums scattered across the plush purple carpet. One is the Bee Gees' *How Can I Mend a Broken Heart*. Yup, my heart is broken.

I keep looking, and then I find it: Roberta Flack. I pull the album from the sleeve, blow on it, then lay it on the record player, lift the arm, and carefully guide it to the first track. Fighting back the onslaught of tears, I flop back into bed as she starts singing "The First Time Ever I Saw Your Face." I fall asleep somewhere during "Bridge Over Troubled Water" and sleep through the day.

Thump… thump… thump.

The bedroom door shakes with the force of each knock.

"Joanie, git up you lazy bum!" It's dad. "How'd you 'spect ta keep a job sleep'n all day?" He slurs as his body slides down the wall and crashes to the floor. "Git up, you good fir nothin' piece-a…"

I hear a quiet hush broken only by deep, steady vibrations of air. His heavy breathing. He must have passed out again. I take in a deep breath and hold onto it as I raise myself up to my elbows and force my body to roll over. That's all I can do today. I'm spent.

• • •

Things have turned ugly. Dad's not working consistently, and he's drinking again. He thumps and crashes as he teeters down the hall, day and night. His grumbles a lot, a broken record about me spending all my time locked in my room. And if I've successfully gotten up, he complains about me being out with my friends and not letting them know I won't be home.

His verbal barbs sting; with narrow, crinkled eyes, one heavy brow slants in wanton, abusive disapproval. His fingers curl into a ball tightly beside him. I swear he wants to hit me all the time. But I'm not a little girl anymore, and I'm not going to stand for it. Like a phoenix rising from the ashes, I hold my ground and fight back. The fighting is constant, but I don't remember everything behind the fog, like the burns on my body. Sometimes I remember, sometimes I don't. All I really know is the fighting.

My father snarls as he explodes from the kitchen chair. His massive fist swings at me, and the punch lands hard in my ribs. The pain is excruciating as I'm propelled to the ground, my lungs hissing for air. His fiery eyes are laser-focused as he lunges at me again. Visions surface of the fight we had when I told him I was pregnant.

I can't do this anymore.

More nimble now that I'm not pregnant, I roll out of the way and let him smash to the floor. Too drunk to get up, his limp body lays sprawled on the linoleum.

Breathless, I run up to my bedroom. The wall shakes as I slam the door behind me and latch it. My back to the door, I slide down to the floor. I can't believe my parents wouldn't take both of us. I gave up my baby, and now I'll have to leave home anyway. What did I give him up for? My heart aches. I wish I would have kept him. Things would have been so different. I would have been a great mom.

Anger shudders through me, but I can't dwell on that right now. Getting up, I stuff some clothes in a backpack.

Each step creaks as I tiptoe down the stairs. He's still there, passed out in the kitchen. I turn to leave and sneak out the back door, making sure it closes quietly behind me.

I can't stay.

I wind up at Jim's front door, an older guy I met somewhere. The door opens slightly and his gaze cruises over my figure. I cock my head and smile sweetly. He steps back, letting me in. My smile opens doors.

I won't be going back to school. I'm a sinner, after all. Damaged goods. There are rules, though, while I'm living at Jim's house. I need to find a better job. My hours at the Seven Dwarfs just won't cut it. I need more money. A nearby restaurant is looking for a waitress, and I start working there. The money is good, but things don't working out between Jim and me. It's only been a couple of months, and I need to leave again. Men aren't reliable.

Evidently, there's a law that says you need to be eighteen to rent an apartment on your own, and you need to be eighteen to get your GED in order to get a better job. It's a Catch-22 and I have a problem: I'm only sixteen.

Sitting at a table in the restaurant, flipping through the *Chicago Tribune* want ads, I find a cute little one-room apartment. It sounds perfect. I go see the owner and try to cut a deal. I can be persuasive when I want to be. I put on some make-up and do whatever I can to look older, dabbing a little extra plum shadow under my eye.

"It was dangerous, and I had to leave quickly," I explain to the property manager. I stand a few feet away, wearing sunglasses, keeping my head down. "I have no identification, but I assure you my birthdate is June 21, 1958."

His brows knit in a frown as he peers over his glasses, inspecting me. Licking his finger, he turns a page, documents it, and asks if I have the deposit. I do.

I'm in! Clearly, he never checks any further.

Next on my to-do list: get my GED. Chin up, shoulders back, I submit the paperwork and admire the clerk's earrings; they really are lovely. She asks for ID. I have none, but I show her a lease agreement with my birth date on it. That will do. I'm able to complete my GED.

Next, I get my driver's license. They ask for proof of my birth date. Full of confidence, I explain my situation and say that I have no identification... but I do have a lease agreement and a GED with my birth date on it. They accept it. Just like that, I'm eighteen!

Now to look for a better job.

With a new home and a new job, I feel like I should be happy, but I'm not. There's a hollow emptiness inside me, a void. I miss my family. Men are a distraction, a guilty pleasure that helps fill the void; after all, we're animals and like all animals we have a need for love that must be satisfied, right? For a brief moment, a man can satisfy me, but it's unsustainable and I'm still unable to feel anything. So I burn and cut to help me feel something, to know I'm alive.

Today I'm bereft… hollow. I grab a knife and slowly draw the sharp metal edge over my pale skin and watch the blood slowly bead, then flow and escape as the skin breaks. The pain allows me to feel human… to feel alive… to just feel.

Six months later, I've moved in with a new guy in Oakbrook and it's great. He's got money and is covering my cost of living, so I only need to earn spending money. I've changed jobs again, making $4.75 an hour doing the books for a candle company at the mall. Having to go to the mall every day makes it convenient to shop, and I love to shop.

Our store is next to a maternity shop, and there's a toy store across the hall. A little baby tam hat catches my eye. My breath fogs up the glass as I stand outside, my fingers tracing some of the clothes and toys in the window.

My mind wanders to Brian and what might have been. My cheeks warm, the corner of my mouth lifts, a tear starts down my cheek, and my heart skips a beat. I draw a long, deep breath and shake my head as I move on, trying my best to forget.

Men help me forget. There are a lot of men, and over the years the thought of Brian becomes a faded memory.

Two years later, I see a job listing for a plastics manufacturer in Chicago. They make polyethylene plastic folders. It's entry-level work, nothing like the work I've done before, but it's a great job and I'm determined to get it. My interview is with the general manager, Richard Gibson, who sports a full head of wavy brown hair and a dimple in his cheek. He smiles a lot but never shows his teeth, and there's a joyful glint in his eyes. I like him right away. He calls me a real crackerjack. I manage to convince him that I'm qualified and start working on the production floor. For the first time in a long time, I feel safe and happy. The fog has lifted.

About a year into the job, there's an internal listing for an IBM 360 operator. I have no clue what that entails, except it will get me off the floor and into the office. I can be exceptional and relentless when it comes to research, so I read all the information I can get my hands on about the IBM 360 and apply for the job. I've never as much as stood next to an IBM, but I can be convincing. The interviewers believe the lie and I land the job as a data inputter/computer operator.

But now I'm in a pickle, since I don't know what to do. I explain to the manager that I'll need to shadow the outgoing inputter for a week, "just to get to know the finer details of this particular machine." The computer is extraordinary. It's huge, three feet deep by four feet wide and taller than me. I'm a bit overwhelmed. Amazingly, one week is enough time to learn the job, and now I have the responsibility to process the end-of-the-day accounts for both payroll and production.

My office is just down the hall from Dick Gibson's, so I pop my head in and say hello whenever I walk by. I'm always busy running around, since I have an endless supply of energy. Dick will soon be marrying his girlfriend Marj. It's kind of strange to me that they're getting married so old, but it's their second time around and they suit each other well. She's so sweet. I just love when she comes to the office to bring him lunch. Their kindness extends beyond work, too. They often have me over for dinner, and she's a great cook.

Dick's always full of advice, good people's advice, the kind that doesn't seem to apply to people like me, the kind I learned about in Catholic school. He often reminds me that my relationship with guys isn't healthy. I guess it's obvious since they just don't seem to last.

My relationship with my family hasn't fared much better. It just seems like it's too easy for them to let go, so I let go, too. We talk on the phone some, but that's about it.

But my friendship with Dick and Marj is different. Somehow I'm drawn to them. They're different from anyone else I've ever met. Brightness shines from them. I hope our friendship lasts, not many of my relationships have.

CHAPTER SEVEN
BEST FRIENDS

A true friend is always loyal…
(Proverbs 17:17, TLB)

TO CELEBRATE THIS NEW JOB, AS WELL AS MY BIRTHDAY, I'VE DECIDED TO BUY A DOG. There's a lot of research involved in buying the right dog, so I scurry off to the library where I'll spend all my spare time until I find the perfect dog for me. I love books.

Standing at the doorway, my closed eyes flutter. My chest rises, filling my lungs with the musty, paper-scented air. My feet are itching to run, but I force myself to hang onto that breath and reminisce about the characters in all the books I've read. The smell of the library calms me; it's old, it's wise, and I'm in awe of the power of the word. Books take me away to a different place. I can go anywhere I desire for as long as it takes me to finish a book.

My neck cracks as I roll my head and march forward. Today, it's research!

As I stroll over to the card catalogue under the staircase, approaching a huge wall of tiny wooden boxes adorned with little brass knobs and brass label holders, the beat of my heart crescendos, anticipation rising. Inside these tiny draws are slivers of paper identifying the topics contained in each: animals, pets, dogs, etc. The card catalogue will lead me to my new best friend.

I scroll through the labels until I find the section I'm looking for and slide open the drawer. I feel the dryness of the paper as I thumb through each card. There it is: dogs. A good place to start.

In search of a friendly, outgoing dog to match my own disposition, I amass a stockpile of volumes and dump them onto one of the long wooden tables. I pull up the wooden chair, adjust my headset, and switch on my walkman. As the music starts, I get underway scouring the books, singing along in a quiet whisper, feeling stronger, more energetic with every note.

Flipping the page, I titter at a picture of a white German shepherd. I think back to my old school days, recalling a picture of a polar bear that kind of resembled it. I love polar bears, not that I've ever seen one in real life. But I'm sure I would love one if I were to see one.

Intrigued, I read on.

Evidently, white shepherds are dedicated and loyal. My eyebrow arches. I like that.

Their white coats pose no further health risks. Good to know. I have a good job, but I don't have a lot of spare money for medical issues.

So they're not albino. Who knew? I had thought they were albino.

Excellent. They don't shed too much. I'm not a clean freak, but I don't want to clean more than I have to.

They're more sensitive and not as aggressive as other shepherds. Bonus. I want a family one day, and it will be good to have an even-keeled dog. My eyes are glued to the page.

When an intruder comes, they don't attack; they merely alert their owners of company. I nod, contemplating my present living situation. It'll be good to know when someone's coming.

Oh, I love this song. Bopping my head, I start to sing again. As the drums and electric guitar intensify, I too become amplified.

These dogs may be shy if not socialized. My whole face lights up as I assuredly tap my finger over that line. Like my mom, I'm social. This dog will definitely be socialized!

These animals need a lot of space and exercise to remain happy. I straighten up in my chair. I want a happy dog, so we will exercise!

They are boisterous barkers. Why of course! I toss my head. How else will they let me know somebody's coming?

I read on… self-confident, ready to serve, protective, intelligent… loyal. My eye twitches as I swallow. More than anything, I need loyalty in my life.

Sold! I love this dog already. Slamming the book closed, I rise from my chair in search of phone numbers for local kennels. I find a phone book by the public payphone outside the library and jot down some numbers. A good day's work is done!

I find myself singing to myself again as I return to the table, but now I'm singing kind of loudly and I'm dancing around. I just can't slow down.

The librarian's coming, so it's time to get up and go! Grabbing my bag, I scurry away, leaving all the books behind. I apologize as I bump into chairs and people on my way out, full of energy.

• • •

On Saturday morning, I snatch the list of kennels from the kitchen counter and dance my way to the car. I have several kennels to visit today, but only two have white German shepherds available. This dog will be my companion for a long time, and I don't want to make the decision lightly. It'll have to be a good fit right off the bat.

My body has a hard time keeping up to my feet as I approach the kennel. Between the barks and howls, one tiny yelp seems to stand out. Could it be? Oh, that's crazy, what are the chances? The door creaks as I pull it open, my restless leg shaking as I nibble my lip and crane my neck to peer through the tiny window in the inner door.

"Hello, you must be Joanie," says a strapping young man in loose faded jeans, a stained T-shirt, and rubber boots. His milk chocolate eyes assess me. "I believe we spoke on the phone."

"Yes, we did." My voice cracks. "I'm looking for a white German shepherd. I believe you said you have a new litter, and there's one or two left to choose from."

"Oh, white shepherds are fantastic animals." His face brightens. "This particular mom and dad are especially well-tempered. Follow me…" He nods as he opens the inner door. "We'll go take a look."

As we stride through the heavy doorway into the kennel, his voice lowers.

"These puppies are only two weeks old," he says, "so it will be a bit yet 'til they can leave their mother."

"I don't mind waiting." The words fly out of my mouth as he opens the gate. I quickly add, "If it's the right fit."

I crack my famous smile as I push through the gate ahead of him, very excited to see what he has available.

Lying on the ground is a beautiful white shepherd mom surrounded by five darling little balls of snow-white fur. Lowering himself to one knee, the young man tenderly scoops one pup up in his hand, stroking its head with his thumb.

He presents the puppy to me. "Would you like to hold him?"

My cheeks turn pink. I reach out, my fingers gathering the puppy into my arms. He's so small and furry. I hold him up to my face and he licks me all over my cheeks, nose, and lips. I giggle with delight. Never in my life have I felt this much love and joy.

Raising my arms straight up in the air, I hold the puppy high. The sun's rays shine into the darkness through a nearby window, blanketing the puppy in bright light, almost divinely illuminating the sheen of its white coat. Weird. I don't even know that I believe in the divine, but I'm transfixed. I spin around and around, drawing him close to my heart, spinning faster and faster until we fall to the ground, cushioned by the hay. The puppy's heart beats close to mine and a rush of warmth washes over me. Breaking free, the pressure of his little paws tickles as he licks the scars on my hands, arms, back, and legs. Then he quietly nuzzles back into my arms to lick my face. He'll light up my whole life, I know it.

"He seems to have taken a liking to you," the young man observes.

"Yes, yes!" I giggle. "Tell me he's available."

"Yup, he is." He grins as he helps me up and returns the puppy. "Shall we get down to business?"

He closes the gate behind him and we head toward the office door. I follow close behind him, moon-eyed. I'm in love.

"I've done my research," I assure him, brushing the straw from my jeans. I confidently square my shoulders. "I'm ready to negotiate."

With a bit of haggling we agree on $400. It's a good price. I've been saving for a while, so I can make it work. I'll name him Azia, after Asia, one of my favorite bands. It just fits.

When he's six weeks old, I'm able to take Azia home and start training him. I want a well-mannered dog who will also look out for me. Azia quickly becomes more than that, my constant companion. He's my best friend.

I've moved on from man seven, eight, and nine… it's now just Azia and me, and life is good. Azia is naturally well-disposed, just like his parents, and so easy to train. Before long he's following my commands: verbal, hand gestures, and finger snaps. His intelligence amazes everyone. If I place a biscuit on his nose, he sits motionless until I signal him; then he snaps his nose, flicking the biscuit into the air, and as swiftly as a lizard his long tongue nips the biscuit into his mouth. His chops then stretch into a broad smile. He tilts his head and cocks a brow, probing for another treat. I wrap my arms around his neck and run my fingers through his thick mane. I could watch him do that trick all day, but I'm conscious of his diet. I won't spoil him.

Azia sits at the door while I get ready to go to work. He's eager to go out and play but knows he'll have to wait until I get home for that. I look at him, amazed. He seems to know when it's time to go for a walk and when I have to go to work. He'll sit on that rug by the door and not move until I'm ready to go. He's so in sync with me. I tousle his head, looking over my shoulder as I leave.

"Stay. I'll be home soon, good boy."

He behaves so well that I decide it's time to take him for a walk in town. We've been practicing near home and he walks right beside me, never wavering. I want to see how well he does without a leash, so I bend down, unclip the leash, and stare him in the eyes as I stand back.

"Heel," I command, holding out the palm of my hand.

He stays.

I take a few steps away, my eyes laser-focused on him.

He doesn't move.

I turn my back to him, walk some more, and toss my head over my shoulder.

He's still sitting there, right where I left him, with a smile stretched from ear to ear. He hasn't budged.

I turn away and watch his reflection in a nearby window. He's just waiting for a signal.

I click my fingers. He gets up, strides toward me, and stops right at my side. He sits again. What a smart dog!

I kneel at his side and rub his ears. "Good boy, good boy," I say, acknowledging his effort. I wrap my arms around his neck and bury my face in his fur.

Azia's awesome, and unlike the people in my life, he's loving and non-judgmental, even on my bad days.

One day I lie on the bathroom floor and blow the cigarette that's glowing between my fingers. Azia whimpers quietly as he nuzzles under my arm. I feel his warm chin against my leg. His sad eyes gaze up, reassuring me that he'll always be with me, no matter what. He never abandons me, and I will never abandon him.

There are times when I just can't find a puppy sitter. I won't leave Azia at home alone, so I bring him to work with me.

"Dick, I need your help," I whisper one day as I peer into his office.

"Sure, Joanie. What can I do for you?"

"I need you to take Azia for a bit and keep him in your office." I've got the biggest open-any-door smile on my face, and so does Azia.

Dick takes a deep breath, then shakes his head and lowers his chin. My smile doesn't diminish; my puppy dog eyes rival Azia's.

"Joanie, I'll take him while I'm in the office, but you'll have to find another place for him when I'm out on the floor. This has to be the last time."

"Thank you, thank you. You're the best! I'll take him 'round back during my lunch." I'm jumping for joy. "You, be a good boy for Uncle Dick."

I give Azia a big hug and scurry off to work. Dick's the best. I've always been able to count on him. He's a solid, stand-up kind of guy.

"Dick, I need your help," I say another day, pleading in a brittle voice. I know I'm about to ask too much. "You need to do me a favor."

Dick raises his head, beckoning me into his office with his quick smile. "Sure, Joanie, what's up? Where's Azia?"

"He's not here today. But I'm desperate to leave now. Can you punch my time card for me at the end of the day? You know I wouldn't ask if it wasn't an emergency. I'll work off the time later."

I grab his hand, imploring for him to agree.

His face drops. "Joanie, that's not right. I can't do that for you. Proverbs 10:9 says, 'Whoever walks in integrity walks securely, but whoever takes crooked paths will be found out.' It's important to have integrity. Why don't you just explain to John why you need the time? He runs the place. He's the one to ask."

"I can't, I just can't." My voice trembles. "I thought I could count on you!"

The icy daggers in my eyes holding back tears, I storm out and return to my office. As I sit at my desk, flipping my time card in my hand, I concoct a plan: since I'm the one who does payroll and I'm the only one who really looks at the time cards, it's not a stretch. I carefully doctor my time card and leave. No one will ever find out. I'm sure of it.

The following day, John and Dick visit my office.

I am let go.

• • •

The room is dimly lit and the soft light of the sconces reflect in the dark mirrors. Overhead, timber beams are anchored by the rich dark wooden walls around me. The sweet burning fragrance of pipe tobacco wafts in the air, mingling with my bourbon's strong oaky notes of vanilla and caramel, a gift from the man at the bar.

With a tender bite of my lip and raised eyebrow, the man in front of me descends the bar stool and approaches, placing a key on the round table next to my comfy wicker chair. Message conveyed and received.

The red pump slips off my foot and I gently caress his calf. He reaches over and his thumb runs along my cheek… his fingers cradle my chin. I shoot back the last of my bourbon, place my hand in his outstretched hand, and follow him to his room.

Any recollection of these events fade with the blue haze of smoke.

My eyes flutter open and I find myself cowered in the corner of a large spa tub. I tremble as a bar of soap falls into the tub; it's wrapped in the exclusive hotel's proprietary packaging. I hear heavy breathing coming from the outer room—a slow, regular, snore.

The phone in the bathroom vanity catches my wandering eye. I quietly exit the tub and make a call.

"Stephen, help me."

CHAPTER EIGHT
AN INSIGNIFICANT FAULT

When you're in over your head, I'll be there with you. When you're in rough waters, you will not go down. When you're between a rock and a hard place, it won't be a dead end —because I am God, your personal God…
(Isaiah 43:2, MSG)

IT'S CHRISTMAS, THE MOST WONDERFUL TIME OF THE YEAR! I'M DRIVING TO STEPHEN'S house, and then we're heading to Wisconsin to see his parents. It will be so nice to spend Christmas with a family, even if it's not my own.

With a glint in my eye, I think back and remember that magical Christmas as a kid when the gifts showed up outside our house. That was before the cutting, the burning… before Brian… before having to leave my family. It was a lifetime ago.

I shudder and take a deep breath. Stephen is wonderful. This is a new start.

I met Stephen after work one day, sitting beside me at the bar. My mind was racing uncontrollably and I needed something to slow me down a bit. A glass of wine usually helps, but sometimes I need something a bit stronger.

Even seated, Stephen's blonde mop towered over me. His distracting smile turned my head and he spoke with a deep modulated tone, soothing but no match for my compulsive rhetoric. His spirited silver eyes seemed full of wit and banter. I liked him right away.

I grabbed his sleeve, bounced off the stool, and asked him to take me home. His eyes widened. He stumbled back and stammered; he's the kind of guy who always tries to do the right thing, but he did take me home and has taken care of me ever since.

On December 21, 1983, I look over in the back seat and find Azia there. "Lie down, boy," I said. "We've got to go pick up Stephen. It's not that far, but you'd better settle in. It's going to be a long day today."

It's a short drive to Downers Grove, and we'll be taking the trip in my 1981 Dodge Omni. I bought the car brand new with sixteen percent interest. I didn't really understand what that interest rate meant at the time; I just knew I loved that navy blue car, and the sense of independence it would give me. I figured I could afford the monthly payments of $170.61. I hadn't thought about the added cost of gas and insurance, so I had to do without a few things, like fresh vegetables. But really, who eats vegetables anyway?

I'm listening to the radio as we pull up. Stephen's still inside, so like a maniac I honk the horn like crazy to the beat of the music.

"Hey Stephen, bring your stuff down," I yell through the open window. "We need to get a move on."

The car rocks, keeping time to my dance moves from behind the wheel.

Stephen gallops down the stairs with one small suitcase. His eyes close, his lips purse, and he shakes his head. "You do know we're only going for six days, right? How do you even have this much stuff?"

I smile and crack my neck as Stephen sighs, rearranging everything in the car to make room for his little bag.

"I can't believe all the stuff that's able to fit in this car," he says, wiping his brow and shutting the hatch. "It's jam packed."

I grin, climbing over the stick shift and plopping into the passenger seat. "Well, we'll have to find room for a little bit more. We're making a quick stop at the mall on our way out. I just want to pick up a few more things for your mom." I giggle, settling in. "She's so nice to let me spend Christmas with you guys. They've just moved, so I'm sure she'd rather not have extra guests right now."

Stephen smiles as he puts the car in gear. "You know, it's not necessary. She loves having you around. Mom absolutely adores you."

"I know, of course she does. Who wouldn't?" I bounce to the music. "But let's stop anyway. I'm so excited to have a family Christmas this year… I want to get something for your dad, too… I should bring something for dinner… Does your mom still have time to read? I could bring her a book. I have a good one at home. I should have brought it… Oh, did I bring Azia's leash? He doesn't need it, but we'll be in new surroundings. I want to be sure he doesn't run off… I forgot to shut off my water. Do you think I should have shut it off?"

Stephen's family has all but adopted me. His mom is the closest thing I've had to a mother since I left home nine years ago. My eyebrows lift at that thought. Somehow it doesn't seem like that long, yet it's also a lifetime ago.

A smile warms my face as I breathe on the window and draw a heart with my finger. On days like today, when my mind is racing and I'm like an Energizer bunny, I know his mom will do her best to try to keep up with me. I don't know how she does it. It's hard for *me* to keep up with me! When I'm in the doldrums, when I don't even have the energy to get out of bed, she sits with me for hours, taking care of me, and making sure I eat, the apartment gets tidied, and Azia gets out for a walk. I love his family. I've missed them so much since they moved out to Wisconsin. That's why it's so important for me to show my heartfelt appreciation with a small gift, or two, or three. I love to shop.

The anticipation has been building, I haven't slept for days and can't stop. The mall is swarming with people who, like me, have left shopping to the last minute. I drag Stephen from store to store, and as we run back to the car afterward I slip on the ice. He reaches out and grabs me by my coat, balancing the bags in one hand and holding my hand with the other so I don't slip again. It's snowing. Those big fluffy flakes that land on your face for a second before they melt. It's a beautiful sight. We're wildly giddy. The holiday season has begun.

I tap my watch as Stephen closes the door for me.

"It's 3:30 already," I tease as he gets into the car. Azia licks my face. "We really should hurry, Stephen. What's taking you so long?"

I glance over my shoulder. The back seat's been folded over to make a long bed for Azia. The gifts and luggage are packed tight, further back in the car.

"It's a six-hour drive to Wisconsin, Azia," I say. "Make yourself comfortable. It gets dark earlier these days. We've only got about an hour before the sun sets."

We're taking the back way, north along Mack Road toward Roosevelt. On the radio, Sergio Mendes is singing "Never Gonna Let You Go," our strident voices cracking as we sing along.

As we approach a turn in the road, snowflakes waltz in the spotlight of the oncoming vehicle. The large, solid car slides uncontrollably into the intersection. Evidently, these back roads haven't been plowed yet.

"Stephen!"

To the left, an oncoming car; to the right, a guardrail to protect vehicles from going over the embankment. We can't stop, so there's nowhere to go but forward.

The color drains from Stephen's face. Rigid, his white knuckles clutch the steering wheel. He braces for impact, his foot wildly pumping the brake, but the tires are unable to grip the icy roadway.

The oncoming car approaches too quickly and I realize we won't stop in time. Frantically, my hands extend out to the dash for support. My legs tangle amongst the packages at my feet.

Like an underwound Christmas toy, everything slows down, frame by frame, each gut-wrenching moment hangs as though suspended in time. The oncoming headlights shine in my face. I blink as each snowflake lands independently on the windshield, slowly melting into a drop of water; the drops collect and slide along the glass, creating little rivers that cling to the edge of the windshield, then stream off it; they're like the tears clinging to my lashes before running down my cheek and falling into oblivion.

Stephen instinctively pulls the steering wheel to the left.

Impact.

I hear a loud explosive crash, like thunder cracking inside my skull, as this pop can on wheels crumples. A loud, incessant ringing reverberates in my ears. The snow breaks through like a million little diamonds cutting my face. My body lifts, suspended in the air, choked by the seat belt. Crushing pain rips through my chest.

As the other car shears towards me, I hear the grating sound of grinding metal. My precious little Omni is collapsing like an accordion, no match for the oncoming vehicle. Both vehicles are now intertwined when we finally stop, having pushed sideways through the rail. We're hanging precariously at the edge of the ravine. It is eerily silent.

Gasping for breath, my eyes dart around; nothing else moves. Searing pain burns in my chest and legs and I try to speak; my jaw loosely dangles off my face, but no recognizable words escape, only unearthly, feral utterances. Warm blood streams down my cheek, a contrast to the stinging cold winter air.

I'm pinned. I can't move. My chest pounds like a herd of buffalo.

An oncoming woman slips as she frantically runs toward us. Like a caged tiger, she paces in front of the car, roaring for somebody to get help, to call the police. Evidently she is the driver of the other—and she is sorry, so very sorry.

My gaze shifts over to Stephen. There is blood everywhere, but his chest is moving. His head turns toward me, his eyelids hanging low over his glossy eyes. A tear escapes and runs down his face, collecting blood as it falls off his chin.

I focus on his lips as he whispers: "I'm sorry. I had nowhere to go."

Azia's strong smooth tongue gently laps up the warm blood from my face as he softly whimpers in my ear.

Each labored breath is crushing. I feel pain… but I am alive.

My heavy, blood-stained eyelashes lower over my vision like a curtain, and I fade out for a moment.

Suddenly, there are people all around. Lots of people. The ringing in my ear is louder, like a sticky doorbell, and beyond it I hear a chorus of voices.

"Can you hear me?" someone asks. "What's your name?"

The face of a police officer comes into view, and a fireman behind him.

"We want you to stay still, really still. You're going to be okay."

The metal next to me vibrates violently. I scream, but no sound comes out. The car shakes, the metal and glass snapping and popping. I realize that my right foot is twisted and pinned between the bucket seat and the floor beneath me. A faulty bolt must have snapped in the collision, allowing the seat to slide forward off its rail. I'm kneeling on my foot.

"Stop, stop," I gasp, summoning every ounce of air I can muster. "My foot, my foot…"

Where is my bottom lip? My wide-eyed glances ricochet from rescuer to rescuer, determined to garner their attention. Do they know where my foot is? Will they cut through it? I need them to see me! With a burst of energy, my heart pumps wildly and I try to pull my foot out, but I can't move it.

The deafening whirl of the generator drowns out everything else as the jaws of life slice through the metal frame of the car, dismantling the vehicle.

I suddenly feel a sharp, stabbing pain in my chest. It radiates to my shoulder and through my back, getting worse with every labored breath.

"Hold on, stay still," the voices call out. "You're breathing. You're okay."

More voices ringing in the distance: "We need the spreader. We gotta pull the dash away from her. Hook it up! Here we go!"

There's more humming, metal crunching, glass shattering, and as the pressure releases from my chest a tsunami of pain flows in. It's excruciating. Like a fish out of water, my throat gurgles in vain for breath as a collar is wrapped around my neck.

"Cut the belt," someone says. "We need to get her out of here."

And with a snap, I fall forward into the waiting arms of a firefighter, my chin hanging loose from my jaw.

A pair of scissors glimmer in the light of the men's rescue helmets.

"Don't cut my coat," I mumble. Why is my jaw hanging? "I can't breathe, I can't breathe…"

I wheeze, gasping for air. First they cut through my coat, then my shirt and bra. They tape a piece of plastic to my chest, insert a needle into my side…

"Don't worry, you're good," a voice tells me. "You're breathing, you're breathing! What's your name?"

I want to yell, *No, I'm not okay!* But I can't seem to catch more than a thimble full of air. I barely manage a whisper. "Joanie…"

My mind wanders back to something my mother once told me: "Always wear clean underwear in case you're in an accident." But this was a special occasion. I was going to see Stephen's family. I hadn't wanted any pantie lines.

Crap, I realize. *I'm not wearing any underwear!*

Finally, I'm loose and rolled to the side as a board is inserted behind me. Cold tape presses against my forehead. The dark sky looms above as I'm hoisted up out of the seat. There are so many men. Good-looking men at that, working together to get me onto a gurney. I feel safe in the arms of these men.

The cool, wet snow falls on my face and melts away. My extricated body relaxes as I sense the weightiness of my arms and legs. My jaw slides to the left. My eyelashes flutter and close with the heaviness of the encrusting blood and snow.

"Ahhhhh!" My scream echoes through the night as an electric pain pulses from my knee.

"That's better," the paramedic above me contends. "Just setting your leg. It was kind of mangled, my dear. Your foot will have to wait until we get you to the hospital. Just let me get the support boards around it and we're good to go."

They lower me onto a stretcher, flashing lights streaming across my vision as I'm bounced swiftly through the growing crowd towards the ambulance. Soon they've hoisted me into the back and we're on my way. Tubes and wires are applied. Someone places an oxygen mask gently over my face and my breathing becomes less labored.

"BP is dropping," the attendant cautions with a flat, controlled voice. But his eyes are troubled. "Heart rate is climbing. We need to get moving stat."

They start an IV drip and I begin to feel some relief.

When we arrive, the hospital staff warms around me like ants. In search of answers, my gaze sprints between the masked faces. The ringing in my ear has subsided at least. One masked face reports that I have six broken ribs and they've punctured both my lungs, causing them to collapse. They've managed to mitigate those injuries and are taking me up to the OR to stitch up my face. Evidently, there's a large gash extending from the right side of my mouth and I'm not able to have an anesthetic because of the lungs. But they'll give me morphine. I've tried several drugs, and honestly I'm loving the morphine. There are also fractures in my tibia and fibula, and compound fractures in the ankle that will also have to be repaired.

As the surgeon sews up my face, I can't help but tell him a joke I made up years ago. My hidden talent is telling the joke without moving my face.

"You better not be moving your lips," he cautions.

"I'm not. You're still doing your job and I'm talking. My mouth isn't moving."

"I can't believe I understood the whole joke without you moving your mouth." He chuffs, shaking his head as he finishes the more than one hundred stitches required to repair my face.

Hours later, I strain to open my eyes, peering through the slit of my bandaged face. The invading light fills the darkness, revealing a figure next to me. Every bone, every crevice of my body screams in pain, rendering me unable to feel the pressure of her fingers on my wrist.

"Do you need something?" she asks.

My feeble fingers beckon. "Uh-huh, closer, closer…"

The young woman lowers her ear to my lips.

"Pain meds," I whimper. "I need pain meds."

"We can't give you anything more for pain," she says in a brittle voice, her hanging eyelids almost covering her sierra brown eyes. "Your heart will stop."

Tears run down my face. "Please, just give them to me or pull the plug."

She shuts her eyes, shaking her head sadly. "You don't mean that."

A sharp pain shoots through my chest. I clench my teeth and grimace. *I can't tell you what I mean, lady, but I got news for you: I do mean this.*

Evidently my family's heard about the accident. It must be all over the news. Marie lives close to the hospital and is allowed to visit. It's the first time I've seen her since last

Christmas when I brought Stephen home. Barely stepping into the room, she shudders. Her face is white as chalk.

"I want a mirror." I stare at her. "I want a mirror!"

"Oh, sure, I have a mirror." Her voice breaks, trying to sound casual. She forces a smile onto her face as she searches through her purse, then helpfully holds up the mirror to me.

I now see that the bandages have been removed, exposing Frankenstein-esque stitches and bloodshot eyes nestled in a hammock of blue and purple skin.

Marie gasps again and pulls back the mirror, but it's too late; my eyes have seen the hideous creature I've become. The image is burned into my retina. If the nurse was right and I didn't really want to die before, I certainly do now. With no will to live, I turn and sob, hoping the tears will wash the image from my memory, at least until I fall asleep.

During the night, I fall into a coma. As a result of the compound fracture, I've developed fat embolism syndrome, a condition that occurs when fat from the bone marrow seeps into the bloodstream and obstructs the blood flow. This condition is often misdiagnosed and fatal if treatment is delayed, but it's been correctly diagnosed and I'm provided oxygen and intravenous fluids to mitigate the problem.

What seems like a moment to me has been weeks for Stephen. I slowly become aware of things around me again: the sound of my heart monitor beeping, and of people talking. I want to participate, to respond, *Hey! Hello! Why aren't you talking to me?* But I can't control my eyes or mouth. It's frustrating. I'm not really awake, but I'm not asleep either. I can't communicate. I'm stuck in this crazy twilight zone for a while, sporadically fading in and out. I recognize my mother, and I hear Stephen's voice, his wheelchair bumping into my bed. Where's Azia? I miss Azia. I hope he's okay.

Eventually I awake, in control of my body again. My eyes open and a soft sound escapes my lips. I move my arms and pull at the tubes. I'm now a slender ninety-five pounds. Stephen's once-calloused hands are now soft, holding mine. Dark circles hang under his milky red eyes as they linger over me. His quivering smile greets me. His first words of comfort? "Azia is okay."

Over the next weeks and months, I endure more surgeries in an attempt to fully repair my internal organs, as well as my mouth and foot. I rehabilitate in the hospital until March, having to learn everything all over again… how to walk, how to speak, how to smile. My facial structure has been impacted, so I'm unable to use the same muscles as before. My cognitive synapses have changed, too. I know what a cup is, for example, but I can't remember the word for it.

The day arrives when I'm released to go home. My heartbeat accelerates as I climb into the waiting wheelchair. Stephen's eye catches a glimpse of my hand, raw from the scratching and fidgeting. I lower my head and pull my hand into my oversized sleeve.

Stephen has fully recovered from his broken leg and busted ribs and he'll be with me, but I'm still scared. I bite my lip. It's numb. And I can't remember things. It's not like it usually is when I can't remember; this is stuff I know that I once knew, but I forget it. It's not the stuff I never really knew.

Stephen wants to help me remember things: appointments, medication, details about the accident, about why I am the way I am… He also wants me to know he'll be there for me. He holds my trembling face in his strong, once-again-calloused hand. A tear strays from my eye, tenderly caught by his weathered thumb as he caresses the scar on my chin. With his other hand, he holds me close to him by the small of my back and gingerly kisses my forehead.

He's always known there's something wrong with me, something big, but we're both lost in the confusion and uncertainty of what it is. Stress always worsens my anxieties, and all the surgeries are adding more stress than I can bear alone. I'm not sure what's happening, but I know I'm beginning to spiral.

The fog rolls in for days and weeks. I can't explain things, like the cuts and burns all over my body. But in all of this, there is one constant: Azia, my steadfast companion. I know I won't get through any of this without him.

Stephen works all day, my leg is in a cast, and Azia needs exercise. I have a leg-lifting contraption, though, so I can get in the car and take Azia for a walk. What a grin he has on his face as he strides leashless beside the car while I drive around the block with my left foot. An active dog, he needs his exercise and I won't let him suffer because I'm hurt.

Azia has also reopened the door to my family. While Stephen and I were in the hospital, they watched Azia for us and fell in love. But who wouldn't? He's the best. They miss him so much that they've been inviting us over. It's good to have family again.

• • •

About a year after the accident, I'm scheduled to have some minimal plastic surgery on my face. I'm pleased to be able to move from the rolling bed to the operating table on my own. As my arms are extended and secured, tubes and needles are inserted. I count backwards and fade…

Hearing voices, my eyes flit open to see masked faces above me. But none of them acknowledge me. The surgeon is wearing special glasses with attached magnifying glasses, laser-focused on the surgery. I try to inhale, desperate for oxygen, feeling heavy, like every orifice is filled with water. I can't move.

My troubled eyes shoot around the room, trying to make eye contact. I'm going to die from this simple surgery. After all the surgeries I've had, this one is going to kill me? I'm dying and they don't notice me. It's Thursday, and they're talking about their weekend.

"She's waking up, she's waking up…"

And then I'm out again.

Afterward, there's a woman waiting with me in recovery. "We heard something happened when you were on the table," she says. "Do you remember?"

"Yes, I remember. I couldn't breathe. I was going to die."

"We want you to know you were breathing the whole time. It just felt like you couldn't breathe." She touches my hand and plants a smile on her face.

What's the frick'n difference? In my mind, I couldn't breathe. I was terrified.

An older, more seasoned surgeon visits the next day. He reassuring me that he's just doing "regular" rounds and thought he'd pop in. I'm puzzled. He isn't the guy who performed my surgery, but he's intent on assuring me that I was breathing the whole time during the surgery. It seems strange that so many people have come in to check up on me. They're so attentive. I feel special in some way, yet it's strange, like maybe something really did go seriously wrong.

I go through multiple more surgeries. I still don't have feeling in my lip and cheek. I can bite all the way down and not feel a thing. It appears I have no working nerve endings anymore. The doctors have tried everything to save my ankle as well, but the decision has been made to fuse it. Evidently this will reduce my foot's full motion, but there's no other way. I don't think I'll ever quite be the same.

Stephen has been wonderful throughout, taking time off work to drive me to my appointments and staying with me through the endless surgeries. Often he drops me off at the pub down the street, gets me situated, and comes back four hours later when he has a break at work to bring me back home. It's tough being laid up for so many years. He understands that I'm in pain, too, and brings me pot when I need it. He joins me for a beer, but that's about it. Beneath his guilt-ridden eyes, he wants to do the right thing and give me the strength to get through. But I don't harbor any resentment toward him. It wasn't his fault.

We take a trip to the east coast in an old, dented, olive green Volkswagen van that has a piece of sheet metal on one side. It's ugly, but the engine's good. Stephen decked it out with a box for Azia to sit on, right between the seats so he can see out the window.

We camp in the woods, and in the evenings we lie on the hood and dreamily gaze up at all the stars. They're amazing. Those stars are just amazing. There must be a God who made them.

The trip has left me wanting more. I want to get married and have children, but Stephen doesn't. It's a rift we can't seem to get around, so mutually we decide it's time to move on… separately.

He saved me in so many ways. I will always miss him.

CHAPTER NINE
CINDERELLA

It is worth nothing for you to have the whole world
if you yourself are lost.
(Mark 8:36, ERV)

IT'S 1985 AND RONALD REGAN HAS WON HIS SECOND TERM. I NEED TO GET AWAY, TO have a fresh start. A change is as good as a rest, after all, and California is about as far as I can get from this life, physically and emotionally. I don't know anyone there, so I won't have to worry about running into someone and feeling like my history precedes me. Maybe I'll even find some new, encouraging friends. One thing's for sure: it'll be so good to get out of these cold winters.

Yes, California it is. I pack up my things and Azia and I head off to California with some guy named Fred. We move into a small house a few blocks from the beach. Fred doesn't stay long.

Azia loves California as much as I do—the warm sun on our faces, the clear blue skies, our toes in the sandy beaches, swimming in the crystal-clear water, the waves crashing over us… it's all so wonderful. My face exudes joy as I breathe in the sea air each morning before work. In the evenings, we walk along the streets near the beach and shop in the cute little stores that dot the seaboard. I long for the bling in the windows, admiring the hues of beautiful sea glass jewelry. And like all good men, Azia follows along.

"Azia, stay, I'm just going into the store. You wait here for me," I give him *the look*, then walk into the store. Azia waits patiently for me outside. He's wearing his leash, but it isn't attached to anything; he's not going anywhere.

My heart melts as I watch him through the window, obediently waiting. He's such a good dog, truly my best friend.

"Can I help you with something?" a helpful clerk asks, craning to see which item I'm inspecting. "Do you see anything you'd like?"

I point to Azia out on the street. "Oh. I was just checking on my dog."

"He's beautiful." She smiles. "And so well behaved, too. How long will he sit there and wait?"

"Oh, as long as it takes. He's used to waiting while I shop." I turn and reach for a lovely pair of teardrop earrings hanging from a coral stand. "While we're on the topic, I do love these sea glass earrings. They're the absolute bomb. Are they set in real silver?"

The clerk opens her mouth to answer when we hear Azia bark outside. Glancing out the window, we see an officer kneeling at Azia's side, checking him out.

"I've got to go, but you can bet I'll be back for these." I hand her the earrings and rush outside. "Officer, I'm right here. He's my dog. Is there a problem?"

The officer stands up tall and puts his hands on his waist. His face slowly appears from the shadow of his cap as he lifts his head, "Well, I can't help but notice this beautiful dog, and that he isn't leashed."

"I beg to differ, officer." I smirk. "He's on his leash, and it's not more than six feet long, like the law requires."

"True." He nods slowly, lifting the other end of the leash. "But this end isn't tied to anything. You need to be sure he's tied up."

"Uhm, actually, the law doesn't exactly say that." I pause dramatically. "It says the animal needs to be in the control of a competent person. I'm a competent person. I was just inside and in control of Azia at all times." I point inside. "Just ask the clerk. Azia's very well-trained and will sit until I tell him to move. Did he move when you approached him?"

"Well, no."

"I rest my case," I conclude confidently, folding my arms, piercing his authoritative exterior with a playful glare and definitive nod.

The officer snorts, admitting defeat. "You're just pulling threads," he says. handing me the leash. "I'll let it go this time, but you're going to have to make sure you have him tied to something on the other end when you aren't right with him. Consider yourself told."

He touches his hand to the brim of his hat, gives a slight nod, and moves on.

"Come on, Azia, let's go to the beach," I say. "I've got a ball!"

Azia runs past me down the street and onto the dog park by the beach. I hobble behind. Wherever we go, kids run to play with him. Azia's a people magnet.

It's a beautiful sunny day. I sit quietly on the beach as the waves softly roll in one at a time. Tail wagging, Azia barks excitedly as he waits for the ball, eyes full of hope. How can I disappoint him? I get up and throw the ball as hard as I can, teetering as I let go. He's a great swimmer. He jumps the waves on his way out and rides the waves on his way back.

I lean back onto my elbows on the beach, directing my face to the sun. The distant pier is filled with people quietly fishing; the soft, warm winds blow into the colorful canvas sails heading in and out of the nearby marina. Azia frolics between the waves with a companion, a black-brown shepherd mix.

"Hey, is that your white shepherd out there?"

Blocking the sun is a tall figure, fit but not overly athletic like the guys on Venice Beach. He lifts his aviators to reveal blue eyes as warm and welcoming as the sky. They capture me instantly. His skin is evenly bronzed, and his self-assured, well-bred stature and plummy, sophisticated tone suggest he's not a farmer or construction worker. Yet he also has a relaxed demeanor, sockless in his penny loafers, suggesting he would fit equally well at a laid back beach party as he would on Wall Street.

I lean in. Who is this mysterious dichotomy of a man?

"Yeah, his name is Azia," I say, then indicate the other dog. "She yours?"

"Yup, she's Jade. I'm Bill. Mind if I sit for a while?" His eyes penetrate me, reading me as easily as a Dr. Seuss book. It would normally unnerve me, but instead I'm intrigued.

"Sure, I'd love some company." I turn my face away from the ocean breeze, my long hair blowing gently over the scar on my chin. "I'm Joanie. We're new in town, and we're in love with the sun and beach."

Bill and I sit on the beach talking for what seems like minutes, but hours have passed. The sky is set ablaze with reds and oranges as the sun sinks slowly into the sea. Our conversation is so engaging. I embrace the breeze on my face and, strangely, the sting of the sand against my scar.

"I've got to head out," Bill finally says, dusting the sand from his khaki shorts. "Might we see you here tomorrow?"

"Oh, sure. We're here all the time." I shrug my shoulders and laugh. "We live here."

"Me too, just up the beach. See you tomorrow then!"

A few days later, Bill's back. It's lunchtime, so we hop into his bright red truck and head out to a nearby restaurant for the best burger and beer I've ever had. I don't cook, and it's been too many days since I've eaten a full meal; maybe that's why the food seems exceptionally good.

We spend the whole day together, following the dogs as they run up and down the beach and jump into the frantic waves. As the sun sets, the air chills and I shiver. Ever the gentleman, Bill removes his bomber jacket and drapes it around my shoulders.

"Joanie, come stay with me," he muses, leaning back with one elbow in the sand. He leisurely tokes on a pipe.

My heart beats so loudly that I'm sure he can hear it. "Are you serious?"

"Yeah. I'm having a party tomorrow night, and there's plenty of room. Everyone's going to stay and crash anyway. Besides, I want you to meet my friends. They'll love your infectious personality." He leans over and brushes the hair from my face. "And your beautiful smile."

"Sure, that'd be great."

My lower lip quivers as I fight back joyful tears. He draws my face in and kisses me.

The next few months are a dream. I wake up each morning, grab a coffee, and stand on the balcony of an enormous beach house overlooking the ocean. I breathe deeply of the ocean air, sip my coffee, and watch the elephant seals laze along the shore.

Bill is the most laidback, good-time guy I could ever imagine. I don't know exactly what he does for a living, but I know we spend a lot of time partying. We fly to Florida and drive down to Key West because he likes Jimmy Buffet and Jimmy Buffet lives there. We don't actually run into Jimmy, but I wouldn't be surprised if we did. Bill seems to know people, lots of people, and I'm blossoming in his company.

After a night of drinking and drugging, I grab the red parrot kite from the bar, roll it up, and stick it in my purse as we leave… just because I can. It's such an adrenaline rush. I'm free, with no inhibitions, no sense of self-control. I don't even think twice… I want, so I take.

Bill holds me in his arms. "I want to introduce you to my family."

A warm glow rushes to my cheeks. I'm not sure if it's from his words or the wine, but I've not been a part of a family for a long time.

Bill's a single-engine pilot and has his own plane. He flies us to Nevada and we drive to his parents' house from the airport. We wind through an affluent neighborhood, the homes hidden behind huge estates, surrounded by solid fences and forbidding gates. We turn right, into one of these large expanses, and a man approaches Bill's window.

"Hello, Mr. S," says the man. "I'll let you in."

"Thank you, Henry."

Henry pulls open the heavy iron gate and we proceed through the barrier.

"Who was that?" I ask once we're through.

"Just a friendly neighbor," Bill insists with a grin that tells me he's lying through his teeth.

As we drive on, I'm not sure what to make of all this. My head pivots from left to right, straining to see what lies ahead. We wend our way down the pine-lined driveway, then over a small wooden covered-bridge veiled in wisteria. My nostrils fill with their sweet aroma, temporarily overpowering the clean pine smell wafting in through the open window.

We negotiate the forested corners, tall trees standing at attention. The sun is barely able to peek through the branches.

Finally we approach a beautiful log-cabin mansion. The home is extraordinary and I tremble as I walk to the door. And once inside, I'm speechless, mouth agape, dazzled by the cathedral ceiling looming over me. Full-length windows frame the picturesque lake and snow-capped mountains outside. Behind me, two rustic staircases surround a fieldstone fireplace that rises up to the heavens.

I quickly turn and look at Bill, who's thoroughly enjoying my awe and wonder.

"Who are you?" I ask, cocking my head inquisitively.

Bill laughs out loud as he grabs my arm and begins climbing the stairs. "Come with me and settle in your room. This is the guest house. We'll freshen up and go see my parents at the main house this evening for dinner." He pauses at the top of the stairs and points down the hall. "Don't worry, I've ordered something for you to wear. Go look, it'll be up in your room."

The dinner dress is fabulous. I feel like Cinderella meeting the king and queen.

Dinner goes well. His parents are lovely and they adore me.

Bill and I are in love. A mere touch of his hand calms me. His voice, unwavering and confident, steadies me when I falter. His eyes draw me into his optimism and joy. I don't remember ever feeling so happy, so whole. I feel complete.

We travel a lot, spending all our spare time together. We take flights to visit his family at their homes in Catalina and Hawaii, and go on ski trips in the Rockies. Well, with my fused ankle I tend to stick with the après-ski in the lodge and wait for Bill to join me. We even fly home to meet my family, who of course love Bill and are happy to see Azia again.

• • •

They say time heals all wounds, and a lot of time has passed. My secrets seem to have been forgotten and I've been accepted back into my family. I also have this wonderful new family of Bill's.

Then, like a California earthquake, my hand tremors as Bill proposes, slipping onto my finger a gorgeous two-carat diamond ring.

The Cinderella story continues. Our wedding will take place on a yacht, and the invitations have been designed to look like passports. I pick out charming nautical outfits, navy blue tops and white shorts for the nephews and skirts for the nieces, deck shoes and all. Dad will wear a captain's hat and the real captain will marry us. There are matching white collars for our darling Azia and Jade, who will be walked up by our best friends Di and Maddie.

With the wedding plans finalized, Bill and I stand on the balcony of our beach house, boundless blue skies reaching over the calm turquoise ocean. I glance over and catch Bill gazing at me. When he touches my hand, my heart races. Finally I have stability in my life. The rhythmic percussion of the ocean captivates us as we stare out toward the horizon, the blue skies exploding into an array of orange, yellow, pinks, and fiery red. As dusk turns to night, the skies reveal a dark sequined twinkling above. I remember that sky from my travels to the east coast with Stephen.

Pondering the grandeur then and now, I conclude there must be a Creator. Nothing so beautiful could just happen.

Turning to Bill, I decide that I truly am Cinderella, at the ball with the prince. But like all fairytales, an underlying darkness pervades the story, and the clock is about to strike midnight.

•••

The heavens grow dark and black clouds billow in from the east. The brilliant blues skies and seas fade to dull steely grays. The humidity presses down, suffocating life. The fresh, salty aroma of the sea and the sweet fragrance of oranges blossoming are overtaken by the earthy musk of the approaching storm.

As darkness looms over me, the California color drains from my face. Word has come of my father's illness, and I need to go help with his palliative care. I don't want to see my father, but I need answers before he dies. I'll have to go back and confront my past.

Bill knows my past. He knows that I've had a son, but he doesn't know it was my father's son. As I look over to him in the kitchen, I hold the letter in my trembling hands, shuddering to think what he would think of me. My world collapses around me. I'm sinking into a dark place.

Bill sees that I'm struggling. His family does, too, and they express their concern. There are times when I disappear and can't be reached, sometimes for hours, sometimes for days. I've noticed a new problem as well: I pop pills to get out of bed, and drink to slow myself down enough to sleep. I have my Bill friends, and I have my street friends. I'm quickly descending a spiraling staircase into a deep, dark place.

When we start couples counseling, the counsellor asks to see me alone after the second session. It's not a good sign. I lower my head and cross my legs, hoping he hasn't seen me shake. My hopes and dreams are slipping through my fingers.

Just two weeks before the wedding, everything is falling apart. Bill holds my hands firmly in his, but it's been decided—the wedding is off while I get help.

"I'll leave you if you make me go," I threaten, my voice cracking. "I don't want to go to counseling anymore!"

I can't go back. Fissures rip through me with each question the counsellor asks me, opening wounds long since thought to be healed.

As time passes, I go into a freefall, disappearing into the streets, vanishing from my own awareness. Linear time morphs into a dotted maze of consciousness… and then I'm not.

Six months later, still having Bill's car and credit cards—he hasn't cancelled them or reported them stolen—I'm frequently travelling back and forth between California and Chicago, trying to hold both worlds together. For months I've been using ATMs to get cash in order to stay in hotels, all the while living under the ruse that the wedding's just postponed until my dad gets better. I worry Bill may follow the paper trail and keep tabs on me, but I never hear a thing.

In the paper one day, I see an engagement picture of Bill and a girl more suitable to his status in society. Her name is Jane. I crunch the paper between my clenching fists, a swell of rage building inside me. Fury crashes over me, submerging me in a swirl of chaos. It was supposed to be me.

My mind kicks into overdrive. I toss the paper, along with my dreams, into a nearby trashcan. What will my family say? I can't tell them. He's the only reason they've let me back into the house. They don't trust me. They think we're getting married. If they knew we had broken up, if they knew about my street friends, I'd be kicked out.

Being inside that house is insane anyway… memories are surfacing and I feel like I'm drowning. Once again, I cut and burn to breathe. I don't see a way out… unless I kill them… I may go to jail… but the state will take care of me, right? I won't have to worry about any of this anymore. It'll make everything stop… I need to get off this rollercoaster.

The situation escalates as my mind billows and churns. I don't even know who I am anymore. Everything's a blur. I meet up with some street friends and they talk about expanding their "business" into Chicago. Am I interested in a business opportunity? The drug trade is very lucrative. I know I'll need quick cash. I accept the offer.

The storm still rages over me. The dark clouds surround me, my mind tossed between what's known and what's shut out.

I've been abandoned. Someone's going to pay. My friends have connections, they say. They can help me, they say…

I buy a gun.

I know my target.

CHAPTER TEN
THE FELONY

Lord, how long will you watch this happen? Save my life from their attacks. Save me from these people who are like lions.
(Psalm 35:17, ICB)

IT'S BEEN FIVE YEARS SINCE I LEFT FOR CALIFORNIA. CALIFORNIA SEEMS A LIFE-TIME ago. Back in Chicago full-time now, I'm driving the father to an appointment. I drive past Roosevelt Road doing my best Madonna impression, my bright pink lips feverishly smacking gum, my wild hair put up with scrunchies, my leather and lace-clad hands grasping the steering wheel.

The father's head bobs as he fades in and out of consciousness. I survey the sad remnant he's become. I don't consider him to be *my* father anymore, just a sperm donor.

"I wanna… make sure… we're okay," he slurs, barely audibly, drool hanging from his chin.

With furrowed eyes, I look over to the hollow form beside me. "Yeah, sure, we're fine."

"I wanna make sure… you understand… I was very sick… in my addictions." His breathy voice is tight. His eyes strain to reach mine.

"I know, Dad. It's really great you're not drinking anymore." I just want to get this over with.

He struggles to speak. "I hope you know… I was never in my right mind… I was always bombed." He wheezes for breath and loses consciousness again.

With these words, a dark cloud is cast over me. My sweaty fingers slide off the steering wheel and my heart throbs, as deep and penetrating as a bass drum. A heavy rock sits in the pit of my stomach. I've pushed the memories out of my head, tightly wrapped them in boxes and buried them so deep inside that parts of me aren't even aware of why I don't want him to talk about this right now.

Something begins to crack. A bone-chilling, shadowy aura emanates from a gaping subconscious chasm inside me and I become aware of the need to suppress and control the situation before it gets out of hand.

A good dose of alcohol will suppress these unwanted thoughts. Crystal meth will rev up my mind with more pleasant thoughts. Pot and valium will then bring me back down so I can try to sleep. This revolving regiment frees me to happily clean the house and take care of the father without opening up any of the old wounds. Usually.

• • •

One more day of cleaning is over, and I've had a few drinks. I'll just take one more pill to help me sleep. My head swivels, then whirls until I fall face-first off the toilet. I convulse uncontrollably, my cheek smashing against the bathroom floor in a pool of urine and spit. My eyes roll back into my head.

I lay on the ground, unable to move or speak. My heart pounds. I worry about Mom finding me dead in the morning. I can't do that to her. It wouldn't be fair. In the future, I'll use these substances with more caution…

With that, I drift into oblivion.

When I wake up, it's morning. I run into the next room where Mom is getting ready for work. I sob, so thankful that I'm alive and breathing.

I wrap my arms around her. "I love you, Mom."

Annoyed, she tears herself away from me and turns without a word, no wiser to my heart-wrenching ordeal.

Things have become weird at home since my return. I've come to realize that if I don't initiate touch, I'll have no touch at all. And so I begin playing a sick game of avoiding all unnecessary touch.

Eventually a year goes by, and I become convinced that humans don't need physical touch at all.

Business is going well, though. I'm a budding entrepreneur. My friends in California supply me with crystal meth, which I repackage into smaller quantities and distribute here in Chicago through a network of local bartenders. Even after shipping costs, I make thousands of dollars per shipment.

The father has been really sick lately and I spend more time around the house, cleaning and watching him while my mother works. This requires some level of touch. But when he touches me unexpectedly, it sends me to another place. I stop dead in my tracks… gasping as images, smells, and sounds rush into my head. I feel my heartbeats inside my ears… my eyes fixate, a flood of perspiration escapes, and then it's over… I can breathe again.

I run upstairs, retrieve the product, and use some of it myself, cutting into my profits. Drugs help lift me out of my despair, even if only for a short while.

Azia and I are upstairs in my room. It's evening, and my mother is home to care for the father, so I'm able to work. After packaging the drugs, I hide the product and put on a CD. I'm singing along with Bette Midler and dancing around the room.

Suddenly, Marie comes through the front door; the screen door crashes behind her. That's odd. What's she doing here? Even over the music, I can sense a commotion outside. Cars are pulling up, tires squealing, doors closing, voices humming…

Everything happens quickly, but for me time seems to stand still.

The front door opens and the voices get louder.

My mother's voice resonates: "She's up there!"

I hear heavy boots climbing the stairs. What the heck? I'm caught off-guard and there's no time to try to hide anything. I drop to my knees and grab Azia, positioning him in front of me as I back myself into the corner. He leaps into protective mode, baring his teeth and growling.

The bedroom door opens and the police enter.

More footsteps race up stairs, and Marie bursts into the room, shouting, "There's drugs and a gun in here!"

I frantically hold Azia back by his collar; he's barking ferociously, keeping the police at bay. Marie struggles past the officers, feverishly searching, her seething eyes fixated as she haphazardly casts my things on the floor. Inspecting a plate on my dresser, she becomes unhinged.

"Here's some of it!" she announces, picking up the plate.

Relentless, she pulls out the drawers and digs through them. Becoming more methodical, she moves over to the closet beside the door where the police are still standing back from Azia's vicious growl. This is where I've just hidden my stash. She pulls out the freshly bagged product and holds it high

"Here it is!" she exclaims triumphantly.

With that, the police take action, intent on finding the alleged weapon. Having seen the evidence of packaged drugs, suggesting possession of a controlled substance with intent to sell, they're convinced Marie is also correct about the gun.

Rushing to me, Marie grabs my arm. "Joanie, we know there's a gun. Tell them where the gun is."

Azia's maniacal toward the police, but he won't attack Marie.

"There is *no* gun," I insist. "Where are you getting this?"

Wide-eyed, I cling to Azia and retreat inside myself. The divine Miss M croons, filling my head. I can't get the music out. If the Divine is watching, why doesn't He come down and rescue me?

I become an outside observer, as if watching a TV show. How did my sister even find out about the gun?

As a burly officer turns off the CD player and continues the search for the gun, the music continues to play in my head. Am I forgiven?

Another officer, this one younger, kneels at my side, just out of Azia's reach, and speaks to me in a soft, controlled tone of voice. He tries to make eye contact.

"Joanie, you don't want to do this," he says. "Let me help you."

"If you don't leave, I'm going to let Azia go," I warn him. I have no idea what to do at this point, but I know I want them to get out.

"Let Azia go," the burly officer responds challengingly.

They've called my bluff. I don't know what to do, but I'm not going to let him go. Azia is the only thing between me and them.

We continue down this road for thirty minutes before I finally relent and give Azia up. Marie takes him out of the room. I'm pulled to my feet and swiftly turned around. My face is pushed against the wall and my arms pulled back as cold metal handcuffs are slapped onto my wrists.

I descend the stairs, officers on either side of me. I search for my family, who are nowhere to be seen, not inside, not outside. I am alone.

The officer lowers my head, shoving me into the back of a cruiser. The neighbors have gathered. I'm numb and my bloodshot eyes stare tearlessly off into the distance. I continue to hum softly, unable to get the song out of my head. It's the only thing that comforts me. How could my family do this to me? I wasn't hurting anyone.

• • •

I spend the next seventy-two hours in the DuPage County Jail, in a big cell with four or five others. I draw my knees up to my chest, pull my hoodie over my lowered head, and tuck myself as far into the corner as I can. My inflamed eyes peer through my unruly strands of brown hair, beneath exhausted eyelids that hang like falling curtains, struggling to stay open.

My hope of getting answers—and getting out—are dashed with every passing moment. I feel frustrated and alone as I gauge the criminals around me. Every part of my body shakes as I clench my teeth, holding my head between my hands, trying to make the pain of withdrawal go away.

Over the next few days, counsellors come, one by one, taking me in handcuffs to a little room.

"Where's the gun, Joanie? Tell me where the gun is."

"You don't understand, I don't have the gun."

"Just tell us where it is."

"I don't have the gun. You don't understand. I'm really sick. I've got problems that need to be addressed. Like mental problems… you can't help me here."

"Well, we're going to need family consent to get you that kind of help. They want to know about the gun."

"I don't have the gun." I'm in tears, pounding the table with my fists.

I've lost track of time, but it's been about ten days. Marie is eventually designated as my agent and signs the documents allowing me to go to the State psychiatric hospital. I'm excited to be leaving jail.

The hospital is dark green. Everything is green. The food's inedible slop. I can't believe I'm in this situation. Was it only last year that I was planning my wedding? I was on top of the world. The evil step-mother and step-sisters have won, but in my story they're my actual family. Who would do this to their child? I fall into deep despair, hopeless, unable to move.

My sister Rose comes to visit, clutching her purse as she slowly enters the room. With every step forward, she glances backward, planning her escape. She is appalled by what she sees.

"We can't do this," she says. "We need to get you out of here."

With this flicker of hope, a weight is lifted. Grasping the opportunity to escape this place, I become remarkably compliant. "I'll do whatever you say. Please just get me out of here, please."

What I had is lost. What I seek is hidden from me. What I need is unattainable. I can't be absolutely sure of anything in my life. I have no purpose, no direction, no future. Even my past is a mystery. The waters surround me, submerge me. Frantic, I claw to reach the surface, but the waters part between my fingers and I sink deeper into the depths, my chest compressing under the pressure.

There's an internal life force that makes you fight for breath even when death seems like the best thing ever. In my case, it comes in the form of a passing orderly who fulfills my request for a cigarette. After lighting it, he continues with his work.

Sinking into the corner, I lift my sleeve and press the lit cigarette against my skin. The burning sensation brings me back to the surface… I can breathe.

The day has come to be arraigned for the felony. I leave the hospital to appear before a judge. My family has found a lawyer who will represent me. I pull the long sleeves over my scars, over the shackles, and enter the courtroom. I peruse the sea of faces and notice Marie sitting beside my mother, all staunch and proper. Their gazes are fixed on the judge. I stop, scrutinizing them with vile disdain. Why would they have come after everything they've done?

"Do you understand what you have done?" the judge asks, leaning in and peering over his oversized black-rimmed glasses from his elevated seat at the front of the room.

My eyes grow three sizes. "Me? No."

I look back at Marie, then quickly return my attention to the judge. His piercing gaze penetrates me, and like a small child I fold my hands and pout. I truly feel innocent of everything, convinced I should be released. All of this is my family's fault. If it wasn't for Marie calling the police, I wouldn't even be here.

"Do you understand what you are being charged with?" the judge continues, flipping through the pages of a report in front of him.

In protest, I rise from my seat. "No. My family started all of this."

My lawyer grabs my arm and shushes me, urgently giving direction, but I ignore him.

"Listen," I continue, "let me tell you what happened—"

"Your honor, I need a moment with my client." My lawyer stands, shouting over me.

"No, you don't. I'm trying to tell the judge what happened." I slap my lawyer's hand and direct my attention to the judge. "You want to know what happened, right? It's my sister—"

"Your honor, I'd like to request a recess so I can confer with my client."

"I think that would be a good idea," the judge says. "We'll recess until tomorrow morning at 10:00." His gavel slams down and everyone stands up.

Immediately, my mother starts screaming. "You realize you just cost us $3,000 because you just can't keep your big mouth shut?"

"Well, it didn't really cost you anything, did it?" I protest.

My family has somehow managed to get access to what's left of the $30,000 settlement from the car accident and they're using it to pay the lawyer. After all these years, I've really only used $3,000 to buy a motorcycle for Stephen—to thank him for everything he did for me during the surgeries. He's still like family.

Marie claws her way over my shaking mother. "We could have gotten this done if you'd have just done what you were told," she yells. "Don't you ever listen to anyone? You were supposed to plead guilty!"

"But what am I guilty of? I didn't do anything. It was you… all you." My face is cherry red and shoulders shake wildly as the bailiff escorts me out, taking me into a little room where I wait, steaming and hissing for someone to come and explain to me why I'm not being released.

My lawyer opens the door, files slipping in his overfilled hands. He pushes his glasses back onto his nose.

"Look, Joanie, I'm not sure what you're looking for, but this is the best you can get," he says. "You're going to have to plead guilty. It's your first offense. I'm sure I can get you a lighter sentence."

"Can't I plead insanity?" I ask, reaching out for his hand. I'm desperate not to go back to jail. "I've seen it on TV. I know there's an insanity defense."

"Joanie, do you know what it takes to get an insanity defense?" He shakes his head. "Why would you want to go that way? This is going to be much better. I'm asking for probation only."

"But look at me! This is it. If you would just do a little bit more research, you could see I *am* insane. It's the truth! Ask my family." Tears stream down my face. I've heard it all my life—I'm crazy. I'm acutely aware that I'm messed up somehow, but I just can't put my finger on what's wrong. I'm reaching out for help. "How did I even get here?"

"Joanie, don't you remember?" His eyes narrow, his head tilts. "You called a psychiatrist and told him you have a gun. You said you were going to kill your father and then kill yourself. He had an obligation to report it. If he knows you're threatening to harm yourself or others, he needs to turn you in."

Sitting back in the chair, my shoulders sag. My face falls as the words come out of his mouth. I'm speechless. Up until this point, I had no idea how serious the charges were. I have no recollection of calling a psychiatrist and saying I was going to kill the father and myself. I would never do that.

I have no recollection of telling anyone about the gun. Why would I? I didn't bring the gun with me to Chicago. Before I boarded the plane home for the last time, I went to the beach with Azia, to a place where Bill and I always went for walks. Just outside the park, there was a sandy area with tall grass that you're not supposed to disturb, but we always let the dogs run around in there to do their business. That day, I had the gun with me and got to thinking that murder just wasn't worth it. Sure, I was mad at Bill, I was mad at the father, I was mad at the whole world… but it wasn't really anyone's fault. Going to jail for life just wasn't going to be worth the momentary sense of satisfaction. Anyway, I was flying home, and how was I going to pack a gun on a plane? So I threw the gun into the grass and ran back down the beach with Azia. The sun glistened so much brighter on the water after that; I felt much lighter and freer.

I don't know why I would have told anyone about the gun… but I guess I must have. How else would they even have known about it? Perhaps… perhaps there's more to me than even I know.

I curl up with my knees to my chest, sink into my chair, and listen.

"You just need to do exactly what I tell you, and if nothing else happens while you're on probation, you can get the charges expunged." A stern look descends on the lawyer's face and his voice deepens. "However, if you don't walk the straight and narrow, you *will* go to jail. Do you understand?"

I imagine what I'm going to have to pay to have this expunged, but I'm docile and nod.

The following morning at the hearing, with my hands folded and head bowed, I obediently answer the judge as I've been told. I'll have to go to the hospital for additional psychiatric care and have thirty-six months of probation. But I'll be able to go home.

Won't that just be wonderful?

CHAPTER ELEVEN
EXPOSED

For the Son of Man came to seek and save those who are lost.
(Luke 19:10)

IN THE PSYCHIATRIC HOSPITAL, WITH THE HELP OF DR. BRAUN AND A TEAM OF psychologists I start piecing together the disturbing things that have happened in my life, discovering so many complex and disconcerting things about myself and my family. I have these blank pages in my life.

When things happen that I can't remember, and it's been a stressful situation, such as when someone is pointedly asking me something, I usually lie, because it's going to take me too long to figure out what the truth is. If you don't want me to lie, just don't ask me questions I don't have answers for. But if I can just step back from things without any stress, I can take the time to travel inside my head and figure out what actually transpired. Ninety percent of the time, I can find the pieces and answer the question. Yet maybe two handfuls of times there are blank spaces in my head that I just don't want to remember, or maybe it's just not important for me to remember. Sometimes I can't even get a spark of the memory back, and telling a psychiatrist that I was going to kill the father and then myself… well, this is one of those things I can't remember at all.

Because I so often make up stories in stressful situations, I'm beginning to realize that it's difficult for people to know what the truth is. While in a session with my sisters one day, being confronted with questions as to whether the father ever did anything to them, and them saying no, I feel bewildered—why did he choose me and not them?

Later, with my mother, we talk about Brian and what happened when I was young. I honestly tell her what I remember, but she doesn't believe me. She leans in, pointing her finger at me. Her usually sweet face crosses and contorts, her voice grating and accusatory. I pull back in my seat, holding back tears and reluctantly acquiesce, renouncing everything I know to be the truth.

"See, she's a pathological liar," Mom says. "You just can't believe anything she says. This is just what Joanie does. She lied to us about Bill. She never told us he broke up with her. She wanted us to keep thinking she was going to be a millionaire."

"I didn't lie," I stammer. "I just didn't tell you everything. There were things you just didn't need to know… we might get back together. I still love him and I know he loves me! We're going to get married."

Of course this isn't true. Bill's engaged to that Jane girl. As much as I hate it, she fits into his world better than I do.

I tremble in my seat, looking back and forth between my mother and the psychiatrist. I just don't know what they want me to say. I'm still haunted by the father telling me that I'll lose my family. I've lost them before, but then I got them back. I don't want to lose them again.

I struggle with the pieces of memory in my head, the pieces I've found deep inside, when I allow myself to search that deep. These are the things I know to be true.

• • •

There's a common room in the hospital, a quiet place where we can play checkers or chess, watch TV, or read a book. Reading's what I like best. I've just finished the book, so I head over to the bookcase to find a new one. As I walk into the crowded room, there's a buzz in the air. Jack's in the corner having his usual conversation with himself. Selma's in her rocking chair, watching *I Love Lucy* as she rocks her baby doll. Two people are playing Monopoly over by the window.

I stand still, unable to move, my feet bolted to the ground. My eyes gloss over and my head's sucked into a psychedelic time warp, swirls and all. Sweat dampens my shirt, under the arms and in the small of my back. My clammy hands wring like an old washing machine. The steady rhythm of drums pounds against my chest.

A slideshow of memories from the distant past flip through my head. I'm home from school. Dad's on the couch with the Monopoly game, ready to play. I dutifully sit with him. I'd choose the scotty dog if I could, but Dad picks the car for himself and hands me the thimble. I'm not free to run, I'm under his thumb. He always makes me pay the money I owe him… but I don't want to make him mad, so I don't always make him pay me. We play for hours and hours, forgetting to eat, not worrying about homework… I don't want to stop playing because of what might happen if he makes me go upstairs… I'm eight years old.

A few nights later, I'm in the common room watching *Family Matters*, the episode where Steve Urkel won't get off the roof. Again I'm frozen, sucked back into the past.

I'm in fourth grade. We live in a house on Monticello Road. The window of my room overlooks the roof of the garage. My brown hair is pulled back into two pigtails with big blue bows. I'm beside my bed, playing Barbies on the floor. I hear his heavy footsteps approach my door, then his body crashes into the hallway cabinet… the family photos collapse and fall. Then comes the thud of his shoulder bumping into the wall beside my doorway. He's clearly drunk. I spring to my feet, anxiously searching for an escape… but he's found me in the closet and under the bed before, so I scramble for another place—a light streams through the window. I gently open the window and crawl onto the roof, quickly closing it behind me. I push myself up against the wall. It's cold, but I feel safe. The only way he'll see me is if he sticks his head out the window… he never does… until that one time. The Lewises from across the street see me and make a concerned phone call to the police, reporting that I'm on the roof and they're afraid I might fall off. That's the end of the best secret hiding place I ever found. Tears roll off my chin, since the only other respite now is Mary Ellen Shanley's house. Her mom knew more then she let on, I'm sure of it. I wish I would have told her what was really going on.

Through talking and drawing, the doctors at the hospital painstakingly work through each of these memories, helping me bring all my past traumas together. It's difficult, but we're making good headway. Soon I'm released to go home and will only have to come back for scheduled visits. I've been given a number to call if I feel anxious in between.

• • •

What is Kuwait? Newscasters on TV are talking about Desert Storm and the Gulf War. Evidently the war is over now, but I didn't even know it had begun. We don't watch news in the hospital and I've just arrived home.

Truly, I'm more concerned about the wars I've been battling in my head, and with my family, than the wars in this Kuwait place.

There's an uneasy silence at home. Dark clouds gather and I can feel a storm brewing. The family has hired a nurse for the father, and I'm not to take care of him anymore. They don't trust me. The raised eyebrows, crossed arms, and dead silence when I enter a room speaks volumes, and the feeling is mutual.

When I'm home, I stay in my room with Azia, afraid to meet the father… afraid to meet anyone.

Carrie is one of the father's caregivers. She's peppy and has a smile that could melt icebergs. Her voice is as calm and relaxed as a summer float in a canoe on a clear lake. She's the rare person I don't mind running into.

"Jesus loves you, Joanie," Carrie tells me. "You know, my Bible study group is praying for you, that God would reveal Himself to you and you would become His child."

I politely return a smile. I really don't know what that means, but I can tell she cares about me and that sparks warmth inside me.

I get out of the house as much as possible when I have the energy, and Azia is a good reason to get out. Today, I'm out walking with him in Lake Ellyn Park. The park has all these smooth white rocks on the beach. I pick one up and toss it a few times to get

Azia's attention. Then I throw it out into the water as far as I can. Azia tiptoes in, struggling a bit to get into the water. He's developed serious hip problems and is certainly not the spry pup he used to be.

But in these times, outside the house, I'm able to reminisce about those better bygone days. This is a perfect day—a few fluffy clouds in the otherwise blue skies, the brilliant green forest leaves in the distance reflecting on the calm lake, the warm sun shining on my face. I wipe my brow with my shirt sleeve. I've thrown a few too many rocks, it's sweltering, and Azia's tiring.

Searching for a cool place to rest, I spot a shaded picnic table next to the pavilion where a group of people are gathered.

"Azia, let's go up to the shade. It's getting hot out here."

Azia looks at me, looks back at the spot where the last rock landed, and looks at me again. He smiles and staggers out of the water, following me up the hill.

I hear a deep voice somewhere behind me. "Are you gonna say hello to an old friend, or you just gonna keep walking?"

I turn around and stomp with a frenzied shriek. Azia barks excitedly, leaping at him. It's Dick! Next thing I know, I've climbed up on him and wrapped my legs around his waist, clinging to his neck as we twirl round and round.

"Hello Dick." I give him a great big hug and eagerly look around for Gram. They're inseparable. It's been years, but if she's still alive, she must be nearby.

"Don't worry, she's just bringing up the rear," he says, chuckling.

I soon notice Gram just a few steps back, buckled over in her tracks, laughing hysterically. Even in the shade, the sun glistens over her head. A feeling rushes over me that I just can't explain, except to say it's a wave of complete joy. It's been so long since I've seen them, yet it feels like only yesterday.

"What are you doing here?" I ask as I notice that there are a bunch of other people with them. "Who are all these people?"

"We're here with our church. Our friend Carrie Shadid was just baptized in the lake."

"Carrie Shadid? Is she a nurse? I think she is one of my father's care givers." There she is; I see Carrie standing at the pavilion, waving at me.

"Carrie is in our Bible study group," Dick explains. "We've been praying for the daughter of one of her clients, but I didn't know who it was. Joanie, we have been praying for you."

Gram comes closer. "Imagine, we had no idea it was you we've been praying for. God works in mysterious ways." She wraps her arms around me and pulls me in so tightly that we trip and tumble over together.

I've heard of God, but He's some far-off entity. Who is this God they're talking about, and why do they talk to Him? Do they think He listens or cares? And if they're praying so hard, why is my life still so miserable?

We exchange phone numbers and I return home, amazed to have found these old friends again. What a coincidence.

• • •

Mom is working, and there's another caregiver in the house with us. I'm not sure who, because I'm sequestered in my room. She must be busy cleaning up downstairs or something.

Hearing a quiet knock at my door, I get apprehensive. I stand up and put my ear to the door but can hear nothing. It creaks as I open it a crack.

The father is standing in the doorway, wearing only his boxer shorts and T-shirt. His head gestures toward the pullout couch and he enters the room.

"We need to talk." He is firm and lucid.

My heart pounds like a herd of wild horses. He walks past me and sits on the couch. I forget to breathe.

"Don't worry, I'm not drunk," he says. His eyes are sunken deep in his pasty face. After years of drinking, the veins in his oversized nose are a roadmap to death and destruction. "You know I can't drink with all these medications they have me on. I'm very sick."

Relieved, I take a breath and sit on the floor, trying to cross my legs. I'm clumsy, unable to really cross them because of my fused ankle. Held captive by his wrinkled eyes, I wait to see what he has to say, hopeful for an acknowledgement, an apology.

"I want to talk to you about what you said in the hospital." He shakes his lowered head. "I'm very disappointed. I thought we were beyond all this, Joanie." He pauses, lifting one heavy brow in disapproval. His weakened body musters some strength and he gazes directly into my frightened eyes, speaking firmly in a thick and unyielding voice. "I thought I told you, you'd lose your family."

Teeth clenched, and blinking wildly to fight back the tears, I shake. I'm eight years old again. He's right. I told, and I've lost my family.

"I'm sorry. I'm sorry..." My voice trembles. "I'm so sorry."

I so wish I could take it all back, and if I could take it back, and then my family won't hate me anymore. Seeking comfort, I reach out my hand. Agitated, he thrusts it off his knee, then stands up and leaves the room. I'm on my own, weeping in my own puddle of tears.

Like a shot, I'm overtaken by a fit of rage. Who does he think he is? I pull myself up onto my feet and rush to the door. Like a wild animal, I pace back and forth. How sick is this? What is happening? Every emotion courses through my shaking body, the anger and sorrow battling in my head taking over my body. I wish I could take back what I've just said. I *am* so sorry—so, so sorry—but it's all his fault! He was the adult. He ruined my life... but if I could take it all back, my family wouldn't hate me anymore. If I hadn't said anything, we would still be a family. I would have a family. I feel like I've somehow gotten lost...

There's another knock on the door. I'm weary of answering the knock, so I take a deep breath. "Yes?"

Evidently some time has passed. Mom is home. She strides into the room, her glacial blue eyes expressionless. "You're upsetting your father. You really need to find your own place. You can leave Azia here, since I know it will be hard for you to find a place where you can go with the dog. We love Azia. He's welcome to stay."

This pisses me off. Yes, Azia is a fantastic dog, but I can't believe they're willing to keep him but not me. I'm her child. Aren't moms supposed to always love their kids? I thought I could count on her. I need her. Where am I going to go? I have nowhere else to go. Don't they know I would if I could?

I stay.

• • •

Outside the snow is falling, but the chill inside is just as cold. The father continues his physical decline, and now that he's not so mentally with it, my plan is to get him to admit something on tape. If I can get some evidence and play it for my sisters, maybe they'll listen. Maybe they'll believe me.

I get out my tape recorder and test the microphone. Who am I kidding? What's this going to do? And how am I even going to do it? I'm never left alone with him.

My heart sinks as I slump onto the floor. There's no hope, no hope for me. I close my eyes, arms sprawled out, and will myself to die. I think about dying every single day. I have for years. I just want to die so bad. I wish I never was… but I am. I don't fade. I just suffer.

The father dies.

During my next psych visit, I can't sit down. I'm pacing around, explaining that I just can't go to the funeral. It's too much. So Dr. Braun tells my mother I won't be at the funeral and that I'll need to see the father one last time on my own, for closure.

The day before the funeral, I'm allowed to go to the funeral home alone. My mother is not happy. I'm not quite sure what she thinks I'm going to do to him.

"Is it okay if I leave him a note?" I ask the lady who has taken me to see him.

She smiles. "Sure, go ahead. I think that would be nice."

I've written a letter, so I take it out and place it in his sweater pocket.

"Would it be weird if I take a picture with him?" I ask.

"No, it's not abnormal. A lot of people do that." She takes a photo with my polaroid camera.

I thank her and leave.

Azia's been sick. He has cancer, and needs surgery. I've scheduled it for the day of the father's funeral. That morning, I take Azia into the hospital and wait for his surgery to finish. I cry at the sight of him; he's shaved and has a long scar on his stomach. It's just horrible. His dark chocolate eyes, once crisp and full of energy, now seem to melt away.

By midafternoon, the staff help me carry his almost lifeless body out to the car for our journey home. When I arrive, I struggle alone with his deadweight, pulling him out of the car and heaving him up the five stairs to the front door. I feel the hum of his soft whimpers next to my chest as I carry him to the living room and set him on the couch. Snuggling beside him, I cover us with his favorite blanket. I love him so much. He's everything to me.

Once settled on the couch, the screen door creaks and Marie steps in. She stomps the snow off her boots. The smell of death follows her as she walks through the doorway carrying a beautiful arrangement of vivid white Easter lilies mixed with carnations in a backdrop of rich greenery. As I breathe in the fragrance, I think of Easter. Why are there lilies at Easter when they smell like death?

Marie stares at me. "Where have you been?"

I prop myself up, half-heartedly greeting her with the most apathetic look. I yawn while peering out under half-drawn eyes. I gently caress my Azia.

"I cannot believe you weren't there," she snaps, putting down the bouquet.

I cock my head and look her straight in the eye. "Azia's sick. He's got cancer."

"Joanie, you could've had that surgery done any time. You choose *this* day. Are you kidding me? Do you know what it's like to bury your father when one of us is missing? Everyone was asking, 'Where's Joanie?'"

"Sorry you had a hard day, Marie," I snip, burying myself on the couch. "Sarry."

Marie huffs, shaking her head as she retreats into the back room.

Rose enters next, her mascara dripping over the red circles that hang under her bloodshot eyes.

"Joanie, you have no right," she rasps in a hoarse voice. "I wish you could think of somebody other than yourself. Do you know what that did to Mom?"

"What good would it have done for me to be there?" I snap back. "There was no reason for me to be there."

I should never have opened my mouth to Rose. I know better.

She leans into me and explodes like a volcano. "Joanie, you are the definition of evil!"

"Huh," I snort. "I'll have to look that one up to see if my name appears in the dictionary under evil…"

I bury my face into Azia's warm neck.

As if choreographed, Ann follows closely behind the others and shares her equally repugnant sentiments about my decision not to attend the funeral. By this time, I'm done. I have no more energy. I take Azia outside for his last pee before bed, then go up to my room so I won't have to encounter my mother.

For the next few months, Azia and I suffer together alone in my room. By the end, he has no energy to even open his eyes as I burn next to him. We fade together.

When I wake, he is still. Azia has died.

I don't shower. I don't eat. I stare blankly into the distance and see nothing…

I loved Azia more than I could ever have imagined loving anyone or anything. Through the most difficult times in my life, he never left my side. He was always so cooperative and loving. I remember dressing him up for Halloween, in sunglasses and hats; he was hysterical. He never wanted anything from me. He always knew when I was sad. His head would be right there in my lap. When I self-harmed, he would watch me with his big eyes, ready to leap into action if anything went too far. He would get upset if I cried out loud. That would just kill him. He knew all my secrets. He was my protector, my confidante, my best friend, and now I truly am—alone.

CHAPTER TWELVE
BLESSED ARE...

For I was hungry and you gave Me food to eat. I was thirsty and you gave Me water to drink. I was a stranger and you gave Me a room.
(Matthew 25:35, NLV)

IT'S 1992, A YEAR SINCE THE FATHER DIED. I'M STILL IN THE HOUSE, AND THINGS between my mother and I have continued to escalate. Dr. Braun and the team at the hospital are trying to help me cope with the finality of the many unresolved issues resulting from the death of the father and the continued coldness of my family. I'm starting to pull things together, but just when I think I've taken a few steps forward, I seem to lose myself again, missing time.

Sometimes I feel on top of the world and just can't stop myself. I have no control. I can't sleep. And then there are the times when it takes too much energy to even lift the covers from my head. I spend weeks in my bed, not even showering. Nobody comes into my room to clean or check up on me; I'm just one more disheveled tarnished article on a heap of soiled sheets and clothes in the now pungent room. Speckles of chip bags and soda cans are the only bursts of color in this drab scene. I reach for the meth, convinced that drugs are the only thing keeping me from falling further into the ghastly abyss.

"I want you to start journaling," Dr. Braun recommends during one of our sessions. "I think journaling will help you clear the cobwebs in your head and allow you to delve in and discover the many facets and hidden places in your world and bring them all together. Find a safe, quiet place where you can write."

I peak at him through my puffy eyes and nod. My whole body sags. I feel heavy, in need of respite from the cage my bedroom has become. I need a safe place. I've been out to visit Dick and Gram a few times. They have a lovely property in the country just down the road in Wheaton.

"Can I use your shed as a retreat?" I ask Dick one day. "It's got a little bench in there. Maybe I could use a corner of that bench to sit quietly and journal for maybe fifteen or twenty hours a week? Just a little break from the endless pressures at home. I promise I won't be a bother at all."

After a bit of convincing, he and Gram allow me to use their shed.

Right now they're on a weekend mission trip. I stand in the doorway of the shed, arms on my hips, full of new energy as I start moving a few things inside. It's just a small pavilion with some windows and gardening tools, but I see potential. With just a few finishing touches, I can make it homey. With newfound energy and vigor, I spend the weekend fixing it up.

When Dick and Gram get home from their weekend trip, I hug them as they get out of their car and escort them into the yard.

"Welcome home," I say, unable to hold back the excitement in my voice. "Don't you just love my little haven?"

Gram's eyes widen as she surveys the work I've done. "Well, you sure have fixed it up, that's for sure. Though it looks more like a home than a haven. Where have my garden tools gone?"

"Oh, I needed to move them out of the way. I put them in a box outside around the corner. I covered them up so they won't get wet in the rain. Don't you just love it?" I beam "I think we should call it Joanie's Place."

It's so nice to have a safe space for myself. I've worked so hard to make it my own.

Dick and Gram look at each other, then shrug their shoulders and sigh. "Yes, Joanie, it's lovely. You've done a marvelous job."

• • •

My mother's not happy that my getaway is only temporary. She keeps pushing me to find a permanent place. This ignites another battle, and things between us become even more hostile.

"Why are you still here?" she demands, slamming down the milk jug on the kitchen table. "You have done nothing but destroy this family."

"Me? How can you say that? I did the right thing. I had his baby!"

"Well, I wish I'd have done the right thing," she snaps back, throwing her hands in the air. "I wish I would have aborted you! It would have saved us all a lot of grief."

My face drops at her words and I burst into unrestrained sobs. I'm cursed. A cold, sharp blade has been plunged deep into my heart. I'm barely able to catch my breath. I wrestle up the stairs, grab a backpack with a few clothes, and leave the house, going to the only place where I know I can find peace… my haven.

It's afternoon when I arrive, raw with fresh burns. I'm bawling and blubbering, barely coherent, endeavoring to explain to Dick and Gram what's just happened at home. They tell me how much Jesus loves me, and how much it hurts Him that I've suffered so much.

They give me a Bible and pray with me. A wave of peace sweeps over me, and for the first time in a long while, I'm calm.

Dick says I can stay and journal, but he insists I can't stay in the shed overnight. They leave to run errands and I realize it's getting pretty late. I bring my bag into the house. The guest room is empty, so I pull back the sheets and crawl into bed. It will be good to have a restful night. I wake the following afternoon.

Finished journaling for the day, I start wringing my hands. I need to keep them busy. I have a habit of counting and sorting things—nothing special, just anything. Like alcohol, it seems to calm me down on my busy days. I do like shiny things, and lately I've been counting and sorting paperclips and hangers. My haven is full of them, floor to ceiling. In fact, I'm finding it a bit difficult to open the door.

After a quick search, I find Dick reading a book in the living room. "Dick, can I ask you a favor?"

He apprehensively removes his glasses. "Sure, Joanie. What's up?"

"I need to clean out my haven. It's a bit cramped in there, and I'm having a hard time even opening the door. Can you help me?"

"Opening the door?" His forehead wrinkles.

"Yes," I say, chuckling. "But once I get in, will you check on me every half-hour to make sure I'm getting somewhere? Dr. Braun is extremely happy with my progress recently and says I need to work on setting boundaries and goals. I need to arrange accountability parameters."

"Sure can, Joanie." He quickly gets up. "Now let's see about getting you through that door."

• • •

I'm beginning to feel like the different parts of my life are starting to come together, like a weight is being lifted off my chest and I can breathe, really breathe, for the first time in so long. I read the Bible they gave me almost every day, intrigued about this God I've heard so much about all my life but don't really know. Genesis is hard to get through, and I don't like the Adam and Eve stuff, but I do like Joseph. His brothers sold him out. I can relate.

I spend a lot of time at Dick and Gram's, but not all the time. I've started sorting through the things at home I want to take with me to Wheaton. I find all sorts of unusual clothes and wonder if it's something I'd even wear, like short skirts and tight tops. I lift up a pair of baggy old jeans, then inspect my old school uniform. Somehow these clothes all look and smell recently worn. I box them up and set them aside.

In the basement, I find some old photographs. I love photos, as they lead me to think about the really nice camera I hope to get one day. My face brightens. Like books, photos take me to wonderful, far-off places. Flipping through, I'm reminded of my early Christmases in Connecticut, the daytrips with the Shanleys, and the trips with

Stephen and Bill. The corner of my mouth slowly lifts until my whole face expands in a smile.

My mother tromps down the stairs and finds me with the photo album—and a war over it ensues. Like an obstinate teenager, my mouth opens and vile words shoot out like a barrage of arrows until the battle's done. Shaking uncontrollably, I pull myself into a ball on the floor. The tiny, brittle girl inside calls Gram, who reaches through; her godly words pull me out of the crisis.

It's Mother's Day. As my final gift to my mother, I leave my childhood home for good.

No matter where I find myself, there are days and events that trigger me, sending me off the deep end, spiraling into oblivion. When I come to, I need to sort through the haze. Even with all the love I feel at Dick and Gram's, trauma is never far off. It lurks around every corner.

My birthday often falls on Father's Day, and it happens again in 1992. Dick and Gram have gone to church. On this day, I just can't make it, so I sit on the front step and write in my journal. I can't eat. I can't talk. I retire to my room only to crawl under the covers and weep. Somehow, in that room I feel a tender comfort.

July 4 is another trigger day. The sound of fireworks usually pierces through my body, but this year, taking a step forward toward recovery, I return to my childhood house with the memory of the abuse I endured there. Standing tall in front of my bedroom window, I read John 14:4: "If you ask me anything in my name, I will do it." I claim my life back, in Jesus's name. I don't know what it means, but I've seen Gram do this before. Somehow, today it helps.

Another day, I tear apart the guest room at Dick and Gram's house. I've lost my cheque book and can't find it anywhere. I once again pray in Jesus's name, asking him to help me find it. To my amazement, it works! Gram's been talking to me about the Gospel of Jesus, but I've been reading from the first part of the Bible, and it doesn't seem to connect.

One day she and I sit together and read about Jesus, specifically the story about the man with the unclean spirit and demons. I'm not sure what it's all about, but I know I've done a bunch of those sins I read about in Catholic school. I must have a filthy, despicable spirit inside me. I think back to a cartoon I once saw with a man; he had a devil on one shoulder and an angel on the other. Well, the devil on my shoulder is always sending me down the wrong road.

"Read Mark 5:5–6 for me," Gram says, caressing the scars on my arms.

"'Night and day among the tombs and in the hills he would cry out and cut himself with stones. When he saw Jesus from a distance, he ran and fell on his knees in front of him.'"[1]

"Does it sound familiar?"

---

[1] NIV.

"I didn't know people in the Bible cut themselves."

"And what did the man do when he saw Jesus?"

"He ran to Him."

"Run to Jesus, Joanie," Gram says. "Run to Jesus. After He heals the man of his unclean spirit, He sends the demons out, and then the man is in his right mind. In Matthew 28:18, Jesus says, 'All authority in heaven and on earth has been given to me.'[2] He can help everyone in His creation."

I just don't understand any of that, but I ask Gram what it would take to be baptized. I'm willing to try anything. Holding my hands, she explains that I should call the pastor of their church. She also reminds me that I can join them at church any time.

I decide to go see what it's all about, but I still have a lot of questions. I feel a battle raging inside me for control. I'm kind of like a spectator on the bleachers watching the fight.

• • •

My demeanor can change rapidly, even in a single day. Sometimes I feel strong and protective, and other times childlike, crying for hours. Still other times I feel sexy and flirty.

One evening, I remove the morning's makeup to prepare for an exciting night out. I'm somehow unfamiliar with the reflection looking back at me in the mirror. The head tilts, and I ponder the image. Not willing to dawdle long, I promptly continue with the regimen, applying a thick coat of foundation to cover a strange, indelible scar. Unhappy with the results, I grab a tint palate and add a layer of powdered blush, creating the illusion of structure to the undefined cheekbones. I then artistically paint a rainbow of color encircling my eyes. They say eyes are the window to the soul, but as I stare into these eyes, I see only the mirage of a distant sea, now nimbly framed with a thick coat of mascara. With the brush, I stroke from the lid to the tip of each lash. Searching through my cosmetic bag, I find the perfect glossy fuchsia lipstick. I slowly run it along my lips, pucker, and blow a kiss to the piece de resistance, finally ready for a wild night on the town.

A night that will be lost to my recollection.

• • •

The clouds gather and darkness covers the green fields as a summer storm barrels through the Midwest. I'm inside looking out as the lightning flashes and thunder roars a mere second after. I feel drawn to walk out into the middle of the field and raise my arms to the sky. The teeming rain quickly soaks through me as I call out, "Jesus, I am not afraid! You are my Savior." The earth shakes defiantly under my feet and I can barely stay standing, but I'm not afraid. I dance and sing in celebration.

---

[2] NIV.

"Joanie, what are you doing?" Gram is calling from the door, holding a towel. "Come inside, there's a storm out there."

Obediently, I walk back into the house. "I'm not worried about dying anymore, Gram. If I was hit by lightning, Jesus is my Savior and I'd go to heaven."

Gram dries my hair with the towel and then wraps it around me. I'm home. I have a new family.

Soon Dick baptizes me in the same lake where we reconnected, back when Azia was still alive. I want to make him and Gram happy.

I want to stay, but nothing in my life ever really sticks. Soon I'm in another battle with my mind.

"Joanie, what's this?" Dick asks one day, holding up a pipe. "I found it in the shed."

"I don't know, I'm sorry." I contort my body to get by him and run to my room.

"You need to let Jesus change your life."

What does that even mean? I thought I already had.

• • •

I walk down the lane to the road to collect the mail, and there I find a letter addressed to me.

"I've got mail!" I shout, jumping up and down, holding the letter high.

As I run back up the lane, I flip over the letter and look at the return address. It's from Stephen. The world around me vanishes into mist as I slide into my room and hop onto the bed, gripping the letter in my trembling hands.

While reading Stephen's letter, the color drains from my face. I lose myself in his words.

A hurricane hits me and I spiral into the vortex. I fall almost lifeless to the bed. For days all my energy is drained. I'm unable to eat, unable to drink. The pattern of the needlepointed pillowcase is etched on my face. I garner all my energy to pull myself up, roll my body out of the bed, and flop ragged to the floor. I blindly gaze into the endless distance between me and the bathroom, eventually dragging myself down the hall.

Getting back might be a job for tomorrow.

Then, like a bolt of lightning, my energy and zest for life returns days later. I doll myself up in those unfamiliar clothes I brought from my mother's house and head out to the bars in town. I need to drink to help me unwind enough to seduce a man, to fill the hollow emptiness that's unravelling me. These hot nights are happening more and more frequently.

• • •

I putter around, alone in the house. Beside Dick and Gram's bed, I find a copy of the book I'm reading with Dr. Braun—along with a letter Dick and Gram have written to him. My trust and faith in them shatter as I flip through the book, reading the detailed notes that reveal their attempt to figure me out.

They think I'm really sick!

Out of control, feeling irreconcilably betrayed, I decide that I need to leave. I pack some clothes, leave a cryptic note, and take whatever I can get a hold of to help me survive on the streets… once again, alone.

CHAPTER THIRTEEN
NOWHERE TO LAY MY HEAD

And Jesus said to him, "Foxes have holes, and birds of the air have nests, but the Son of Man has nowhere to lay his head."
(Matthew 8:20, ESV)

UPTOWN SOMEHOW FEELS SAFER TO ME THAN DOWNTOWN. MY EYES VIGILANTLY DART back and forth as I stand in front of a hotel across from Truman College, my backpack hanging loosely off my shoulder. A few garbage bags at my feet contains all my worldly possessions.

Darkness closes in on me with the setting sun and I anxiously try to light the cigarette in my trembling hand. The flash of a disposable lighter briefly brightens the entry, enabling me to see a haggard guy, maybe about my age, grinning eerily at me, half his teeth missing. Using his light and taking a puff of my cigarette, I make casual conversation with him. I'll call him #26, but surely he's much further down the line than that.

He likes me, invites me into his room, and having no place else to go I apprehensively follow him up. It's dark and dirty and the smell of urine in the hallway stings my nostrils. The paint flakes from the walls and cockroaches scurry around the sink. A lone mattress sits on the floor in the corner. No sheets, just an old wool blanket tossed on it. It's the kind of place that makes you want to take a shower and wash your clothes after having just been there, but it's a roof over my head, and for that I'm grateful.

Evidently it's a men's hotel and I'm not supposed to be there. I manage to sneak in and out undetected for about a month before I end up at the YMCA. The YMCA is a good place to be. They offer help for homeless people with mental health issues, but they also have rules. I need to take the prescribed meds, which make me feel spaced out and nauseous. My stomach just can't handle it. I palm the drugs, tricking the workers into believing I've taken them. But eventually I get caught and have to leave.

After that I head to the emergency room staff. The staff there have come to know me because of my regular urinary tract infections, and they direct me to Grasmere Residential Home.

At Grasmere, time stands still. I have access to a psychiatrist who says he's helping, but I still can't seem to grasp hold of myself. I fall into a deep abyss. There's news of a bombing in Oklahoma; kids have been killed, drawing me into the endless hours of coverage on CNN.

Everything else vanishes. My identity fades. I don't recognize myself, and I seem to be taken over by an unknown force. In moments of lucidity, I find even my meagre belongings have disappeared in the night. I don't feel safe. The weather's turned, and I'd rather be out anyway, so I leave.

On the streets, I always carry a cup so when I see people of some means, I can panhandle for small change. I'm amazed how many people do give something. There are two types of people who give: those who don't want to see you after they've put the money in the cup, and those who really do want to see you and have compassion. There's something special about those people.

"Hey sweetie, how are you doing tonight?" a man asks.

I quickly lower my head and slink down low, sure that he wants something. "Good?"

"Give me your hand." He pulls a $20 bill out of his wallet. "I want you to look at me."

My eyes narrow and darken. The edges of my mouth drop. Why do people immediately think I'll do anything in desperation?

He puts the wallet away with one hand, then slowly reaches out his other hand and patiently holding it under my clenched fist. I slowly loosen my grip, opening my tiny hand over his enormous hand; it's so big and strong that I'm sure he could carry the weight of the world in it. He places the $20 in my dirty hand, closing my hand tightly around the bill.

"I want you to promise me you aren't going to do drugs," he says.

I look up into his dark, soft eyes. They twinkle like Gram and Dick's. There's something special about him. For a moment, the joy and peace I felt with them sweeps over me. I can hear Gram's delightful laugh, and my muscles relax. My sullen lips quickly turn into a grin.

"Oh no, of course not," I assure him. "Thank you. You're a saint."

Turning away, I place the bill deep in a pocket. When I look up, he's disappeared into the looming fog.

I keep my promise. I don't spend his $20 on drugs. Instead, with an extra spring in my step, I head out to McDonald's for a small burger and fries.

As I begin to think about food, my shrunken stomach growls. I glance down the alley and see a friend, Shanice, dumpster diving. I'm happy to be getting a fresh meal. Surprisingly, I've had some real Grade A meals from behind a nearby five-star restaurant, and usually I won't hesitate to score the bounty from the top of the garbage. But today it will be McDonald's, and it will be fresh.

• • •

Heroine scares me. Besides, my own mind already gives me as much escape as I can handle. More actually. Fortunately, marijuana and alcohol also seem to do the trick in calming me down when I start to switch and spin out of control, though they make me feel listless and tired.

In the small groups where I hang out Uptown, narcotics aren't readily available. Terry's an older Irish guy who loves to tell stories. I love to watch his thick red beard bob up and down as he regales me with tales of days gone by. But when we hang out, everything's very shallow. It's no big deal when people come in and out of your life. You can't hold on to friends… you can't hold on to anything.

Toot is a big, heavyset woman who's really sweet and loving, with an infectious laugh that makes her whole body ripple. But boy, it doesn't take long to learn that people can be really nice to you one minute and then steal from you the next, or turn other people against you and jerk you around. I mean, I'm already on the streets; how much more can I be shunned?

The hardest part of being homeless is having lost all my stuff. I carried it with me as long as I could, but I trusted so many people… and you can't trust people. They make out to be friends, then leave and take your stuff with them. I was once beat up for just seven dollars and change. It's a hard lesson to learn, but possessions aren't the only things that get lost on the street.

• • •

I see a lost child sitting in a corner, slumped over, trying to sleep in the shade. The poor girl looks a mess. I should go and help her out.

I lift my tired body off the ground, and suddenly the child moves with me. That's when I realize she's just my reflection in the glass. There are no mirrors in this world, only reflections in windows.

I'm drawn to this echo of myself. Red circles outline the bottom of my eyes. Deep, dark shadows below them indicate either a lack of sleep, too much marijuana, or a combination of both. These hollow eyes are void of personality or character. The face is crowned with an indistinguishable mane, more resembling a tangled bird's nest than hair.

Unsettled, I lean closer, searching the reflection to find some remnant of the person I once was. With two fingers, I trace the scar on my chin, confirming it.

In the window, I notice a familiar figure approaching from behind. I shade my eyes to get a better look. It's Mrs. Carr, my mother's friend from St. James the Apostle Church. She's a social worker. Wishing to melt into the reflection and disappear, it registers that there's no chance she'll recognizing the dirty, unkempt, emaciated shadow I've become.

For a moment, I consider turning around to say hello in the hope that she'll bring me back to my former self… but I can't. That spark, that extroverted, outgoing part inside me, has faded away. Yet for the first time in many months, a smile cracks my weatherworn face, brightening it a shade as I feel strangely comforted by this familiar face.

● ● ●

Today's a bright sunny day. I'm singing in the streets, making everyone's day a bit brighter. I woke up this morning with a fabulous bunch of ideas. Well, I hadn't actually fallen asleep, so I guess I didn't really wake up today at all.

On my way to the library to find some books, I remember that it's my birthday. I stop at a bakery window and look at the birthday cakes… chocolate would be my favorite. Chocolate reminds me of Azia… oh Azia. I should go to the dog park and see if I can find an Azia-like dog… it won't be as great as Azia, but it's something to do

But oh yeah, I was going to see if they might give me a piece of cake… or maybe I could find an old cake in the dumpster. Ooo. The dumpster smells today. Beer… yeah, beer's a good idea. I turn the corner and find a liquor store.

● ● ●

Memories of Azia comfort me as I sit and watch the dogs play. Faint and dizzy, I feel exhausted. I scout around, but there's not much relief from the heat here, so I walk south toward the beach. There are fewer tourists on the beach than usual, a result of last year's baseball strike making fans less enthusiastic to attend games in the area. Still, the hot weather brings out the locals in droves.

Kicking off my filthy, smelly socks and shoes, I revel in the cool, wet sand squishing between my toes and strip down to a T-shirt and shorts. The mothers glare at me, and it feels like being naked and exposed in a hailstorm, every wedge of ice a crystal dagger cutting into my skin. Guardedly, they turn their children's playfully bobbing heads away, their gasping voices resonating and echoing across the water.

My pulse is weak and racing, my skin cool and moist, and I'm desperate for relief. My tired bones shake with a rush of energy as I enter the cool water. I wade deeper, my body collapsing with gratitude, my skin tingling as goosebumps burst out. Feeling cool and clean, my spirits lift enough to believe I'm just like these other revelers.

I return to my pile of clothes, lay down, and soak up the sun.

"Hey Joanie, you really have become a woman of color!" a woman calls. "You're bright red, like a fire truck!"

I realize the voice belongs to Toot, who chuckles as she presses her stumpy finger against my arm, leaving a white circle on my translucent red skin.

My eyelids slowly open. I had fallen asleep, and now all the other sun worshippers have left the beach. My body burns like fire as the sand rubs against my brittle skin. My blisters break and ooze, causing clumps of sand to adhere to my leg.

"Oooooooo, I can't move," I cry out.

"Better get a move on. Cop's coming. He ain't gonna let you stay here."

The sun's setting, but the nights aren't much cooler than the daylight hours, even with a remnant of a breeze coming off the water.

The police make regular rounds to ensure nobody sleeps on the beach. He's making his way to us, so I grab what's left of my belongings and Toot and I move on to find shelter in a nearby gutter.

I find an old collapsed potato chips box on the ground, and a smile comes to my face. A memory jumps to mind—jumping around gleefully with Mary Ellen on her pink canopy bed, munching on chips… Mrs. Shanley never got cross when we played like that.

Making space, I lay the cardboard box on the hard cement where we finally settle in for the night. I hold tightly to my torn blue backpack and hide my right hand, firmly gripping a knife for protection while I listen for intruders and wonder how many more hours I'll have to wait until I get a chance to eat again. Every day, I'm just wishing to die.

Drool runs steadily from my mouth, down my hollow cheeks, and pools on my forearm. I slowly rouse to the welcomed sun shining on my face, the circles beneath my eyes darkening with each sleepless night.

I have no idea how long I've been laying on this sidewalk. With nothing to do, you'd think I would have all sorts of pent-up energy, but sleep is the only thing I crave—and yet a good rest is the one thing that eludes me.

I know what I have to do now, but I'm unsure if I have the strength to do it. With my tattered bag on my back, I drag myself to my feet and begin down the nearby alleyways, tripping over empty bottles. A sludge of beer and urine mixes with last night's rain and washes up on my feet, quickly seeping into my shoes at the juncture where the tops are tearing away from the soles.

I lift a garbage pail lid and wretch as the smell of last night's fish and chips wafts into my nose. There's nothing in my stomach to expel. Demoralized and depressed, and somehow still determined to find enough food and water to last a few more days, I shuffle with today's dinner down the alley back toward my little corner under the overpass where I'll hide until I absolutely need to move again. At this point, necessity is the only thing spurring me on. It seems I have an innate instinct to survive even when all I want to do is die.

There aren't a lot of places where I feel comfortable using the bathroom—sometimes a fast food restaurant, or the local college. I like big open spaces, and it horrifies me to walk into smaller, confined places like gas stations. But sometimes you just gotta go.

Passing through the doorway of a gas station, I watch the person behind the counter intently, wanting to catch when they look up at the first sign of my *aroma*. My greatest fear, more than being seen, is to be smelled before I get to the restroom. I'm ashamed, sad, and angry at the person I've become.

Once safely in the restroom, I pick up the bar of green soap from the ledge. I'm reminded of a commercial where the bar of soap is cut to reveal the layers of protection within. My cuts, too, protect me. And like the suds that are washed down the drain, the pieces of the person I once was are caught up and washed away in the life-storm around me.

I hate myself… I want to escape… I just don't want to be.

• • •

Through the barred windows of an Uptown hardware store, I check the clock in the storefront. It's 1:30, I need to get around the corner to Grasmere. Between the hours of 2:00 and 5:00, they open their doors to visitors.

When I get there, my old psychologist is at the front door. I don't want to be recognized and asked a bunch of questions, so I pull my hoodie over my lowered head and move quickly to the community room to get lost in the fray.

A cloud of grey-blue smoke lays heavy in the room, each gasping breath filling my lungs with the oxygen-deprived air. Each blink of my eyelids scratches my eyeballs like sandpaper and the whites of my eyes turn red and cloudy. A gathering tear lets loose and runs down my cheek. The phlegm from my lungs loosens and expels with a deep, wet cough, but I'm grateful to get out of the cold and rest comfortably for a bit.

Summer's faded to fall. The beaches are long forgotten, the days shorter, and the once busy streets are deserted as both tourists and locals seek refuge from the impending winter. Only the few with no one to share Thanksgiving with are left wandering aimlessly, moving from one watering hole to another. We homeless are left huddling over warm sewer grates.

Even on the street, survival requires cash. The trick to making money is a shell game of moving around just enough that people take notice, not blending in so much as to become part of the landscape, a fixture. At the same time, you don't want to become the proverbial guy at a certain corner. I don't worry too much. Most people are too busy to notice anyway.

The lake's far too cold to swim in, so the best way to get clean is save up some pocket change to get into a fast food restroom, a somewhat hospitable environment to rinse my wretched mouth and freshen up a bit. I feel like I'm making strides when the manager stops to talk to me. While taking care of business, he brings me some extra fries and lets me stay a bit longer than usual.

After freshening up, feeling unusually energetic, I go "shopping" for shoes, until I'm recognized by a staff member and am unceremoniously asked to leave.

During the day, the library becomes my sanctuary. It's the place I go to lose myself in a good way. In secluded corners, I find love in a racy novel or get taken to a more desperate time with *The Color Purple*. Sometimes I just flip through the dog-grooming books, reminding myself of Azia. Inevitably, the book drops on my chest, raising and lowering with each sleepy breath.

When I wake, a short stroll over to the friendly librarians scores me an apple or leftover half-sandwich. I eagerly wash it down with cool water from the public fountain.

● ● ●

Snowflakes glide down from the sky with a twinkle, camouflaging the darkness and grime of the city in a winter wonderland. A crisp ring resonates in the streets behind the *ho-ho-ho* of a Sally Ann Santa standing under brightly colored Christmas lights. The sidewalk is covered by a thick white blanket of snow, each flake distinguishable as I watch them land on snowbanks lining the streets.

Steam rises up into the frigid air, not relevant to most people, but to me it signifies a warm grate. Oh how I wish Azia's warm body would be here, keeping me warm. But then, I would never wish this blight on him.

It's becoming more difficult to find safe places to stay for the night. With no unoccupied grates in sight, I begin a quest for food—scrounging, urban foraging.

I suddenly buckle as a sharp pain blossoms in my side. My haggard, sullen eyes and sunken cheeks tell the story of days spent worrying about where to sleep, where to eat. With cold, cracked fingers, I struggle to open garbage bins in search of anything edible. Every step sends an electric shock from my frozen wet toes up my legs; they scream in pain, begging for warmth.

I follow the blue and white hospital signs. The screeching wind has picked up and I squint, my ice-clad eyelash hairs protecting my eyes from the pelting snow. I eventually distinguish the red and white brick of the Methodist Hospital of Chicago.

A gust of the stiff wind blasts through and thrusts me to the ground. Searing pain shoots from my fingers; they seem to shatter like an old porcelain cup against the unforgiving ice, a streak of blood left behind. Crawling to a nearby bench, my arms and legs tremble as I heave my weakened body onto it, resting for a moment before continuing toward the hospital.

The hospital doors slide open, and I walk inside to find the registration desk. A triage nurse takes my vitals and tells me to sit in the waiting room. My raw, frozen fingers struggle to remove my running shoes, caked in the melting slush that now forms puddles beneath my chair. My socks, held together by threads, fall heavy, splashing into the frigid umber pool, exposing feet colored a rainbow of yellows, blues, and grays. Though my blistered and bleeding fingers tingle, my feet are hard and feel no pain.

A young boy sits between his parents. With an anguished look, they listen to the nurse's kind words as she carefully unwraps the boy's hand to expose a bloody gash. Quickly moving out of triage, they leave behind a bloody towel.

I reach across the seat, snatch the warm cloth, and wrap it around my frozen feet. I shove my stinging hands deep into my armpits under my opened coat. For a long time, the penetrating pricks and needling are unbearable; tears stream down my face from the shooting pain I feel as my appendages warm. Like a child, I whimper quietly in the corner.

Hours later, the sensation of warmth returns, bringing with it a more natural color.

With a strident, slightly annoyed voice, the nurse finally calls my name. Evidently, I was in the washroom when she called for me earlier. I'm escorted to a small observation room and wait there for what seems like hours before I'm seen by a doctor. I've recovered sufficiently by this time and given a stern warning that it's dangerous to stay outdoors in this cold. He says I should consider spending the nights in a shelter, then provides me with pamphlets and directions for some local facilities.

Just like that, I'm returned to the streets. What am I going to do with the pamphlets, build a fire? It's been a good day and I've discovered that I enjoy waiting in the ER. I think I'll be sick more often. I wonder how long I could sit in the waiting room before someone would make me register with the triage nurse. I'm pretty good at hiding.

Pacific Garden Mission is the bomb, but it's hard to get in. It's quite far, in the Near West Side, and I certainly wouldn't wander around in that neighborhood without an escort.

Bob's a big, burly guy. He's homeless, too, and often goes to the Pacific Garden. Today he's invited me along. As we approach, a huge sign illuminates the red brick building: *For the wages of sin is death.* A shiver runs up my spine. A part of me dies on the streets each day. Am I suffering in payment for my sins? Just beyond is another sign: *Christ died for our sins.* And then, further down: *Jesus saves.*

I'm paralyzed for a second as a ticker-tape of images flip through my mind: Easter at St. James the Apostle Church, a cross draped with a purple cloth, the baby Jesus, my little Brian, Azia, brilliant sunsets, the grandeur of the night sky, the Bible glowing on the nightstand, Gram's soft hands gently holding mine, our heads tenderly touching, her grey hair tangled together with my brown, the water cascading off my face as I spring up out of the baptismal waters. Jesus is there, and for a split second I feel Him.

"Joanie," Bob says, shaking me. "Are you coming? We need to get into line."

With a blink, I shudder and return to the moment. Bob grabs my arm and drags me through the snow to the entrance, all decorated for Christmas, and we fall into the line. After an unusually short wait, we're in for the night, greeted by a group of the friendliest people I've seen in a long time.

I return as often as I can, each time drawn in by the kindness and love of the people who work here, providing food, clothing, rest, and somehow hope.

A bright red and green pamphlet draws my attention to a nearby counter. "Do you think you may have a mental illness? Are you having a hard time accessing your medication?"

Yes, yes, I do, I think, drawn toward the pamphlet as though by a magnetic force. I grab them, almost toppling over in my attempt to reach. The inside stamp directs me to the Community Counseling Centers of Chicago. I know I need to go there.

Sometime later, the sliding doors of the counseling center open and I walk in, approaching the woman behind the counter.

"Hello," she says, her eyebrows jumping above her sunny eyes. "Do you have an appointment?"

"No, I don't." I raise the brochure. "It says I should come."

She grabs a pen. "That's okay. Do you have insurance or are you on public aid?"

"No, I don't have either."

"Where do you live? You need an address to get public aid. Do you have an address?"

"No. Is that going to be a problem?"

"Not at all." She smiles, shaking her head as she grabs some papers. "I'm just going to need to get some things set up. We'll fill out these application forms together. Do you think you can come back in a couple of days? Then I'll have you all set up."

I shrug. "Sure I can. What else am I going to do?"

I return two days later and meet Lori, an exceptionally tall woman whose kindness exceeds her height. She spends hours with me, patiently getting the details of my life and completing piles and piles of paperwork. My mind's so scattered that the pile seems overwhelming. I could never do it alone.

On my third visit, I'm escorted into an office with dark wooden shelves filled with thick leather-bound books, their spines stamped in gold. It's the first sunny day we've had in a long time and dust particles shimmer as they dance in the stream of light shining through the window.

Dr. Childers is poised in a brown leather chair behind her desk. The thin wired glasses, propped high on her nose, frame her gentle blue eyes. Her rosy cheeks glow in the sun.

I sit across from her, window to my back, her eyes looking deep inside me. A strand of blonde hair falls delicately over her face as she purses her lips, both edges lifting evenly in a warm smile. Her head tilts to the side and she furrows her eyebrows; she listens intently until everything and everyone around me seems to fade away. Soon she's calling out to people, dictating orders and formulating a plan to get me off the streets and onto public aid. All the while, her eyes never stray from mine.

After nine months of living on the streets, I'll be happy to start 1995 indoors. For the first time in a long while my shoulders lift back and I sit up straight in my chair. I feel lighter, not so far into the abyss.

I feel hope.

CHAPTER FOURTEEN
WAR AND DEATH

This is not a wrestling match against a human opponent. We are wrestling with rulers, authorities, the powers who govern this world of darkness, and spiritual forces that control evil in the heavenly world. For this reason, take up all the armor that God supplies.
(Ephesians 6:12–13, GW)

WITH MY WHOLE BEING, I'M LIVING THROUGH WORLD WAR III AND I'M NOT GOING TO win. I shrivel under the pressure of my imploding head, my clenched teeth unable to open, like an old rusty vice grip in need of oil. Drool runs from my mouth and I'm unable to loosen the grip to provide some relief.

My eyelids flutter as I try in vain to open my crusty eyes and focus. My arms and legs are limp and throbbing in pain. I feel bruised and beaten from a battle, fighting with my inner self.

With little control, I crawl into a ball and am overtaken; the grieving child inside cries incessantly for help, then with steely eyes, the stiff-necked obstinate teenager within emerges with explosive, uncontainable wrath. The hairs on my arms are singed by the glowing red ember of a cigarette, sending a sulphuric smell into the air. Needing to retreat, I use every ounce of energy I can muster to draw in my legs and lift my arms up around my head. I try to calm myself with fruitless, self-consoling words, but I'm on the front lines of an unwinnable war.

I arrive at the hospital with twenty-eight burns on my body—my neck, my feet, even the back of my arms where I won't see them. I'm convinced I didn't burn myself, yet they're fresh burns. And as sure as I am that I'm not responsible, there is no one else to blame.

I succumb to the truth: no matter what happened with my family, I am the problem. I'm sick. I'm mentally ill and my family's right not to be around me.

"What's wrong with me?" I ask Dr. Childers, my eyes transfixed on her. "Why do I seem to lose control? Why can't I pull myself together?"

Unflinching, she carefully counts the burns. "That's what we're going to try to figure out."

"It's extremely frightening. It's so hard to stop, as if there's this organized chaos inside me battling for control. I want to know what it is, so I can look it up and figure out how to fix it."

I'm determined to get a foothold in the bunker within my soul.

"Well, we don't need labels." She pauses, drawing in her pink lips, her brow wrinkling contemplatively. "Your body has been designed with certain coping mechanisms. You've had some very difficult experiences, but we're going to figure this out together."

"Is it normal?" My eyebrows triangulate, hopeful. My eyes are as wide and honest as a child's. My chin draws up as my bottom lip pouts.

Finished counting, she lowers the sheets covering me and gently holds my hand, speaking quietly. "Yes. For what you've gone through, it's normal for you."

The corners of her eyes moisten. She's struggling to hold back tears, but her voice is confident and reassuring. "Now let's get you stronger and back into that rooming house we found for you. Eventually we're going to find the right regimen, the right cocktail of medication that will work for you." She pauses. "But first we need to manage the lost time, that dissociation. I'm going to arrange some art therapy to help tackle it."

Art therapy? What does that even mean? She registers me in a day program for adults with mental health issues. Artistically putting the puzzle of my life together, I see that during bleak, stressful times, the pieces get dark, and many are lost and broken. But in the times when things are good, all the bright pieces are there and fit together. I stand back and look at the picture; I can see I'm not crazy.

Still, pieces from even yesterday's part of the puzzle are broken or lost for a time. It's disconcerting. I don't want to be lost; I want to be whole, to be bright and radiant.

Dr. Childers has assembled a team of specialists to help in my recovery. Colleen is my psychologist. The strength contained in her tiny physique is mind-boggling. As I meet with her, I'm left exposed and unconcealed as she explores for fresh, undetected emotional lesions. Our appointment is scheduled for an hour. Two hours later, overcome and drenched in a floodgate of tears, my body is convulsing, pulled in a tight little ball. I'm trapped in a choke point under her desk. Colleen sits patiently on the floor, lying in wait just outside the barrier of the desk, her voice soft and attentive

She begins her reconnaissance mission.

"Joanie, I'm here," she says. "How are you feeling? When you're ready, you can reach out for me. I'm here to help you up."

Suddenly, Colleen's cloudy figure transforms into the father. My grown-up self melts away with the color in my face, leaving only the trembling eight-year-old inside me emerging with wide, terror-filled eyes, scrambling and recoiling. My struggle? Wanting to die and battling to survive.

"Daddy, don't touch me." I kick out my feet violently, demanding to retreat deep under the desk. "Leave me alone. I want to die."

Retreating, I pull my knees close to my chest and wrap my arms around them. I wait. My whole body writhes in pain as I shoot daggers from my bulging eyes.

Careful not to advance too quickly, though not deflected by her waiting patients, Colleen begins a slow and steady offensive of encouraging words. "Joanie, remember where you are. I'm Colleen. You're in my office. You're in a safe place."

After what seems like hours, this barrage of inspiration slowly begins to tear down my defenses. Still wary of an ambush, my eyes tightly closed and the corners of my mouth drawn, I shudder. Tears stream down my face, soaking my clothes.

"I… I wanna come out… but I'm afraid."

Seeing a weak point, she infiltrates. Palms up, her hands slowly enter the no man's land between us, careful not to breach my blockade too quickly. "Here I am. When you're ready, just take hold of my hand. I've got your back. I will support you."

Measuredly, my breath slows. The muscles in my arms relax, allowing me to loosen the grip around my legs. My lashes flicker with the invading light and the shadow before me slowly transforms back into Colleen. My cold, clammy hand shakes as it reaches out and slowly touches her unwavering hands. I'll need her physical touch to help guide me from my stronghold under the desk. But she's breached my stone fortress. My fortifications melt and crumble around me as she continues to barrage me with affirmation, reinforcing my beaten spirit.

Unhurriedly, she rises to her knees, reinforcing herself. It's an unconditional surrender from me: my deadweight falls into her waiting arms, her gentle voice assuring me that she'll safeguard my troops. She eventually lifts me up out of the miry trench, and I stand on firm ground, physically and emotionally supported by a friend.

There is no medication to deal with this part, the baggage I carry. These types of exchanges happen several times as I battle with my past over control of my present, in the hope of building a unified and victorious future. Each time I stand a bit taller, shoulders squared, chin up, feeling lighter, amazed that all this can happen by merely trusting someone. Through it all, I know there's nothing I could do to Colleen to make her leave me. I've always yearned for this kind of positive physical contact.

•••

The days are long, the air thick and heavy. My ankle aches as I limp from house to house collecting census information. Little droplets shimmer at the ends of my dyed-red hair before letting loose and dripping with a splash. Sweat drips from every pore, dampening each sheet as I stand at the doors, tediously taking information about who's living at each house. My internal thermostat has been broken for as long as I can remember. I've found a new freedom making $15 an hour with the Census Bureau, but on days like today it's almost unbearable.

My walls of distrust have been crumbling ever since coming off the streets and into the SRO. I'm letting people in and building relationships. Manny, an African American man who lives a floor above me, works at one of the nice restaurants downtown. His name is actually Victor, but I call him Manny; he's about five years younger than me. I love the way his long curly hair falls on his face. I've opened my heart to him. His dark eyes are usually framed by misty red sclera, either from drugs or the hours he spends over the hot stove. This is the first long-term relationship I've had since Bill, and I'm all in. He's a great guy.

I roll a joint. "Manny, you don't do coke anymore, right?"

"No, no, Joanie. I used to, but not anymore. I've got a good job. I'm clean now." He lights a joint of his own and takes a long drag.

After we're done drinking and smoking, he's so tired and chill that he stays over for the night, leaving early the next morning.

I've been given more responsibility at the Census Bureau. I'm a manager now, so I want to look nice. I search through my extensive jewelry box one day, looking for my gold necklace and bracelet, but they're missing. Where could they be? Dumping all the jewelry on the bed, I separate each item in the pile, coming up empty.

I glance at my watch. I need to go or I'll be late.

I close the door tightly behind me, jiggling the key out of the keyhole, just as Damon opens his door across the hall. I live in this building because I'm on social security. My gig with the Census Bureau is only temporary. But Damon isn't on social security; he pays rent for this dump. He sells newspapers every day on different corners of the city, making about $35 to $40 a day. Fantastic money. He's a true entrepreneur. He knows where his customers will be and what they want to read. He smokes cigarettes, pot, and drinks everyday, too, so we've gotten to be good friends. We use together—or at least we used to. He says he found Jesus or something.

"Damon, you'll never believe what happened," I tell him. "I've lost that gold necklace and bracelet I got last week. You know, I paid $50 each. I just can't imagine how I lost them. Did you see anything? Who could have gotten into my apartment? You'd better lock your doors. There's a thief in the building!"

"Joanie, Victor took it." Damon catches himself, trying not to laugh as his eyes narrow.

I step back, throw my hands on my hips, and shake my head emphatically, "Ah. No, no. Manny wouldn't do that."

Damon's wisdom has been earned, though. It's evident through the silver strands glimmering in his dark curly hair.

Glaring into my eyes, he speaks with unflinching authority. "Yeah, he would. You need to get a grip, girl. He's an addict."

I give him a backhanded wave, then raise my chin in defiance and storm down the hall. I know Manny wouldn't take anything from me. He loves me. I refuse to believe it.

On the bus to work, I mull over the morning's events, yawning and pulling up my comfy pants. I just can't seem to wake up these days. I hope Damon isn't mad at me after that outburst. I've been feeling a bit off, flying off the handle all the time. I've gained a bit of weight, too, and can't fit into my jeans anymore.

I'm concerned I may be going through the change of life, so I've made a doctor's appointment today during my lunch hour. I read the doctor's name on my reminder card and smile: Dr. T from Transylvania, Romania. He just makes me howl, and he finds me very interesting. I enjoy entertaining him.

To add insult to injury, I've recently discovered that I have diabetes. The doctors want to keep an eye on it. Personally, I really have no interest in following all these diabetes rules, but Dr. T will have to do a blood test today anyway, so I figure I'll kill two birds with one stone.

"Joanie, have you noticed any changes?" Dr. T asks as he takes off his stethoscope and hangs it around his neck, making notes in my chart.

"As a matter of fact, since you mention it, I think I'm going through the change of life. My mother started early, too. It must be hereditary. Is it?"

When he turns around, the look on his face is something I've seen before. He brings a chair over and sits in front of me, knee to knee. He reaches out for my hand.

"Joanie, you're not going through the change of life," he says in a soft voice. "You're pregnant! And with your diabetes, there's a good chance there will be complications if you don't take your blood sugar more seriously."

He spends quite some time listing the challenges I'll face, but I really don't hear anything much past "You're pregnant." I stare into space, his face fading into the white walls behind him.

From the little that does come through, it sounds like I'll have a big baby, like twenty pounds or something!

He pauses and puts his hand on my shoulder. "Joanie, do you want this baby?"

At his touch, I snap back. My voice quivers as I strain to regain focus. "I had a baby once, the only other baby I've had, and I had to give him up for adoption. I'm not young anymore. I'm forty-two. This may be my only chance."

A lonely tear breaks loose and runs down my cheek. I wipe the tear and my running nose with the back of my hand. I want this baby more than anything.

Dr. T nods. "Then let's send you to the hospital and get you checked out."

He also reassures me that if this is what I want to do, he'll help me get through the physical challenges; but if I don't, I don't have much time to change my mind.

In the hospital, I'm a mixed bag of emotions, one minute crying, the next laughing with the nurses. Wringing my hands, I pace the room, wondering how I'll be able to take care of myself and the baby. On the other hand, the excitement of finally having a child of my own makes my heart race and puts a spring in my step. I love children and have always imagined a normal life, living in the suburbs with my husband and child. This could be my chance.

But who's the father?

Manny's heard from Damon that I'm in the hospital for observation since I'm pregnant. He drops in for a quick visit.

"Hey Joanie, hope you get back soon. It's not the same without you." He struts into the room with a wink and a glint in his eye. His demeanor quickly changes, though, when he lowers his head and comes close. "Uh, I'm a bit low on cash. Think you can spot me $40 or $50? I'll pay you back at the end of the week when I get paid. It's just a little tight this week."

Manny's jittery. He licks his thick lips. His eyes dart between me and the door.

I always want to help out, so I rummage through my purse. "Well, I wasn't planning on coming here, so I don't have any cash. Just my debit card."

"No problem. Give me your code and I'll give it back when you get home." His eyes have grown two sizes, and his teeth sparkle behind a big grin. He snatches the card from my hand, biting his lower lip.

How sweet. I flush as I give him the code. *Maybe he'll buy a gift for the baby,* I think to myself.

But the money isn't for a baby gift, and instead he just cleans me out. During the short time I'm in the hospital, he takes $2,450 of the $2,500 I've saved from the Census job. I just can't believe it. He only leaves $46 in the account.

Once again, it's Damon who convinces me it's not a clerical error at the bank. Manny really has taken all the cash.

How could I not know? I've been involved in the drug scene. I know what drugs do to people. My head drops as I look at the bank book, my shoulders sinking. I put my hands on my stomach and realize this is Manny's baby. He's the father, and oh what a baby daddy he will be.

I keep making regular visits with Dr. T., trying to keep my blood sugar levels under control, but I'm totally out of control, continuing to swell. He's freaking me out. I'm just learning how to control my own levels, let alone with a baby inside me.

Panicked, I visit Dr. Childers one day. She's helping me wrap my head around all these emotional challenges and working on my relationship with my own mother.

"Joanie, how late did your mom work most days?" she asks.

"Sometimes pretty late, when she had to close up shop. She worked hard. They really needed her there."

"All night?"

"No, she was home at night. Sometimes she'd get in just before I heard my dad stumble up the steps and down the hall. Sometimes she'd have been sleeping for a while already."

"Did he stumble in quietly?"

"No," I scoffed. "He'd smash against the walls in the hall, even when he tried to tiptoe in."

"And your mom never heard him… go into your room?"

I'm quiet. There's a steadily increasing thump in my chest as my heart tries to escape. I gasp for a breath and cradle my stomach. A mother of a young child listens intently in her sleep. She must have heard something. She must have known.

Dr. Childers reaches out. "You've put your mom up on a pedestal, Joanie. You need to bring her down and deal with the whole truth."

Though my mother has always denied knowing that anything went on, Dr. Childers shows me there's no way she couldn't have known; she was in the house, I was little, and she would have heard. Evidently, I need to acknowledge and accept that she's flawed, too. But is she as flawed as me? Coming to this realization lightens the heaviness inside me.

Throughout the next week, I re-evaluate other things, too. It's beginning to register that my baby's father, who is now suggesting we get married, is a drug addict who has stolen all my money. As much as I'm grateful to Dr. Childers for finding me a place to live, the ten-by-ten-foot room at the SRO isn't suitable for a child.

Manny says he will take care of me and the baby, but he's shown me what kind of person he is. I recognize that neither one of us are competent enough to care for this child.

Without discussing it any further with Manny, I've come up with a plan and present it to Dr. Childers.

"You said how beautiful this baby would be, and in any other situation you would take the baby," I say. "Why won't you take my baby? You don't have any of your own and you're engaged to a great guy. Won't that be a great way to start your marriage?"

I'm pleading, dead serious as I try to find a solution to my problem. I have only one motto in life: don't hurt a child. I'm desperate and running out of options.

We have a long discussion about the ethics of her taking my child, blah blah blah. The bottom line is, she won't take the baby. I'd have to go through the whole pregnancy and delivery process, plus I'd have to be sure my blood sugar levels remain normal, or I'll hurt my child. Even if I go through all this, I'd have to give up the baby—again. That would kill me.

I pace the streets, calculating the pros and cons. I really don't see an option. I'm on my own, and Manny isn't going to support me in deciding to kill his child. I can't see anywhere else to go.

Unable to get a good grip, I wipe my sweaty palms and pull myself up onto the bus. My muscles are tense as I take my seat, alone. I flashback to another bus ride, and my heart races. I struggle to take a breath… is this what a heart attack feels like? People around me have their heads down, buried in their newspapers or phones. Desperate for any sign of support, my eyes dart around in search of anyone who will raise their head and make eye contact. I'll talk to anyone. I look, and I wait, but there are no troops to rally around me. I'm alone.

I stumble off the bus and slink toward my destination. Picketers stand at the fence yelling, "Murderer!" Others pray. I stop short, staring at them, my red cheeks drenched. Don't they know how hard this is? I want to retreat and escape, but I have no choice. I have nowhere to go. I've surrendered my own desires to keep this child and decided that I need to solve this problem. This is the only solution. This is going to help, right? I make a run for the door.

They say a big city is a lonely place. You rub shoulders with a million people every day, but it can be the most isolated, solitary place. We live anonymously, not really knowing anyone. That's how I feel at the abortion clinic. I feel abandoned, left alone to fill out the paperwork, alone on the surgical table, alone in the pain… and let me be clear, there's pain. As the vacuum sucks the fetus, my baby, out of my body, I'm shaking and screaming… alone. It's horrible and painful. My hopes and dreams are pulled apart and destroyed.

At home, phone in hand, lying on the bathroom floor, shoulder to the ground, knees pulled in, I call Dr. Childers. Then I wrap my arms around my legs and sob. Tears flood down my face until there are no more tears. They're spent from the physical and emotional pain coursing through my body.

After everything I've been through, I have never felt such a crushing weight pulling me down. I'm gasping for air, drowning in guilt, with no light and no hope, having broken the one principle I've always clung to: never hurt a child. This is the deepest, darkest time in my life. There's nowhere to go from here.

I call Dr. Childers on her direct line three times that night. It's unusual for a doctor to provide that number to a patient, yet each time she answers. I feel a distant spark splitting me open, striving to ignite something that will stir a flame in my soul. She has saved my body, but my soul is empty.

Through the day and into the night, I just lie there, limp, bruised, and beaten.

I killed my baby.

PART TWO
REDEEMED

CHAPTER FIFTEEN
DADDY

The Spirit you have received adopts you and welcomes you into
God's own family. That's why we call out to Him, "Abba! Father!"
as we would address a loving daddy.
(Romans 8:15, Voice)

IT'S BEEN A GREAT WEEK AT DICK AND GRAMS, BUT NEXT WEEKEND IS MY WEEKEND TO die. On the bus to Chicago, the woman next to me leans in and asks, "Would you like God to be your Father, your Daddy, Joanie?" She taps my hand. "Won't you take Jesus as your Savior?"

I have a hard time with the concept of a "father." The only two examples in my own life are the father, who also fathered my son Brian, and Manny, the father of my second child, a lying, stealing drug addict. Neither paints a picture of strength, support, or love in any way, shape, or form. And a "daddy"? Well, daddy just isn't in my vocabulary at all.

Yet as I sit on the bus next to a complete stranger, with my *Left Behind* book in my lap, ready to give up on life, I find myself looking up, beyond the top of the bus, out to the blue skies above, praying to God… my Father… my Daddy.

"God, I don't have much good to say about fathers, but this woman next to me tells me You're greater than any father," I pray. "She says You love me and sent Your son Jesus so I would be free from everything that separates me from You. I don't like rules much, and from what I've seen the Bible has a lot of them. But she says I don't have to worry about that because You love me so much that You're gonna meet me right here where I am. I know I'm a sinner and need to be forgiven. I'm sorry for sinning. I accept Jesus as my Lord and Savior. I need a good Father. Will You be my Daddy?"

I've heard about God and Jesus my whole life, but this time it's different. It's September 10, 2000, at 5:07, a week after my intended suicide weekend. Something is changing inside me. I have a desire to get to know this God: the Father, Son, and Holy Spirit. My heart does a tango. I'm dancing inside. I feel a burning inside I've never felt before, a burning that tells me I'm alive. But this burn doesn't hurt; instead it seems to *heal* my hurt. I feel lighter and sit straighter. My face feels tighter, like I've gotten a facelift.

I'm intrigued, somehow drawn to understand all this better, to understand Him better. Vignettes of my life float above me, the battles I've fought. If I reached out, I'd almost touch them. Why is it so unbelievably meaningful to me that the God who created me knows me so well, that He is going to meet me right where I am? Of course He will. Even though I can't believe some of those things I've heard, even though I've just killed my own baby, with all this crap that's happened, why is this so crazy to believe? I heard it at school. I heard it from Damon. I heard it from Gram. But it never really sunk in.

God, You love me just the way I am!

I can't contain my excitement. Thoughts and questions flow out of me until the woman next to me excuses herself. As she steps out into the aisle, I glimpse her glowing face, a tear clinging to the outer edge of her eye, a dam holding back a lake of tears that with one blink would send a flood streaming down her flushed cheeks.

"Joanie, I'm so happy for you," she says before she disembarks. "The angels in heaven are celebrating that you've decided to follow Jesus. But remember what I said: it's easy to decide but hard to keep. It's going to take a bit more work. Promise me you'll find a church and tell your friends Damon, Dick, and Gram."

I nod, and as she touches my hand a warm rush radiates from my fingers up my arm. She turns and leaves the bus.

Sitting back in my seat, I let out a deep sigh and rest my head. Then it strikes me, who *was* that woman? I didn't even get her name. But I'm quickly distracted with thoughts of home and telling Damon about what's happened. These next hours on the bus can't pass fast enough.

Damon grew up in the notorious Cabrini-Green housing projects with his mom, dad, and seven siblings. Evidently his father had another family, but Damon only found out about them later in life. He had also been through the jail system and knew a thing or two about real life in that part of Chicago. Though no stranger to violence, he knew that growing up in Cabrini-Green also required a person to have deep bonds of community and mutual support in order to survive. To this day, he's very close to his sister Ruth, who lives with her son in the South. He loves them. When he talks about them, his voice softens and his whole body relaxes. He often goes to see them for Christmas, and during one of those trips a few years ago he "came to know the Lord."

As I lean my head against the window, the warmth of the fall's evening sun bathes my face. I close *Left Behind* and ponder Damon's decision. It's just like the woman said: "It's easy to decide but hard to keep." The first time Damon decided to have faith in God, he didn't keep it. When he came home from that trip, he started watching this rich, black preacher guy on Sunday mornings, and I'd watch it with him. I just thought this guy was doing all right for himself, so maybe this God really was something.

Well, Damon tried doing the right thing, but soon he was back to his old self.

The sway of the bus lulls me as I reflect back. Last Christmas, Damon went down to visit his sister and found Jesus again, but this time it was different. Something changed. Normally when he came back from one of these trip, he brought back great weed, and I remember waiting for him to return. I called and called him, anxious to hear back. I knocked on his door for days after he was supposed to come back, and finally one day he opened the door.

"Damon, you're home. How long have you been back?"

"Uh, I don't know. A couple of days maybe." He was squinting from the little light in the hallway. His putrid breath was off-putting. He was a mess. His stained shirt was half-tucked into his wrinkled pants, the buttons mismatched.

"Damon, do you have any weed?" I asked, breathlessly.

"You know what? In fact, I do." He stepped into his room and began looking around. He took a long time searching his tiny ten-by-ten room, opening cupboards and drawers, until he finally stopped. He lifted a little baggy, giving me a big grin.

"Here it is. Come here."

My heart skipped a beat. I licked the drool gathered at the corner of my mouth and nibbled my bottom lip, bouncing at the thought of rolling a joint. But Damon had other thoughts. He walked over to the bathroom and dumped it into the toilet.

Even now, all these months later, I gasp a little at the memory. I can picture that day as clearly as ever.

"W–what are you doing?" My eyes popped out of my head as I looked down into the toilet, shuddering as I watched the buds float in the water.

He smiled ear to ear as he flushed it down. "I have to show you something."

I just couldn't believe it. Dazed and mortified, I fell back and landed on the floor like a deflated balloon, ready to cry. Then I got so mad that I jumped to my feet, grabbed him by his dirty, wrinkled shirt and began shaking him. "Damon, have you lost your mind? What have you done? What have you done?"

"Joanie, I've given up smoking weed." His face shone. Just like the woman on the bus, he had the biggest smile I'd ever seen, which is saying something for Damon; his teeth are his most recognizable feature.

I fell back, chuckling. "Yeah right, like that'll ever happen."

"And I've given up smoking cigarettes." When he said this, his voice cracked, as though he were trying to persuade himself as much as persuade me.

That's when I knew he was really messed up and must just be doing some new weird drug.

Damon lay back on his bed, his chest slowly rising and falling. His eyes didn't flutter wildly under his eyelids like when he had his other highs. He seemed strangely at peace.

I'll admit, I was in shock and didn't believe it for a second, but over the next few months Damon was an absolute jerk to me. He wouldn't do anything but work, get fast food, and sleep. I didn't like him anymore. He wasn't a nice person. I remember thinking that if this was what it was like to find God, I didn't ever want to locate Him.

It took a couple of weeks for the reality of what had happened to Damon to really sink in. He wasn't going to get any new pot. I was on my own.

Six weeks later, he finally started resembling a human being again, though it took about six months for him to be completely right. At least I could sit down with him in his room, at that same little table by the window, to have a talk.

"Joanie, I was with my sister Ruth when I realized I'm going nowhere in my life," he told me. "The only way it's going to change is if I give up this addiction I have."

Then he started telling me about Jesus. At the time, I was thinking, *Okay. This is going to wear off.*

But it hasn't. This time he's still doing the work to hold on to his faith. I think maybe Damon gave up too much at once, though, what with going through withdrawal at the same time. That's why he was such a jerk.

And yet every Sunday his door would open as an invitation for me to come in. Then he'd go to the dive downstairs and get food so we could eat and listen to that TV preacher together. It was good food, too. A whole breakfast. I was always eager to go.

• • •

The bus pulls into the Chicago station and I gather my things and step off the bus. Won't Damon be surprised? I can't wait to tell him. I can't wait to tell everyone! I'm so happy to be alive, to feel.

Wait, what? I'm happy to be alive? My eyes dance a little and the corner of my mouth twitches playfully. Yes, I'm happy to be alive.

I bounce up the stairs of my building, running to my room, feeling like Tigger but more likely resembling a sad Eeyore after sitting on a bus for hours with my fused ankle. The keys aren't cooperating as I try to unlock the door, and Damon opens his door to see what the commotion's about. As excited as I am, he'll have to wait a minute.

"Just wait there for a sec," I say as I get the door open and fall into my room.

I head directly for the freezer and pull out a plastic bag. Damon is now at the door.

"Damon, do you have a lighter handy?" I ask. He sighs and shakes his head. "Oh yeah, you don't smoke anymore!"

I grab my purse, pull out my lighter, and light the fifteen copies of my suicide note, placing them in the metal garbage pail. We watch together as they're consumed into embers.

"Damon, I'm a sinner and need forgiveness," I say. "I've accepted Jesus as my Lord and Savior. I have a good Father now."

Damon starts to cry and gives me a big hug. We talk for hours. We count on each other a lot, and now I see how much I've needed him in my life. I have no one else so physically close to me who cares for me so much. When I'm depressed, the people downstairs don't know how bad off I am, but Damon does. He makes sure I eat, shower, and get up. He's never given up on me and has never asked for anything in return. It's like God put him there.

After Damon leaves, I call Gram and Dick. I can barely hear them, because they're jumping up and down, cheering my decision to follow Christ. It's been a long time coming.

Like Damon, I've decided a lot of times. I even got baptized once, but it was only to make Dick and Gram happy, hoping they'd let me stay with them a bit longer. I didn't know then that I had to work to keep my faith. But it never really meant anything to me then, so I wouldn't have really tried.

• • •

Gram mails me a New Living Bible so we can start studying it together. I hold the brown paper package tightly against me, my face flushed, my heart nearly beating out of my chest.

Sitting at the table by the window, I place the package on my lap and carefully untie the twine to reveal a red, leatherbound book. I close my eyes, lift it up to my face, and slowly draw air in through my nostrils. I hold my breath for a while before exhaling leisurely; there's nothing better than the smell of real leather.

Oh thank you, Gram, I think. *I'm overjoyed.*

On the left page of each book in this Bible is an explanation about the author and the state of the community he lived in to help me understand the context, but the coolest thing is that on the right is a decorative letter I can color. With my twelve colored pencils, I feverishly color as I read through each chapter. I call Gram to apologize, feeling bad for what I've done. The Bible is a holy book and even putting it on the floor is a sin. How much more sinful must it be to color it?

"Gram, I know when I was in school the nuns would say how important the Word is and you shouldn't put it on the floor. I get it's important, but I've been coloring it and I feel absolutely awful. It's just the letters are so pretty…"

Gram giggles. "It's okay."

"But you don't understand. I'm doing it a lot." I'm sure she'll be angry that I've ruined her gift with some sort of blasphemy.

"Make it your own Bible," she says instead. "God doesn't care you're coloring it as long as you're reading it, too. Memorizing it is even better. That way, when you don't have a Bible handy, you can still turn to God and remember what He's said to you." Her voice is as soft and smooth as Aunt Bee's butter pecan pie. "You should try memorizing, too."

I'm just happy that coloring in my Bible isn't blasphemy, and reading it makes God happy. Placing the Bible on the round table next to me, I begin to flip through the pages. For the first time, my eyes are opened. I can really see and understand. I'm also excited that the *Left Behind* book is part of a series; I can't wait to read them all.

Not everything in my life changes right away. There are still days when I want to die, when I feel empty and want to burn to try to feel something… anything.

I decide to take Gram's advice and resolve to memorize scripture before I let myself burn. Today it's a long, difficult verse. As my eyes follow my finger along the page, I'm convinced that I don't really need to burn so much this time.

All in all, it goes well. Eventually I'm memorizing verses and not burning at all. As I read, I become more aware, more cognizant… more *here*. I ponder the Lord knowing and loving me, and Him seeing me hurt myself. I sniffle and wipe a tear, imagining how sad that would make Him. I read about Holy Spirit inside me, in my heart. I don't want Him to be in a place that I'm going to hurt, because if I hurt myself, somehow I'm going to hurt Him. I burn myself less and love Jesus more.

• • •

I've still been seeing Dr. Childers regularly and Colleen three times a week, each time revealing my skin as they look for evidence of new mutilation. Dr. Childers has been on vacation, so it's been a few weeks since I've seen her. She lifts the hospital gown draped over me and counts only three burns, and they're all older burns that are already healing. There are no new signs of self-harm.

Quietly I change back into my clothes and meet her at her desk.

"Joanie, what's going on?" she asks. "There are no fresh burns. I'm so proud of you."

"Well, I found out about Jesus," I say, beaming. I'm pleased I've made her proud.

Pushing her chair back, her voice cracks a bit as she calls out to her receptionist. "I'm going to take a bit longer."

Then she stands up behind her big desk, comes right around, and pulls up a chair right beside me, like we're equals. Her eyes glisten and her cheeks brighten to a rosy pink.

She reaches softly for my hand. "Joanie, I'm so happy for you. Tell me everything."

I take all the time I need to tell her what happened: the suicide letters, Gram and Dick, the book, the woman on the bus, the prayer. Dr. Childers shares that she, too, is a believer, but she wasn't allowed to share her faith with me because of an oath she took when she started working for the community centers. Now that I've opened the door to the discussion, we can share our faith stories and pray together. We talk for a long time.

Each morning I sit by my window with a cup of coffee and read the Bible. Each verse reveals a new truth about this God who loves me so much, this God I knew about but didn't really know. As I get to know God, a warm calmness flows over me from deep inside, strengthening and regulating my heart, pumping life-sustaining blood through every part of my body, bringing with it a sense of peace and joy that bubbles inside like the mania I once tried to control. This joy is so strong and dynamic that I'm incapable of containing it. I want to share it with everyone I meet—in the grocery store, in Dr. Childers's waiting room, in the hospital, on the "L", everywhere.

Romans 3:23 says, *"For everyone has sinned; we all fall short of God's glorious standard."* I sinned. My dad sinned. My mom sinned. Those many men I was with sinned. Even Dick sinned; he's not perfect. We all make mistakes.

Romans 6:23 says, *"For the wages of sin is death, but the free gift of God is eternal life through Christ Jesus our Lord."* I deserve death and destruction for my sin. I deserve to burn, because like everyone else I'm not perfect.

Romans 5:8 says, *"But God showed his great love for us by sending Christ to die for us while we were still sinners."* God knows how imperfect I am and He still loves me that much. My own family couldn't love my imperfections. It blows my mind that He does.

1 Peter 2:24 says, *"He personally carried our sins in his body on the cross so that we can be dead to sin and live for what is right. By his wounds you are healed."* The sins of the world have to be paid for, and Jesus did that. All of our sins and imperfections have already been paid for. It no longer matters what I've done, or what other have done to me. I just need to look forward… I just need to look up.

Ephesians 1:7 says, *"He is so rich in kindness and grace that he purchased our freedom with the blood of his Son and forgave our sins."* His grace, His power, has cured me. How much more can He do? What am I capable of through His power?

John 3:16 says, *"For this is how God loved the world: He gave his one and only Son, so that everyone who believes in him will not perish but have eternal life."* He just wants me to believe. He wants me to live!

1 Corinthians 6:20 says that *"for God bought you with a high price. So you must honor God with your body."* In return, He just wants me to glorify Him, to honor and worship Him? That's not hard, I can do that!

Acts 4:12 says, *"There is salvation in no one else! God has given no other name under heaven by which we must be saved."* No one else is worthy to pay the price. It could only be a perfect God; it could only be Jesus.

2 Corinthians 6:18 says, *"And I will be your Father, and you will be my sons and daughters, says the Lord Almighty."* I have a new Father, the best father.

I've always loved a good novel. As I sit here and probe the chapters of my own life, though I know it's true, I confess that it reads like a piece of fiction. I also know that it doesn't define me; God does.

Looking back, I see God's hand reaching out to me through His creation, through people around me, even through Azia. He's a Shining Light I just never recognized. Dr.

Childers assures me that though all my troubles have certainly played a role in who I've become, Jesus has overcome these experiences and will use them for His glory and honor. In Christ, I am a new person. The old has passed and a new life has begun.

    This is where my redemption story begins.

CHAPTER SIXTEEN
TRANSFORMATION

*Don't copy the behavior and customs of this world, but let God
transform you into a new person by changing the way you think.
Then you will learn to know God's will for you,
which is good and pleasing and perfect.*
(Romans 12:2)

OUR BODIES ARE CREATED WITH COPING MECHANISMS FOR SELF-PRESERVATION. Through periods of my life, I've suffered from severe trauma and stress. Had they stayed in my consciousness, the trauma would have destroyed me. In an effort to protect me, my brain compartmentalized it into boxes and hid it deep inside me somewhere.

From time to time, this trauma seeps out of its box and sends my mind into protective mode in order to defend itself. These natural defenses kick in to shield my memory until it can get the trauma safely back into the box. My brain dissociates in and around the time of the trauma, which is why I have lapses in memory and why I lie to people to try to fill the gaps. I become very confused.

Dr. Childers and Colleen say it's important for me to deal with the traumas in each box so they don't pose a threat anymore. They want me to open each box in a safe and protected environment and address what's inside, then slowly integrate these memories back into my consciousness. They promise that these lost memories are nothing to be afraid of, and they're always going to be there to help me understand myself better.

These are the battles I've been waging under the desk with Colleen—and at times, with Dr. Childers. Though I'm gaining ground, it's still a difficult war. But with Jesus on my side, I know I'm not fighting it alone anymore.

Still, I feel like a caged animal that's been set free. I'm still pacing in circles, afraid or somehow unaware I can run.

Less and less, I find myself under the desk or in a corner awaiting rescue as I battle the demons of my past. My team's tactics have been working, but evidently there has been some talk in the psychological community about controlling and limiting touch in therapeutic relationships. I've been doing so well that Colleen asks if I would be willing to meet with a panel that will be writing policy to explain the need for touch in our therapy and how I would be impacted by a no-touch policy.

The thought of a no-touch policy immobilizes me. "Oh Colleen, if you can't touch me, how are we going to get me out from under your desk?"

"Well, we're going to talk about that, and I would appreciate it if you would come with me to speak to the panel."

Eager to support her and explain my need for touch, we enter the conference room together. With a deep breath, I walk in and take my seat beside Colleen. In front of us is a long table filled with professional-looking people sitting straight in their seats, pen and paper in hand, peering at me over glasses perched on the tips of their noses.

Like a child, I sit with my sweaty hands clasped together on my wildly shaking knees, only daring to raise my head and speak when called by name.

At the end of the meeting, the members of the panel stand, shake my hand, and thank me for coming. I stand a little taller and smile a little brighter as I leave, having contributed to the development of future policy on the limits and boundaries of touch in therapy across the nation. I hope it will help others like me. This is a significant, meaningful moment in my life. I have value. I can make a difference.

• • •

Through my continued therapy with Dr. Childers and Bible studies with Gram, I have a growing desire to get to know God, even studying on my own in my room. I imagine Jehovah Father, Jesus Christ, and Holy Spirit; there are three of them, and yet they are one. He knows who I am. He gets me.

As the first tear rolls down my cheek, my whole world changes and the scattered puzzle pieces come together in my head. I'm not alone. I never have been. Another tear follows and soon I'm sobbing. A sense of joy overcomes me and I drop to my knees, my body shaking as I laugh uncontrollably… He gets me.

For the most part, the boxes have been unpacked and repacked. My need to burn has vanished, and for the first time in many years I feel the pieces of myself come together. I'm becoming a whole person. Still, there are weeks when I'm slothful, when just getting out of bed is an impossible task; the next week, it's like a confetti bomb explodes in my head and I spend all night trying to collect the colored paper.

Dr. Childers thinks she may have an answer.

"Why do I have to go to the hospital?" I ask. "You said there's nothing medically you can do for my mental illness, that you can't give me medicine to fix it and you're doing what you can with therapy."

"Joanie, this isn't going to sound right to you, but because you're doing so well, now is the time you may need medication."

"I don't get it. If I'm doing so well, why do you want to give me medicine?"

I slump back in my chair and pout, wondering why she wouldn't have suggested this months or years earlier and saved me a whole bunch of heartache.

"This big, huge problem you've been dealing with for so long is melting away, and now we have to look at what we're left with," she explains. "There's something underlying going on, a metabolic issue we need to address."

She reviews the large team of therapists, social workers, psychologists, and psychiatrists who have been working with me throughout the last few years.

"You can't reach your full potential until we take care of this medical part of it. I'm going to take care of the medical part now." She leans in and looks at me wistfully. "You're not going to be who you're meant to be, who God wants you to be, until we deal with this final piece." She pauses to make sure she has my full attention "Do you trust me?"

I imagine what it would be like if all I needed was a simple pill to help me feel happy all the time.

"Of course I trust you," I tell her.

"You know I don't like labels, but this time I think it's important that you know what you're dealing with," Dr. Childers says. "You have a condition called bipolar disorder. I need you to trust me enough to go to Northwestern for two to four weeks, so we can determine the underlying problem causing it and find the special combination of medication that will help you."

I nod my head in agreement, but two weeks is disconcerting. This doesn't sound like it's just a matter of taking a simple pill.

A month later, I'm still in the psych hospital, a guinea pig as they undertake the huge task of discovering the right cocktail of medication for me. I've been on a mood stabilizer that messes up and elevates my liver enzymes. Though they don't ever want to stop a medication cold turkey, in this case they have to because I need surgery to have my gallbladder removed.

They wheel me into a private room at the regular unit in the hospital. I fade in and out of consciousness, peering through the slits in my eyes. I manage to see a woman who's always sitting beside me. Why won't she just leave me alone? I want her to leave so I can escape from this nightmare.

I've always prided myself on my manipulation skills. In my more lucid moments, I do my best to distract her: go get me food, or a doctor. But she just won't leave.

A week later, I'm back in the psych ward. The opportunity to escape has eluded me.

After three months, I'm off all the drugs and need to start again from the very beginning. With the first drug, my hair falls out. Devastated and enraged, I throw plates of food, full bedpans, anything I can get a hold of. I throw them at anyone who comes near me. The crashing, clanging, and shrill screams just bring in reinforcements. I fall to the floor, exhausted, rolling back and forth, pawing my head with clenched fists like a playful kitten washing her head. But there's no whimsy here, only an anguished attempt to hold the pieces of my head together amid the volcanic eruptions in my skull. The demons inside my head are making a desperate final attempt to get out and regain control of my life.

"God, where are you?" I scream.

The orderlies grab my kicking feet and pull my arms behind me. I'm captured, hogtied, and sedated, then placed in the *quiet room*. I wail and gnash my teeth like an animal, lifting my shoulders in a futile attempt to reach my arms and gnaw my way out of the restraints.

I didn't bring my Bible to the hospital, because I was angry at God when I went in, and now I'm beyond angry… I'm livid. Here I am, believing in Him, and look where it's gotten me. I thought my life was supposed to get better, but I can't stand Him after this.

Hoarse from screaming and cursing, spit spews from my mouth. How jacked up is He to let this happen to me? I hate Him, revile Him, for putting me here.

Frantically, I search the room for something I can use to kill myself, anything to end this wretched war, but I'm restrained, unable to reach anything. Every day I've been plagued with a thirst for death, an ache to commit suicide. It's been with me as long as I can remember.

In the midst of my complete despair, the Bible verses I memorized to squelch my desire to burn spew out of my mouth.

"My God, my God, why have you abandoned me?" I call out in anger. "Why are you so far away when I groan for help? Every day I call to you, my God, but you do not answer. Every night I lift my voice, but I find no relief. Yet you are holy, enthroned on the praises of Israel."[3]

Words of comfort follow.

"Come to me, all of you who are weary and carry heavy burdens, and I will give you rest. Take my yoke upon you. Let me teach you, because I am humble and gentle at heart, and you will find rest for your souls. For my yoke is easy to bear, and the burden I give you is light."[4]

In anger, I reply.

"How long, O Lord, will you look on and do nothing? Rescue me from their fierce attacks. Protect my life from these lions! Then I will thank you in front of the great assembly. I will praise you before all the people."[5]

More words escape in comfort.

---

[3] Psalm 22:1–3.
[4] Matthew 11:28–30.
[5] Psalm 35:17–18.

"When you go through deep waters, I will be with you. When you go through rivers of difficulty, you will not drown. When you walk through the fire of oppression, you will not be burned up; the flames will not consume you."[6]

The Father continues to speak.

"'For I know the plans I have for you,' says the Lord. 'They are plans for good and not for disaster, to give you a future and a hope. In those days when you pray, I will listen. If you look for me wholeheartedly, you will find me. I will be found by you," says the Lord. "I will end your captivity and restore your fortunes. I will gather you out of the nations where I sent you and will bring you home again to your own land.'"[7]

I'm eased by the words of Jesus.

"Don't let your hearts be troubled. Trust in God and trust also in me."[8]

Finally I call out, "If everything I've believed this past year is true, please just take me." With that, I let go of every muscle. The burden of all the baggage I've carried my whole life is suddenly lifted. I know Jesus and I'm not afraid. I know that if I die, I'll be with Him.

A wave of calm comes over me. He has used Scripture to speak to me. God is with me, even here, changing me from the inside for His purpose.

I am released back into the regular population and given a new drug. "Happy Joanie" is back, the outgoing jokester, laughing and finding humor in everything. I like this Joanie, and other people do, too, but it always escalates and goes too far. Each idea is followed by a better, more exciting idea… ideas I share like a yappy little mutt.

With this constant drive to do too much, sleep evades me. My brain just can't shut off. At home, I'd have started to drink or take drugs to slow my brain down, but here at the hospital those resources aren't available, so I just keep spinning and spinning, out of control, not able to get off this incessant teacup ride. Subsequently, I feel physically ill.

My mouth doesn't stop. I eat, I talk, I eat, I talk. A piece of chewy steak gets lodged in my windpipe, and I start choking. I comb the room, eyes bugged out, being ignored because I constantly rattle away. I run over to a male orderly, pulling his arms around my waist to do the Heimlich, but he isn't getting it. Suddenly people are yelling out, "She's choking, she's choking!" He finally gets it, grabs me, and forces me to expel the piece of steak.

He's saved my life. We now have a special bond.

This orderly is my only friend in the hospital. I don't have any friends outside, and my family… well, they don't even know if I'm alive. I sink deep into my chair and cover my head with a blanket. I'm the only one here who never gets a visitor. Everyone else has visitors who bring them treats. I'm all alone.

---

[6] Isaiah 43:2.
[7] Jeremiah 29:11–14.
[8] John 14:1.

There's a kid staying in the hospital with me. His name is Tony and we've talked a couple of times. I like him. When his family comes around, they bring him an entire Italian dinner. He's notice that I'm always alone; my lost puppy dog eyes may have helped him notice.

One day, his big, gregarious Italian family offers me some tiramisu. My chin quivers at this glimmer of hope.

• • •

It's September 11, 2001, and the world stands still, gripped by the news from New York, Washington, and Pennsylvania. I spend countless hours mindlessly watching events unfold on TV. The world outside looks to be just as depressing and lost as my world is in here.

But as bad as it is, I'm almost relieved to be inside where I'm protected.

With the most recent drug, a heavy fog sets over me. With a slow and steady gait, I shuffle along the floor, like gritty sandpaper. All my senses are stifled and smothered. My view is obscured by a low-lying, yellow-grey mist. I hear the swooshing of blood passing by my ear and all the smells are suddenly ambiguous. I smack my lips at the taste of the stagnant air.

• • •

Dr. Childers meets with me to discuss my release from the hospital. I feel trapped inside the psych hospital, unable to catch my breath, but the thought of leaving is even more terrifying. I'm on so many drugs now that I feel nothing. I'm dead inside.

"You're not going to leave me like this," I say, tugging at her sleeve. "Look at me. I'm nothing. I don't have a personality left. I'm taking these drugs, but I don't laugh. I'm not happy. I'm not talking to anybody. I feel numb."

My hand falls dramatically to the table.

"Well, I think we're going to have to try different doses and give it some time," says Dr. Childers. "You need to trust me."

But so far I've been given eight mood stabilizing drugs with corresponding antidepressants to offset them. Depression is so much worse than mania. Sometimes doing one thing in a day is all the staff ask for, and I can't even do that. How could I survive at home alone?

Not long after that, the doctors decide that I'm stable enough to return home. The concoction is working and I've accepted having bipolar disorder. I've even embraced the medication. My life's less of a rollercoaster now. I'm never as happy and excited as I used to be, but it's manageable—and so is the sadness.

I've been trying out a few churches, but I don't feel especially comfortable in any of them. I'll keep trying. I page through the latest book in the Left Behind series, *Desecration*, and I find it riveting. I can't wait for the next one.

Manny wants to be in my life. But I don't trust him.

"I still owe you money," he says. "Let me bring it over."

"Yes, you do and I want my money back."

But he doesn't have the money. He just wants a roll in the hay, or something else just as nefarious.

A verse comes to mind: *"Therefore, if anyone is in Christ, the new creation has come: the old has gone, the new is here!"* (2 Corinthians 5:17, NIV) The old me is gone.

"Manny, I'm so involved in the Lord right now, there's no way I could see you unless the Lord stamped you on the head and said, 'I want you to see him.'"

"Where do I get that stamp?" he asks.

Like a flattening tire, a slow steady stream of air passes through my lips. I can't say Manny isn't persistent, but I need to let go of the past to move forward with my Father.

I shake my head and hang up. I won't talk to him again.

• • •

"You need to quit smoking," Damon tells me. He's pleased that I've ended things with Manny and has been encouraging me to take more big steps in faith.

"Shut up!" I fold my arms and turn around, not even listening anymore. I remember Damon's withdrawals and want no part of that.

He positions his head in front of my face. "It's not godly. God doesn't want you to do that."

"Show me in the Bible where it says I can't smoke," I say, pushing the Bible across the small table toward him.

"Joanie, Holy Spirit's living inside you." He reaches over and places the tips of his fingers over my heart.

I slam my fists on the table as I stand up. "Don't you even do that! Now you're making me feel like Holy Spirit is coughing and I'm giving Him lung cancer."

Squeezing my eyes shut, I grit my teeth. I feel convicted inside. God doesn't want me to damage my body, His temple.

My fists relax. I need to quit smoking and make other changes, too, like not getting drunk. I plunk back into my chair and let out a huge sigh. Scripture memorization got me through my urges to cut and burn, and they'll get me through this, too!

I don't have thoughts of suicide anymore, so I get worried when I think about it again. I shake those cobwebs out of my head and realize it's nothing more than a thought about a distant memory. I'm amazed that my thoughts of killing myself have really gone away. Those seeping boxes aren't a problem anymore. I don't disappear or lose time. It's good to be whole.

I stopped meeting with Colleen once those boxes were packed up, but I still see Dr. Childers from time to time. I'm at the point where I'm able to acknowledge my mental health and know enough to recognize the signs when I need to get help, before I begin to spiral.

Today she and I are meeting to plan my move to the West Side. It's time to leave the SRO and get into some new housing. All the social workers agree that I need more space to live healthily. I just need help finding the right place.

A light catches my eye, and I see that Dr. Childers is wearing a ring on her left hand. With keen scrutiny, I study it while she's writing. Jewelry's something I notice, and I haven't seen this ring before. She tracks my gaze, her eyes disappearing behind her beaming cheeks as she turns the ring to reveal the five-karat diamond. It's huge.

"I've met someone," she says. "I'm stopping my practice for a while to make a home and have some time off." She checks my reaction to this news. Though I'm sweating inside, I'm mostly just happy for her. I'm trying to hear her out. "Since you're moving to the West Side, we wouldn't be able to continue working together anyway. You won't be in my area. You've come so far, Joanie. You're not the same person who came to me all those years ago. This is happening at the right time, you're so ready for this."

Rebuttals flow through my head fast and furious. Without cutting me off, she lays out the steps we will take: I have her number to call in an emergency, and I already know that I won't call it unless I absolutely have to. If she doesn't answer right away, I know she'll call me back. She always does. And eventually I won't have to call her anymore.

Like always, she's right.

I've been transformed.

PART THREE
RESTORED

CHAPTER SEVENTEEN
TESTING GOD

"Bring to the storehouse a full tenth of what you earn so there will be food in my house. Test me in this," says the Lord All-Powerful. "I will open the windows of heaven for you and pour out all the blessings you need."
(Malachi 3:10, NCV)

THIS PLACE IS SO BIG. IT HAS A BEDROOM, A LIVING ROOM, A KITCHEN, AND BATHROOM — and I have closets. It's clean and there aren't any bugs. It's wonderful. Damon and a couple of guys from the SRO are helping me move in. I feel so bad for them, seeing how wonderful this place is.

"I don't ever want you going towards Central Avenue," Damon says sternly as he looks out the window, pointing down the road. His customary smile is shrouded by pursed lips.

I'm still going to medical appointments in North Side, and he's concerned about the stops I'll take to get there.

"Whenever you go anywhere, I want you to come back to Laramie," he says. "Take the Green Line back to Laramie on your way home. When you leave, walk toward Laramie, not toward Central. You don't wanna be there."

Evidently, Central and Washington is a big crime corner.

His eyes narrow and his voice lowers an octave. "Promise me you'll always do that."

"Yeah, I can promise you that." I shrug, not understanding all the fuss, but I'll listen to Damon's advice; his considerable urban experience has made him a wise man.

I stand next to him looking out the window at the field of flashing blue lights in the distance, an uneasy feeling growing in the pit of my stomach.

It's a bit unnerving being on my own without Damon. He's been family for so many years. I'm in a tunnel, so branching out is difficult. Everything's new and hard. Even finding a grocery store or church is challenging. The Pentecostal churches I've been to are quite different from the Catholic church where I grew up; people shout, wave their hands, and fall to the ground. A quick glance around the church and it becomes apparent I'm the only white girl—in the whole neighborhood, in fact. I'm in the hood. On the surface, I certainly don't fit in, but when I start talking to people they realize I'm just Joanie, a new Christian who lives down the street and wants to be part of the family of God. But it's hard not to feel like I'm some sort of project for them.

Once again, Dick and Gram, with their computers, come to the rescue all the way from Ohio. They do a Google search around my location to find churches. I don't trust them or this Google thing, convinced they don't really know where I live.

I peer out the window as I talk to them on the phone. "I'm on the West Side," I say. "This is like really deep. I don't see a lot of white people, you know."

"Yeah, yeah. You're not that far from the suburbs," they assure me. "You're just a few blocks away."

A police car squeals past my window, people be jamm'n, boom boxes blaring. I'm unconvinced. Without a car, relying on public transportation, I may as well be in Ohio with them. Clearly, I'm not close to the suburbs.

"We have a friend Nikki who lives in the area," Dick says. "She goes to a church called Judson. Take down this address and find your way there. It's really not that far from you. Call the Transport Authority and check it out."

Dick's persistent, so I scribble the address on the back of an envelope, totally unconvinced I'll ever use it.

I hang up, flip through the phone directory, and call the Regional Transport Authority of Chicago to find a route to get to this Judson place. Evidently, I have to go to the end of the Madison Line, take the Austin bus to one block north of Division. I plan for a long trip, an hour and a half in the direction Damon told me to avoid.

It's Sunday morning and things are quiet in the hood. I get up early and catch the first bus. In five minutes, the bus stops; I'm trying to explain to the conductor that I need to get to the end of the line to get to the suburbs, and he's trying to convince me that this *is* the end of the line. In all, the trip took only fifteen minutes. I've arrived at Judson Baptist Church very early.

Approaching a big medieval-type brick building with turrets and everything, I stand before two sets of big wooden doors, side by side, and I'm not sure which to open. I glance at my watch. It's way too early to just aimlessly follow someone in.

With a deep breath, slowly exhaling, I pick the left one and open it. The heavy door creaks, and squinty-eyed I explore the dark hallway.

A shadowy figure moves into the light.

"Hi, I'm Arthur Jackson," says the tall, middle-aged man who greets me. He extends his hand. His ebony eyes, set behind dark-rimmed glasses, show more of a smile than the subtle lift of his mouth. His beard and dark curls are clipped short.

I smile back. "I'm Joanie Brusseau."

His firm grip cocoons my hand. "Welcome. Have you ever been here before?" His powerful voice fills the empty space. "You're a bit early."

"No, it's my first time… there was a bit of a mix-up with the buses."

"No problem. Thanks for joining us today. Why don't I help you find a seat?"

I follow him upstairs to the loft, where I sit down as he excuses himself. The white walls of the ceiling are framed with dark wooden beams supported by wrought iron rods, bearing six cast iron lanterns. The sun streams in through a beautiful stained-glass window behind the pulpit. The glass depicts a red cross, the central focus surrounded by an array of yellow, green, turquoise, and blue rectangles. The image draws me in, a reflection of Christ in my own life—His blood shed on the cross, bursting through the scattered boxes of my old life, giving me light, a new life to shine for Him.

A group congregates in the pews below me as the service begins. Their diversity extends beyond race, with families young and old alike, people in smart three-piece suits and ensembles picked up at the thrift store. The congregation is a clear reflection of both communities along North Austin Boulevard: Oak Park on the west, the birthplace of Frank Lloyd Wright and Hemingway, predominately white and affluent, and on the east a neighborhood with a reputation for drug-dealing, gang activity, drive-by shootings, prostitution, and economic failure. It's safe to say not many enterprises have the intestinal fortitude to open shop here, but Judson has. Like the Jews and Gentiles of the early church, these communities have found a common ground of worship through Christ. I'm amazed this can happen. It's so uncommon, almost unnatural.

Arthur leads the choir, his robust voice so deep and smooth that it fills every crevice of the room with triumphant rejoicing. As the echoes still ring in the loft, he turns to introduce the speaker for the day. Evidently this speaker has written a book, so his words carry some sort of authority.

During the service, they ask if there are any new people, and I quickly raise my hand. I'm immediately surrounded by people who introduce themselves, welcoming me—not in a weird overbearing way, but a genuine caring way. Bola, a sweet African woman from Nigeria, takes down my number. She'll call me the following day to invite me to Bible study on Wednesday.

I'm so excited that someone from the church takes the time to call. I feel so special and make sure to go.

On Wednesday, Arthur opens the church door and we walk in together for Bible study.

"Nice to see you again, Joanie," he says.

"Oh, you're Arthur. The choir director, right?"

This time his grin smiles as big as his eyes. "Nope, I'm Arthur the pastor."

"Oh." A sheepish smile overcomes me. I lower my head and walk through the door. If he's the pastor, who was that guy speaking on Sunday?

About ten other people have gathered in the small room, and they all share stories and prayer requests.

Caught up in the moment, I blurt out, "I'm living with a guy who's not my husband, and I'm really trying to disengage from this relationship." I become the center of attention. "His name is Mike and he's really nice, but we're not married and I really need him to leave."

Mike moved in a short time ago. I just seem to need a man around. I know it's not what God wants, but I'm lonely.

"Yes, Joanie, that's good," someone says. "We can pray for that."

Their heads bob like a flotilla of ships on a stormy sea, a thunderous voice among them booming out, "Lord, help Joanie realize she's living in sin!"

My throat tenses and I struggle to gulp. If I don't get Mike out, I could die and not make it to heaven. I just want God to find Mike another place to live, because I know this lifestyle isn't what the Lord wants for me.

I look around the room, gnawing on my bottom lip. These people's faces aren't tight and condemning like my family's. They're bright, and the corner of their eyes crinkle behind the smiles on their faces. A rush of love and acceptance fills me from my toes to the ponytail on top of my head. I've arrived home.

Soon after, God finds a new home for Mike.

• • •

Damon and I talk on the phone every day. Our relationship is so strange but special; he's the first man in my life who's never tried to sleep with me.

"So Damon, you keep telling me I have to tithe ten percent and the Lord will provide," I mention. "You know, I have meds and other things to buy. I don't have an extra ten percent."

"How much short are you?"

I quickly do the calculation in my head. "About $30 a month."

"I'll put the $30 in your account."

"Okay." I start to rattle off my account number, then I stop and slam my hand on the table. "Damon, you can't do that."

"Why?"

"You said the Lord's going to provide this for me. Why are you putting it into my account?" I shrug. "You don't trust the Lord?"

"No. I want you to think about this, Joanie," he says with a slow and steady voice. "When have I ever lent or given you money?"

"Never."

"What am I doing now?"

"You're *lending* me $30 and you're going to put it into my account."

"How long have we known each other?"

I reflect on that. "Five-plus years."

"Have I ever loaned or given you money before?" he says with a little less emotional control.

"Never."

"What am I doing now?" His voice is straining now.

"You're doing it."

"Are you not getting it? The Lord is putting it on my heart to provide!" he shouts in exasperation.

Leaning back, my mouth twisting, I ponder his words. He insists that I should trust in Jesus and let Him help me, but I discover a new problem.

"If I pay you back, I won't have money for the tithe the next month."

"We'll worry about that then," he insists, hanging up the phone.

As I suspected, for the next two months I don't have the money to repay him. He forgives the loan. Then one Sunday the church announces that they're in need of a director for the upcoming summer kids camp. Aside from my job at the Census Bureau, I haven't worked since I left California. With my history, I'm convinced I won't get the job.

But I do. It pays $10 an hour. It's so much money to me, aboveboard, upfront legal money. The people at church are so encouraging, telling me they're happy I'll be directing Camp 4:12. And it's a fantastic experience. I've always loved children but have felt somewhat unworthy because of my history with my own. But God's love flows out of me for them. It sparks something deep inside me. Maybe the old really is gone and I really am new.

I ask Pastor Jackson if I might be able to speak to the congregation about how God has been working in my life. Those eyes smile again. I then walk up onto the stage, the morning sun streaming through the vibrant stained-glass cross, the array of colored boxes bathing me, encompassing me. I look out on the congregation, my family, then take a deep breath and read Malachi 3:10—"Bring the full tithe into the storehouse, that there may be food in my house. And thereby put me to the test, says the Lord of hosts, if I will not open the windows of heaven for you and pour down for you a blessing until there is no more need."[9]

I hold an envelope up in the air for the whole congregation to see.

"In this envelope, I have all my cheques from working in Camp 4:12," I say. "I haven't cashed one. My friend Damon has been helping me understand about tithing and trusting God to provide. I have a lot of medical issues, and when I first started tithing I wasn't able to make the full tithe because I had all these medical bills to pay. Damon helped me top

---

[9] ESV.

it up so I could tithe on the whole, and told me to trust God to provide. Soon after, I got the job with Camp 4:12. I'm not sure how God has done it this time, but I've tithed on this money." I wave the envelope, catching the pastor's eyes. "And I haven't cashed a single cheque… but I *am* going to cash these."

Thunderous laughter breaks out filling the sanctuary.

After the service, Kajaria runs up to me. She's like a sister to me. Her mother, Janie Yarborough, has become my church mom. I call her Ma-J, but at Judson she's known as Big Mamma. It's a title given with great respect within the community. Ma-J's an extraordinary woman with great insight and a great love for Jesus.

Kajaria, holding me by both my shoulders and in a booming voice, as strong and powerful as her mother's, says, "Because of that testimony, you had all of us at the edge of our seats. The way you talked about it, you've convinced me and so many other people. I could see heads nodding all through the congregation. I feel convicted to do the same."

Another couple who were visiting also tell me they were blessed by my testimony and feel convicted. They will test the Lord and tithe.

Three months later, Pastor J brings me into his office. He has exciting news to share with me.

"Joanie, this was our average giving four months ago." He shows me the number on the paper in front of him, then flips the page. I can see that the number has climbed significantly. "And these are our average givings for the last three months, all because the Lord spoke to you, and you spoke to the congregation. This is how God works in people's hearts through testimonies."

• • •

In the fall, there's a call in church for people to take the Perspectives course. It's a mission course that can be taken for general interest, certificate credit, or even college credit. I have no idea what I'm getting myself into, but I decide to take it for college credit.

The Bible is so detailed and I'm amazed there's a whole course on just twenty verses in Genesis 12. The class is so hard that I'm almost pulling my hair out. There are about thirty people in the class, and a different missionary speaks each week.

Using a fine-point pencil to do my homework, I try to only write down the important points from the textbook, but I end up almost rewriting the whole thing. There's just so much good information in it.

For the required final assignment, I choose to study the Fulani, an unreached pastoral people of the Sahara.

On my way home from class that night, it's late and I take a cab. This is safer for me than taking public transportation.

I notice that the driver has an accent.

"Where are you from?" I ask him, looking over his shoulder.

"Africa."

"Oh. Do you know anything about the Fulani?"

He pulls over and stops the car. "I *am* Fulani!"

"Are you kidding me?" I nearly jump over the seat. This can't just be a coincidence.

For the rest of the ride, this man bubbles over while talking about his home and the people he's left. Even with his thick accent, I'm able to glean enough information to receive an A on my project.

That's when I discover there's $500 available toward a mission trip to Kenya for anyone who successfully completes the course.

"Kenya?" My eyebrow lifts as I consider the possibility.

CHAPTER EIGHTEEN
A NEW PERSPECTIVE

And let us not grow weary while doing good, for in due season we shall reap if we do not lose heart.
(Galatians 6:9, NKJV)

I'M AMAZED AT WHERE GOD HAS ALREADY TAKEN ME IN FOUR SHORT YEARS, AND I'M a bit apprehensive as I examine my airline ticket, totally unaware of how this will change my life.

Everywhere I go, friends pepper me with questions.

"Where are you going?"

"Africa!"

"What are you going to do there? Are you going on safari?"

I'm going to Kenya, but all I really know is that it's in Africa. I don't know much more about Africa except that it's known by some as the "dark continent." And as for the safari? Well, I don't know.

Inevitably their response is one of fear and disbelief: "I could never go. It's too far. I'd be so scared. You're so brave." Though I share their concern, I know that God is with me. The excitement of going on an adventure with Jesus soon quells any apprehensions.

Three months later, I'm on the longest flight of my life, over twenty hours, heading east to Africa by way of London to Nairobi, Kenya. Pastor J is leading a twelve-member team from the Chicago-Detroit area to the Pan African Christian Exchange (PACE) Ministry in Nyahururu.

Wachira and his wife Glenda Ngamau are missionaries in Kenya. They met in the United States at the Rock of Salvation Church in Chicago. Wachira is from the Kikuyu tribe and had been attending Bible school in America to prepare for the ministry when they met. They later married and Glenda left her family in Chicago to follow Wachira to his native Nyahururu. Together they began PACE Ministries, providing education for nationals while uniting Africans of the diaspora through missions. While Wachira's busy as the ministry director, Glenda raises their three children and coordinates the outreach programs for the visiting teams. I've seen their family photo on Judson's missionary wall. It'll be good to finally meet them.

Every few seconds I check my watch, each time disappointed that the hands have barely moved.

Like sheep, a string of people disembark the plane when we arrived, each with $50 in hand to pay for their visa. An immigration inspector waits at a desk collecting this money and stamping passports. The passport is opened, he inspects it unflinchingly, then glances up, his eyes scanning to ensure the photo is a good likeness. I smile, open my mouth to speak, but then pause at his contemptuous glare. I snap my mouth shut. I need to take the officials here very seriously.

Acquiring this passport has been quite the headache for me. My initial application was rejected because apparently I didn't exist. I applied for a proper birth certificate in order to prove who I was, and after some investigation I discovered I wasn't Joanie Brusseau, born June 21, 1958. In fact, I'm Jean Denise Brusseau, born June 21, 1960. I was sure this must be a typo, since I've been called Joanie my whole life and for twenty-one years I've been using 1958 as my birth year. It takes me a while to remember that I changed my birthdate when I was sixteen. Oh, I feel so young again!

My passport is stamped and returned without acknowledgement. No grunt, no wave, no anything. With some trepidation, I slink away down the stairs to pick up my luggage, almost sure I'll be surrounded by a Kenyan SWAT team because I've left too soon. I breathe easy as I join my group, unchallenged, and wait in another line to have the contents of our luggage checked. Everything's good, and all the luggage is amazingly accounted for.

Once we walk through the sliding doors, Pastor J embraces a slender man waiting for us.

"Karibuni sana," says the man with an incredible smile. He has a sparkle in his eyes. "welcome to Kenya, Rafiki."

His name is Irungu, and I can tell we will become fast friends.

Irungu and Maina YM, another Kenyan man who's quiet but strong and sturdy, gather up as many bags as they can carry, then move out toward the parking lot and fill the white vans that are waiting for us. Stepping through the sliding doors, I immediately feel the heaviness in the air, like a hot Chicago summer. An unusual aroma fills my nose, a hint of ginger, cardamom, and cloves masked by the diesel fuel of the many honking vehicles swarming the roads and sidewalks around the airport. I jump back as a small car drives up on to the sidewalk to pass another vehicle stopped to collect passengers. I smile, realizing that regular rules don't apply here. This is a strange new world. I'm going to love it.

With a spring in my step, I make my way out to the vans. My face sinks a bit when I see that only the two front seats are cushioned. Oh well. Our destination shouldn't be that far. With a sigh, I crawl into the back and sit on a hard plastic seat draped with a grey wool blanket.

"There's bottled water in the back if anyone needs a drink," Maina YM calls out as he finishes loading the van. "It'll be a long, dusty ride."

I happily tap the tray of water bottles next to me. I'm always so thirsty. I only wish they had ice to go with it.

Nairobi's a bustling city, with no rhyme or reason to the people's driving. Lorries, essentially just big trucks, drive over sidewalks if the roads are too busy. Irungu chuckles as I catch him driving through a red stoplight.

"It's just a suggestion," he says. "Here, we drive with the traffic and if nobody stops…" He shrugs and tilts his head.

Heavy smog hangs in the air and street vendors run to open car windows, pushing trinkets into the hands of people inside, asking for shillings or American dollars as they shout out, "You buy, you buy!"

The road to Nyahururu is long and punishing, with potholes so big you could easily lose your car in them. There's no soft shoulder, only a harsh six-inch drop from the bits of paved road to the dry, hard dirt below. It would be nauseating if not for the breathtaking sights.

As we leave the city, rustic wooden stands dot the pine tree-lined roads selling everything from fruits and vegetables to sheep skins and handcrafted grass baskets. Many have small water holes cut into the deep red earth nearby. Ducks and chickens run freely into the streets. The small towns along the road have colorful open air homes and shops. Motorcycles, or boda bodas, whiz by. Dozens of young shepherds watch their flocks of sheep and goats in the rich green grass while the older nomads wear bright red wraps, watching over herds of skinny cows.

We pass by a large pull-off overlooking the expanse of the Great Rift Valley and are assured we will make a stop later in the trip where there's a much better view of this area that's otherwise controlled by lions, hippos, and water buffalo.

I'm in a constant state of amazement and often catch myself with a gaping mouth, eyes so wide that an elephant could fit through. Herds of zebras run across the distant savannah. A few baboons wander the roadside, looking for scraps of food. A pat of pink flamingos fly over us as we pass by Lake Naivasha, and I get a glimpse of Mount Kenya in the distance. The vast blue skies meet the luscious greenery of the red earth, broken only in the west by a thin curtain of clouds sweeping down from the heavens, bringing rain to the land below.

I've been doing the toilet dance for a while. Three hours into the journey, we stop for a much-needed break before the more difficult part of the trip.

"More difficult?" I question Irungu as I fall out of the van.

He smiles and shrugs. This is rather concerning, as my bottom is already pretty sore. My ankle is stiff and I desperately need to stretch and take a walk.

"Men's toilets over there, ladies are this way," Irungu says. "If you need a seat, you may need to wait. I recommend you hurry. We only have a ten-minute stop here." His smile is directed at me.

"Need a seat, what's he talking about?" I ask one of the ladies on our team. "We're women. Of course we need a seat."

A colorful wrap is wound around the woman standing on the flimsy boardwalk used to keep people up off the mud. She hands out toilet paper as she directs women to the appropriate toilets. Afraid of being left behind, bouncing from one foot to the other, I tell her that either toilet will do.

As the door closes behind me, I discover the purpose behind wearing skirts. There's a hole in the floor with muddy shoeprints on either side to indicate where your feet go to successfully expel your contents.

"Are you kidding me!" I screech. "How are you supposed to do this?"

My cries are met with a quiet snicker outside. With resolve, I place my shoes in the mud, pull down my pants, squat, and release. Warm liquid streams down my leg into my shoe.

"Oh, brother," I snort.

More laughter from outside.

My ankle is fused at a perfect ninety-degree angle to allow me to stand and sit, but it's not designed to allow my knee to extend over my foot, in order to successfully squat; thus, I'm unable to properly use the traditional Kenyan toilet. Hanging my head, I silently return to the van, taking my cramped, uncomfortable seat at the back.

Other crude stick structures dot the road ahead, farmers selling their wares. White polypropylene bags of goods lay unattended nearby and unguided donkeys pull water tanks on simple, rustic carts. Between the small communities, groups of women carrying young children on their backs hoe the rich red fields.

Irungu turns off the main road. If the first part of the journey was the major thoroughfare, this less-kept road is certainly the road to perdition. Many areas have only patches of pavement. Irungu's left with no option but to sway back and forth between them, leaving me dizzier and more nauseous than any rollercoaster I've ever encountered. The acacia trees take over the rural landscape, baboons and herds of zebras never far away.

After a while, Irungu calls for us to look to the left as a herd of majestic elephants stroll by in the distance. Those looking carefully catch a glimpse of a giraffe popping up above the trees.

The air thins out as the van climbs up the mountainside. As promised, we reach the overlook of the Great Rift Valley and the Menengai Crater in the distance. We admire the local souvenirs, while Irungu and Maina YM stand close by making sure we're getting a good deal. Haggling is not only accepted, but expected in this culture. I admire the craftsmanship but cringe at the thought of haggling and asking them to accept less than it's worth.

We continue to Nyahururu, quite a big town compared to the others around it, and soon reach the front gate of Wachira and Glenda's home. It's been an exhausting day and I'm ready for a rest and a comfy bed. We're taken to our rooms and shown our beds; they have a definite indentation, indicating they've been well worn. I lay on the bed and nestle in. They're comfortable enough and I quickly fall asleep, resting through the night.

After a filling breakfast of tea and chapati, a local flatbread, we arrive at the Pan African Christian Academy. They opened their doors in 2000 for first graders and have added a grade every year since. Three rows of wooden desks fill the room. Two children wearing red sweaters sit at each green desk, their feet flat against the dusty dirt floor, their coats hanging neatly on hooks at the back of the room.

I look out the window and notice a young boy, about ten years old, peering inside. "Wachira, who's that boy outside looking in? Why isn't he in the classroom?"

"His name is Peter Maina," Wachira explains. "His grandmother can't afford the school fees, so he sits by that window each day listening to the teacher and taking notes." He then directs my attention to the window sill. "See, some of the teachers have provided him with a notebook and pencil."

"How much is school?" I asked, amazed that this boy would choose to sit by the window rather than play outside.

"There is a public school system in Kenya now, but his grandmother would still have to pay $10 a semester for his school uniform, a workbook, and a pencil. PACE Academy is a private school. We have tuition fees as well."

"Where does he live? Who's his grandmother?"

"So many questions." Wachira laughs. "I'll show you when we get home for dinner. They live just outside our compound."

Wachira and Glenda live with their younger children in the parsonage on a large piece of property beside the church. Their compound is surrounded by a strong wall, protecting the solid brick home and gardens from the elephants, baboons, and hippos who pass through to find food and water in the dry seasons. When elephants break down a section of the wall, they remember it and know it's a weak spot through which they can more easily breach a second or third time.

Peter and his grandmother have no such stronghold to protect their little shack and garden, and as a result they more often suffer devastation due to the hungry wildlife.

The grandmother's house is visible from Wachira and Glenda's home, but it's not just a hop and a skip over the fence; it's a ten-minute trek, hobbling around the gate and trudging through the uneven terrain to get to the door.

When the tiny door opens, I get my first peek at true poverty. I've been homeless on the streets, lived in the hood, and thought I knew poverty, but I'm not prepared for this. Flies buzz everywhere and a putrid stench lingers in the stale air. The walls of this simple two-room shack don't fully meet the uneven dirt floor below, and the orange glow of sunset shines through the thin walls.

A withered old lady stands at the door. At 5'5" I'd tower over her upright body, but hers is curled over a cane, her shaking hands grappling to support her fragile frame. She struggles to lift her head, but as she does a sincere smile greets me, and with great enthusiasm her trembling hand invites me in for tea, a common custom in Kenya to show hospitality to guests. The sparsely equipped shelf suggests I'm her first guest in a long time. I bend way down low to get through the doorway and not hit my head as I enter.

She supports Peter by selling milk from the lone cow that's left a minefield of patties in the yard, attracting the hordes of flies. Peter's father was a drunk and his mother left them; she's the father's mother, and doing her best to raise her grandson with what little she has. There are no beds, just a polypropylene bag on the ground with a light blanket carefully placed over it. There's no indoor toilet or kitchen, either, just a well-placed hole and a firepit in the yard.

She pours a cup of chai tea into one of two cracked cups from a worn wooden shelf. Meanwhile, Peter shows me his artwork, a drawing of the world. He's drawn the continent of Africa with all fifty-five countries labeled. I sit up in my chair, having had no idea Africa had so many countries. I kind of always thought of Africa as one big country. It would be an amazing drawing for anyone, but for someone who has only been to school by peering through a window, it's astonishingly accurate, with the United States properly placed to the left and Europe and Asia drawn well to scale.

In the corner of my eye, I get a glimpse of the grandmother as the last bit of milk drips into the cup of tea. Unbothered, and with a smile that would fill a much larger face, she serves me the tea and they both watch intently as I gratefully nod my head and sip.

Peter speaks English well and interprets as his grandmother speaks of her days as a cleaning woman for the white colonials who lived in Wachira's house when it was the parsonage for the church they came to build. Evidently the house hasn't changed much; there are so many bedrooms, each with a bed, as well as an indoor kitchen and bathrooms with running water.

Peter sits up taller in the little stool, his soft, youthful voice speaking with great strength and pride as he explains how she and the other Kenyans had to fight for their independence when she was a much younger, forty-year-old woman. As he regales me with stories, I glance at his grandmother; this woman, who I first saw as frail, with one foot in the grave, has transformed into a resilient woman of great faith. If God would allow me to be even half the woman she is, I'd be a Ruth or an Esther—"for such a time as this," as the Bible says.

Peter gets up to light the kerosene lamp, prompting me to look down at my watch. It's just after six, but the sun has set and I haven't brought a flashlight. It's time to go. Taking the lamp, Peter escorts me to the gate of the big house. With dusk, the flies have stopped buzzing. I have no cues to avoid the minefield left by the old lady's cow.

Glenda opens the door, looks at my waterlogged face, then quickly glances up to see if it's raining. There's not a cloud in the sky tonight. My heart's been broken by what I've seen, and I've been crying. I feel an undeniable urge, a calling, to do something to help this family, to show them God's love.

"Glenda, I need to tell you something," I say. "I'm on social security. I make $750 a month, and there's no way I could've afforded this trip. But my Christian family at Judson explained how God would supply what I needed. He has. I wrote a letter explaining what God's already done in my life, and after that I was given enough money to get here. I saved an extra $50, to bring small gifts back for those people who sponsored me…" My heart's on fire. The burn is igniting something inside me I just can't ignore. "But I need to redirect that $50 to help Peter."

"I can help you with that." Glenda nods as she wraps her arm around my shoulder and brings me into the house. "Tomorrow. Today, you need to go to bed and get some rest."

Like Ma-J, she's a strong woman in her own right, and God's using her in ways I'm sure she could never have imagined.

The next day I'm in my glory shopping at the market.

"Are you sure I'll be able to get all this?" I ask, clenching a dozen souvenir spoons for my sponsors. The exchange for Kenyan shillings is outrageous and confusing to me. "It's going to be too expensive. We're at 4,000 KSh already. I don't have that much money. I can't afford that."

"You're fine." Glenda chuckles as she has Irungu box everything up and bring it to the truck for us.

Later that evening, I bring Peter my old Bible, some blankets, books, and pens, and for his grandmother a shawl and a cooking pot.

But what comes next astounds me.

"I have one more thing, Peter," I say, the corner of my mouth lifting in a grin. I place a piece of paper on the table. "Let's fill out your PACE Academy application together."

He looks bewildered. "School application? I can't go to school."

"I've paid the tuition for you. You start on Monday." Barely able to contain my excitement, my eyes begin to mist. I wipe my nose with the back of my sleeve.

"Will you help me?" Peter asks. "I don't know how to read much."

His eyes dart between me and his grandmother as he debates whether to switch to his mother tongue and explain what's happening to his grandmother, or hurry along with the completion of the application.

"What's your birth date?" I ask after filling in his name and address.

"Birth date?" Peter looks blankly at his grandmother. His smile quickly fades as he realizes his eligibility has expired as quickly as it came. "I don't have one."

"What do you mean?" I stammer, not understanding the dilemma. "Everybody has a birth date. When were you born?"

With a lump in his throat, he sniffles and wipes his eyes. "I don't know."

Looking between their long faces, I can see that we aren't going to get anywhere this way.

With new resolve, I soften my voice. "What would you like your birth date to be?"

"What's your birth date, Joanie?"

"June 21."

"I want mine to be next to yours."

"June 20 it is!"

Now he can count how many years go by. I may live in the hood and survive on social security, but I now realize how much I have, how rich I am. If I can tithe on $750, surely I can do without a little more. I can put aside an extra $25 or $30 a month to provide for Peter, and maybe send him to college.

CHAPTER NINETEEN
DON'T BLOCK THE BLESSING

Do not stifle the Holy Spirit.
(1 Thessalonians 5:19)

…fan into flame the gift of God…
(2 Timothy 1:6, NIV)

COLLEGE. BITING MY BOTTOM LIP, I APPREHENSIVELY PONDER THE POSSIBILITIES. Wachira says I need a degree to work in Kenya. I'd never really thought of it before, but why not? In God, I'm a new person. I totally can do this.

I look around my little apartment with its used furniture. Nothing is really keeping me here. No car, no mortgage… no family. Picking up a pen, I complete the application to get a legitimate GED with my actual birthdate and plan for college.

I begin my three-year journey, taking classes toward earning my Bachelor in Education at Northeastern, studying right through the summers without a break. I work day and night. It's so busy and I have so much homework that I'm overwhelmed. I just can't believe it. I press on, though, knowing that God has something great in store.

And then it hits me, like a ton of bricks.

There's a strange feeling in my ear, like it's clogged even though there's nothing in it. I'm having a tough time hearing in class. It's annoying, but I can live with it.

Then, like a front loader dumping a full load on me, the ground beneath me shakes and spins. My head feels like it's swiveling on my neck, like a plate being spun on a stick. Walking like a drunk, I try desperately to hang on to anything within my grasp, but everything's just out of my reach.

Instinctively, I tug at my ears, clutching my head in a futile effort to still myself, to stop the incessant, unabating ringing in my ears. I've heard this ringing before—during my car accident—but this time it's not going away. I have Meniere's disease.

Like Job in the Bible, who suffered so much, I claim scripture:

Why did I not perish at birth, and die as I came from the womb? ...For now I would be lying down in peace; I would be asleep and at rest... I have no peace, no quietness; I have no rest, but only turmoil. (Job 3:11, 13, 26, NIV)

My face is red with weeping, dark shadows ring my eyes... (Job 16:16, NIV)

My spirit is broken, my days are cut short, the grave awaits me... My eyes have grown dim with grief; my whole frame is but a shadow... (John 17:1, 7, NIV)

I know that you can do all things; no purpose of yours can be thwarted. (Job 42:2, NIV)

The Lord relieves my suffering enough for me to continue my studies. Meniere's disease will always remain with me to some extent, like the thorn in Paul's flesh that God wouldn't take away.

It's winter, it's dark, and I've just stepped off the bus after my night school class. Two men hide in shadows of the streetlights. The thugs own the streets here. One of the men, a tall skinny guy, is from my building. I've seen him around before. But I'm not sure who the burly guy next to him is. I've heard people from the building call the skinny guy Larry, but out on the street he's known as Blade. No one uses their real names.

"Are you straight?" the burly guy asks from the darkest corner where he leans against the brick building, cigarette hanging from his mouth. He's flipping a shiny object that looks a little too much like a switchblade.

"Um, yeah, sure," I respond tentatively, thinking he's asking if I'm clean. I don't do drugs. At least, I *hope* that's what he's asking me.

"She's straight, leave her be," Blade says.

He steps out of the shadows so I can see his colors. He gestures, and then the burly guy pulls his shoulder back just enough for me to pass by and enter the building.

People at church ask me if I'm afraid of living in the hood, but I rest easy; these guys are the hand of God protecting me. They may be scary to everyone else, but I sense they've got my back.

After graduation, there's a dinner. Evidently I can bring guests. I'm so excited, but I just don't know who to ask. Who will I bring? Friends from school or my church family? Soon enough I have a table of ten filled with classmates who've spent endless hours studying with me, and without whom I'm sure I never would have graduated.

"Joanie, you're summa," one of my friends exclaims in amazement, reading the brochure on the table.

"Summa? What's summa?"

"You got all As?" another friend asks.

I scowl, disappointed that I haven't done better. "No, I got one B."

"One B? Why were we helping you? You should have been helping us?"

My younger friends are in stitches, realizing that they've been one-upped by the eldest student of the class.

Like an unstoppable flow of lava, a barrage of tears carries my makeup down my face. I make my way up to the stage through the crowded room, high-fiving as many elated supporters and classmates as I can, passing by tables like an exuberant baby gorilla. One thoughtful student hands me a tissue, but I only manage to smudge the makeup further.

I stand in front of the cheering crowd, bouncing uncontrollably, raising my hands and exploding into a chorus of "Whoop, whoop!" after receiving the medal bestowed with the title. I am most certainly not a quiet person. For the first time in so long, I feel overwhelmed with an irrepressible feeling of euphoria. I breathlessly leap and dance, unconcerned with my unstable ankle.

For a split second, the fog approaches, and I worry my mania has returned, but the delighted faces of everyone around me gives me encouragement. I deserve this. I've worked hard. I return to the moment and soak it all in. I had no idea how well I'd been doing. I've now graduated with distinction, the highest honor of my graduating class. God is so good!

That night, I wear medal around my neck, my fingers caressing the thin metallic disc in my hand. I pause to contemplate its symbolism; it means so much to me as a token of what God has brought me through, an indication of where He's going to take me from here. I'm an adopted daughter of the Father, freed from my dark past by His Son Jesus, filled with His power through Holy Spirit. I know I'm capable of conquering any mountain in my path, perhaps even Mount Kenya!

• • •

Pastor J will be moving to another church in the area. Before he moves, he talks to me about an opportunity to work as a teacher for missionaries at a college in Machakos, Kenya. Now that I have my teaching degree, I make plans to go. I've committed myself for one year but have no idea how I'm actually going to get there or support myself once I arrive. However, I've seen how God has already worked miracles in my life. I'm learning to have faith that He will provide for anything His Spirit has put inside me to do. I just need to fan the flame and it will burn. This is the burn God has always wanted me to feel, so I know I'm alive.

Ma-J is helping me grow my faith. With bowed head, fingers tangled in my brown roots, I slam my elbows on her kitchen table, futilely trying to construct a support letter to send out to my friends.

"Ma-J, I just can't ask people to support me while I'm in Africa," I say. "It's not their problem God wants me there. How can I ask people here to support me when they have families of their own to take care of and I know they don't have extra?"

Ma-J towers over me, hands on hips, her voice strong and confident. "Don't block the blessing." Her furrowed forehead and stern eyes mean business. "Don't be too proud to take what people want to give you. God gives everyone different gifts. He has a purpose for each of us and we need to work together for that greater purpose. Sure, some can go, but others can't—and by giving what they can, God allows them to participate in the Great Commission. Read 2 Corinthians 9:7–8 for me."

I pick up my Bible and read:

Each man should give as he has decided in his heart. He should not give, wishing he could keep it. Or he should not give if he feels he has to give. God loves a man who gives because he wants to give. God can give you all you need. He will give you more than enough. You will have everything you need for yourselves. And you will have enough left over to give when there is a need.[10]

"Now read a bit further down," Ma-J insists. "Start at verse twelve and read to the end."

This gift you give not only helps Christians who are in need, but it also helps them give thanks to God. You are proving by this act of love what you are. They will give thanks to God for your gift to them and to others. This proves you obey the Good News of Christ. They will pray for you with great love because God has given you His loving-favor. Thank God for His great Gift.[11]

"If you don't take the money God puts on their heart to give, then you're blocking the blessing God has in store for them. You want that?" Ma-J shakes her head as though to say, *Oh no you don't.*

Obediently, I write and send the letters.

Some time later, I stand at the mailbox, holding a response to one of those letters in my trembling hand. Sniffling, I try to read the letter through the misty lenses of my eyes.

Damon has committed to support me with $10 a month while I'm in Kenya. We always had a kind of negative codependency on each other when we were living across

---
[10] NLV.
[11] 2 Corinthians 9:12–15, NLV.

the hall from each other. It's amazing to me how God's now bringing that dependency full circle to His glory. Like me, Damon has also gone back to school, getting his Masters in Drug and Alcohol Rehabilitation. He's planning to upgrade to a PhD, so he'll soon be Doctor Damon.

I had delivered my letter to him in person. It was so good to see his smile again and talk about how God's been working in our lives. He lives in a retirement community now on the Near North Side. After twenty years without a driver's license, he's got both his license and a car, but boy does he drive slow. We went out for lunch; I can't believe he's still alive with all the cars that were honking behind him.

I'll miss seeing him while I'm gone, but I'm so thankful for his continued support.

• • •

Sitting on my bedroom floor, Kathy and I are elbow-deep in boxes as I pack up my life.

"Maybe I've bit off more than I can chew," I say, shaking.

On this summer day, my palms are moist and droplets are collecting on my forehead. But it's not the heat or the diabetes causing me to perspire today. I've started purging and packing. The stress of letting go of all of my past as I head into an unknown future is taking a toll.

"C'mon, Joanie," my friend Kathy teases, laughing as she holds up an old pair of jeans. "Straight-legged, faded jeans haven't been in style for twenty years. How long's it been since you've worn them? Do you really think you'll ever wear them again?" Next she points to several tracksuits with price tags still attached. "And what's with these parachute suits? You have them in every size and color imaginable. Don't look directly at them. They could blind you."

Kathy and I met when I was the director of Camp 4:12 at Judson. Her church's youth group came from Canada on a mission trip to join our staff from camp. She's helping me clear out my stuff before I move to Kenya.

"Why do you have so many of the same outfit?" she asks. "More importantly, why have you kept them? Clearly you're never gonna wear them."

A huge lump lodges in my throat, stalling my reply. "They're the bridesmaids outfits from when I was going to marry Bill on the yacht."

"Oh." Kathy lowers her head with clenched teeth and recoils. Then seems to regain some confidence. "But you are trying to purge. You really have to decide what you need and what you can do without."

A tear grows in the corner of my eye as I'm flooded with memories of Bill, Jade, and Azia. Then I relive the disappointing end to my wedding plans.

"How about we put this on the look-at-it-a-bit-later pile for now." She stacks them on the already waist-high bundle of clothes. "But we're really going to have to decide on some of this stuff today if you hope to get this done by the weekend."

I sit with a glass of ice water, surveying the mass of boxes and bags that have come to clutter my tiny apartment. Over the years I've stored my things in a lot of places, and today I've brought them all together to condense before I leave for Africa.

A large suitcase pushed back in the corner catches my eye. I shudder, and the ice tinkles rhythmically in my glass. I feel goosebumps raise on my arms.

The secrets of my past are hidden in that suitcase.

"What's in there, Joanie?" Kathy's eyes follow my gaze.

I realize there's no way out now. I have to address it.

"Those are my photos," I whisper. The suitcase is so jam-packed that it looks like the seams are ready to burst. "You take your chances opening it. The lid may fling off and photos will explode all over the room like a jack-in-the-box."

She opens the suitcase, it pops, the photos scatter, and we buckle over, laughing hysterically.

There are thousands of photos in that suitcase. I gather twenty or thirty, reminiscing about the good times and brood a bit over the difficult times. I'm getting a bit misty.

"You're sure you're okay?" she asks, a looking of concern descending on her face. "I mean, to go to Africa? Will you be able to call your doctor if you need her? Will you have what you need, like medication, or don't you need it anymore?"

"Oh yeah, I still need my medication. You know I take insulin for my diabetes. I have everything I need for that. I still take medication for bipolar as well, even when I feel good and start to think I don't need it anymore. Just as I embrace my insulin for my medical health, I embrace my medication for my mental health. I know I can't go without it. As for the rest, God's healed me a hundred percent. I'm good."

As Kathy lets out a sigh of relief, I quickly realize it'll take much more time than I have to sort through all these photos. I've found some family photos and tuck them away. It'll give me some closure to send them to my mom and sisters. We haven't been in contact in years, aside from me creeping them on Facebook. They haven't moved. Though I've forgiven them, I just can't open myself up to the chance of being impugned again. Dr. Childers has assured me that though forgiveness is a pathway to freedom and healing, that doesn't mean I'll forget, and it doesn't always lead to reconciliation. That's okay.

I prepare to mail the photos while Kathy drags the suitcase aside. It'll be stored for another time.

By the end of the weekend, my belongings, like my life, have been amalgamated, boxed up, and distributed or trashed. I'm ready to go.

● ● ●

Roy and Toni are dear friends of mine from Judson. Roy's a doctor, tall with a full head of straight white hair. Toni's got an infectious laugh; I love spending time with her, because we make each other belly laugh.

They have a huge backyard, and this afternoon they're hosting a commissioning party for me. More than a hundred people from church have shown up to support me. I'm so blessed to have this new family. God has rewarded my faithful giving. Toni has prepared some of her famous dishes, and I'm just buzzing around, saying my goodbyes.

I reach for my new camera at one point to take one more picture of Ma-J... but it's missing.

"It's gone!" I cry out and begin frantically searching for it. "The camera's gone!"

I'd been saving for this camera a long time by taking on extra babysitting work. I babysat whenever I could, even soliciting babysitting jobs when no one was asking. One couple I'd solicited asked how much more I needed to earn, and I told them it was about $120. They just gave me the cash and told me to get the camera already.

I picked up the camera three days ago—and now it's gone missing. We look everywhere, but can't find it.

Dejected, yet staunchly believing that even these little things are important to God, I sit down beside Ma-J and pray, "Jesus, help me find the camera."

"What about Damon?" Toni recalls. "Didn't you just drive him to the bus depot?"

I suddenly remember that I gave Damon the camera to hold while we were driving. "Oh no," I say. "I think I put it on top of the car when I got out to hug him goodbye."

I'm usually a good driver. Not super slow like Damon, but good. Not today! I'm all over the road trying to get to the corner of Division and Austin and back again, my eyes scanning right and left, inside bus shelters, outside, around bushes, everywhere.

But I can't find the camera anywhere.

Shuffling sadly, not wanting to make eye contact with anyone for fear of a flood of tears, and unable to speak through the enormous lump in my throat, I return to the party empty-handed, a forced smile on my flush face.

"You should call Damon," Ma-J suggests with an unusually quiet voice. "He should be back home by now."

Nodding, unconvinced and barely able to lift my feet, I trudge back into the house and make the call.

"Damon?" I say in a brittle voice when he picks up the phone.

"Joanie, thank God you called. I didn't have Toni's number, but I have your camera!"

I jump up out of my seat and dance. "Thank you, Jesus!" I shout.

I quickly make plans to collect the camera before returning to the party. It's the last time I'll see these friends before I leave for Africa in three days.

• • •

On my last day home, I have a nervous stomach. My fingers twirl around my newly dyed red locks as I make a few calls. The first call is short and sweet; I call Rose to let her know how God is working in my life and where I'm going to be for the next while. She's glad I'm happy and lets me know that our mother has a new job at a department store.

I also need to talk to Dr. Childers one last time before I leave for the mission field. We haven't spoken in quite some time, and I want to let her know how much she's meant to me, without overstepping our boundaries.

I take a deep breath and call, hoping she hasn't changed her number.

"Thank you for sticking with me, and with therapy, and for getting your degree, because a lot of people give up," she tells me. The richness in her tone hasn't changed. It's still strong yet delicate. I know she was the hand of God on me through those difficult years.

"I DID and now I'm done." I inhale a slow, deep breath and hold it momentarily, allowing it to nourish my lungs before I recline in my chair and slowly exhale. I'm content. With Jesus, I've overcome so much.

"I think you're done, too, Joanie," she says, sounding joyful and satisfied. "I never had a doubt you could fly. You've done so well. May God continue to bless you."

As we hang up for the last time, an old memory verse comes to mind, from Matthew 25:21: *"The master answered, 'You did well. You are a good servant who can be trusted. You did well with small things. So I will let you care for much greater things. Come and share my happiness with me'"* (ICB).

He's done so much for me already! I feel pure joy. I'm truly content. But I've also learned that my God is not a contented God; He's always looking for ways to help me grow. I sense a new adventure around the corner, and if I know my Friend, it's not going to be boring.

What does He have in store?

CHAPTER TWENTY
MY HEART'S DESIRE

Do what the Lord wants, and he will give you your heart's desire.
Let the Lord lead you and trust him to help.
(Psalm 37:4–5, CEV)

IT'S THE FALL OF 2007, AND I'M AT A COLLEGE IN MACHAKOS HOMESCHOOLING TWO kids from one family and helping out with math and science classes for another family. The campus compound consists of about twelve homes for full-time professors and several three-story buildings for classrooms and administrative offices. Their terracotta roofs pop next to vibrant blue skies wrapped in ribbons of wispy white clouds. Round blue and orange ice cream parlor tables and chairs dot each porch. The buildings are laced together with brick pathways and groups of umbrella-covered picnic tables framed by colorful gardens and hedges between rich green grass.

My classroom is in the newest building. It's exciting to prepare themed units in which we read books, conduct math and science experiments, do art, and spend Friday afternoons at the movies. The electric pain shooting through my knees from our lunch-hour hopscotch games would be a useful science lesson, if I could pull back the skin. Though I know I need to be careful with what's left of my one good foot, I'm working for Jesus and I'm all-in.

On Parents Day, both sets of parents come to see the work their kids have been doing. It should be a good day, but I don't feel the joy… I'm not happy.

I'm lucky enough to be staying in the Bonel family home while they're gone on furlough. I even have house help. I've been told that if you're white and don't have house help, you're looked on poorly, since the help only costs three dollars per day.

I pay Mbulu five dollars and you'd think it was a million bucks. Mbulu is helping me understand Kenyan culture. She helps me immerse myself in it by inviting me to her home on the mountain each weekend. They call it a hill, but looking up from the bottom I see a mountain before me; trekking the narrow ridge along the pathway to her home confirms it: a mountain it is. I'm so thankful that my foot allows me to maneuver around the delicate footings going up. But on the way down, fighting the forces of gravity, it's much harder. I hold onto her shoulder with one hand and tenaciously grip the wall beside me with the other to successfully navigate the unyielding ridges with my limited mobility. I've become close to her whole family, spending Sunday mornings worshipping with them at their church in the hills.

Not many of the staff at the college spend much time outside the campus walls, but I do. That's where my heart is, with the people of Kenya. I leave the compound and walk along the dirt road into town to do my own shopping. The streets are crowded. Wooden shops are topped with corrugated metal roofs. They sell colorful clothing, bottled water, DVDs, and cell phones. Vendors rest outside their shops on brightly colored plastic chairs, using red Coca-Cola crates as tables. Everyone seems to have a cell phone; it's much more prevalent here than it is in the U.S. I'm shocked that they even transfer money to each other by cell phone. There aren't as many wires overhead, and perhaps there is no need; there are so few landline phones.

At the gate of the hospital, a crowd is gathering in front of a sign that read "Kick Polio Out of Kenya." Nearby, a man has collapsed on the ground and the crowd is waiting to see if he will get up on his own. The onlookers include men dressed in slacks and button-down shirts, women wearing heels and skirts, and children in their school uniforms. An unattended motorcycle lays on the ground, as its rider, a security officer, runs through the gate toward the hospital, perhaps to get help.

Down the road, green wooden kiosks line the roadside, umbrellas shading the vendors from the bright afternoon sun while matatu and motorcycle drivers seek shade beneath the trees in front of the old church. A flurry of vendors call me to buy their products; I'm white, so they assume I can afford anything. I pass by a man sitting in the dirt asking for spare change as young, emaciated children who should be in school run into the alleys with bottles of cheap alcohol.

There's just so much more that should be done, and though I don't know what to do, stepping out of the compound is a good place to start.

Georgette Short teaches the missiology class at the college. She's a short Scottish woman with long white locks and a bit of a crooked smile, her eyebrows are so light that they're hidden behind her wire-rimmed glasses. Georgette is the happiest person I know, next to Gram.

We laugh wildly whenever we're together, but today I've come for some solemn council. We sip tea together on the porch of her small home next to mine.

"Joanie, you're so glum."

"Georgette, I just feel so bad. God brought me ten thousand miles to this place, and I'm just not happy."

She leans in and lifts her eyebrows. "And why do you think that is?"

"Most of the staff here never leave the compound. They seem so entitled. The kids I teach are entitled… their parents are entitled…" I scan the grounds to make sure we're alone, then hold my hand out to signify the youngest girl and whisper, "I feel so bad just for saying this, but you-know-who is just such a pain in the ass."

Georgette laughs out loud. "It's okay to feel that way Joanie." But then she lowers her voice. "You may not be the only one who thinks that."

"I feel like I'm being picky. This is where the Lord has me and I need to make it work. I'm never going to find happiness if I can't find it where He wants me."

"Joanie, the Lord wants to give you the desires of your heart. He says so in Psalm 37:4."

"Hmm." That is news to me. "My heart has had a lot of desires. Is He sure He wants to go there?"

"Well, as you let Him work in you, He changes your natural human desires into something that will honor Him. He made you, Joanie. He made you with certain gifts, talents, and desires. He knows what they are, so you don't need to lie to Him."

"Well, that makes sense, I guess," I say. "But look at everything I've done to get here. I've finished college. My whole church is supporting me. This is what I wanted. Now I get here and I'm going to be unhappy with it?"

I throw my hands up, exasperated.

"I want you to focus on something," Georgette says. "You are happy in some aspects. When the weekend comes and you're able to get off this campus, and not be with a bunch of people from the developed world, but get to spend time with the nationals, I see joy when you come back. After having slept on a board without a bathroom, you have so much joy." She raises her hands. "It's just in here that you seem unhappy."

I cringe as I contemplate her words. "What does that even mean?"

"It means this isn't your place," she reassures me with a touch of her hand. "There's something different for you and you just have to open yourself up to find the place where the Lord wants you."

● ● ●

We're off school for the month of December. Wachira invites me to visit PACE in Nyahururu on December 11 and meet James and Heidi Roland, who are in Kenya from the U.S. to help Wachira start the Pan African School of Theology. Most local pastors have no formal Bible education, so Wachira, James, and an African American woman named Dorris are working together to equip these Kenyan leaders.

The people at the college are worried.

"Don't go," they say. "Do you know how far Nyahururu is? It's a five-hour matatu ride. During the holidays, things are worse. People are going to steal from you and the matatu prices are going to go up. You're putting your life in your own hands by going."

Because of this, I decide that I can't risk it. Next time I'm on the phone with Wachira, I give him the bad news.

"I can't come," I spill out. "It's too dangerous."

Wachira is a good listener and he takes some time to respond. "Joanie, I would never bring you out here if there was ever any thought or concern for your safety."

Wachira, a multitasker, regularly has two or three conversations going on at the same time. He's usually barking out orders to someone in the hall while conversing with another person sitting across from him. But today I'm pretty sure I have his full, undivided attention.

"I'll have Jim and Heidi call you," he assures me. "We will be there to meet you. You'll have all the instructions you need." Then he adds, "Bring an extra $30 in case anything happens, like if the matatu price goes up. But I don't think it'll happen."

A matatu is a fourteen-seat van that acts like a bus. In Kenya, people always stop to pick people up, and there's always room for "one more person." I've been on a matatu with twenty-three passengers. It's a funny thing for Kenyans to say there's "no room."

"Make sure you're in the front seat," Wachira advises me. "They can't overstuff the front seat.

This reminds me of my first trip to PACE, sitting for hours on the hard seat covered with a woolen blanket.

Some days later, my leg quivers as I stand and wait at the bus station, humming praises to Jesus. I'm concerned, but it's not a frozen-in-my-tracks fear, just caution.

It's a bumpy five-hour ride during the holidays, but I'm in my element, immersed with the nationals, chattering about family, friends, and the upcoming election. I'm thrilled to have secured the front seat, meaning I have the attention of everyone in the matatu. There's an excitement in the air. All my fears have vanished.

Hours later, I arrive in Nyahururu, a busy village with so many people milling about. Chickens and goats run on the street. How am I going to find this Heidi I'm supposed to meet? I stand in the street, caught up in the swirl of energy around me. I then feel a tap on my shoulder, and I don't have to guess who it is. Of course it's Heidi. There aren't any other white people around. We hug and immediately I feel a sisterhood, a deep connection with this young mother of four.

Like Caroline Ingalls in *Little House on the Prairie*, Heidi is at ease in Kenya. She leads me through the market, conversing in Kiswahili with her favorite merchants and picking up some last-minute items for dinner.

Then we drive home to meet her children. Little William, Peter, Sophia, and Maria run up to our car like little monkeys, greeting us with their clever chatter. They present me with the freckled array of wildflowers they've spent the morning picking. Sunshine floods my soul and hope blooms inside of me as they guide me, hand in hand, to the guest room to show me the drawings they've made. A tear collects in the corner of my eye at the "Welcome Joanie" artwork crafted in colorful crayon. In the details of the sparsely furnished room that's been specially prepared, I find the joy that's been eluding me at the college. They don't even know me, yet they've taken painstaking effort to decorate the room and welcome me. It's precious, absolutely precious.

Back in the kitchen, Heidi shows me the oven that she and the children have made with scrap materials they've scrounged up. They've made cookies in it. It took several attempts before they were successful, and they taste heavenly.

Heidi homeschools the children, but two days a week they attend PACE Academy, taking part in this developing school. They wear the same uniform and study with the local children who are taught by rote memorization. It's amazing. The girls, who are older, now have a good understanding of what their dad is doing here and how special it is. They're learning Kikuyu and are trying to teach me the singsong inflection of this local language. They tell me that *Ūka haha* means "Come here."

"Oka ha ha," I call out, pronouncing it the way I heard it.

When I'm done, I expect the children to rush over. But they don't move.

"O ka haha," they sing, and then all the children turn around and come over.

"What's the difference?" I stammer.

"It's the singsong, Joanie. You don't just say it. You sing it!" They giggle until I finally start singing the words.

Wachira takes me to PACE Academy several times during my four-day visit, showing me all I could be doing here. We tour the dorms where the forty-five needy or orphaned kids live. Jim and Heidi tell me about spending time with them on weekends. It stirs my heart to see this place again and hear the amazing stories.

When I think about having to return to Machakos, my heart sinks, like the stones I once threw to Azia in the lake. It's not my heart's desire to return there.

During our evening devotions, I share my struggles at the college, as well as the joy I've found here. The Rolands encourage me: "Seek out God's will in the joy He provides."

• • •

I remember seeing Peter's grandmother in Nyahururu, her weathered body crunched over her walking stick as she painstakingly shuffles to town, taking a few steps then pausing for a breath. There's almost an audible crack as she raises her head occasionally to be sure the way is clear; then, as unmanageable as a bowling ball, it drops and she teeters on.

I remind Wachira that I need to make time to see Peter and his grandmother while I'm here. He takes me there directly, using the opportunity to stop by his home on the way and pick up some documents.

"Peter, I'm staying in Machakos now," I tell the boy when we arrive for our visit. "It's a five-hour matatu ride from here. When you want to come and visit me, you talk to Wachira. He has the money."

I realize that if I give the money directly to Peter, he'll use it for food—and it would be hard to argue with that decision.

• • •

It's my last night and the children take me for a walk in the neighborhood along a dirt road. There aren't any cars, just wide open space.

At the end of the road, we encounter two kids, one with a bucket of water and the other a bucket with a hole on the bottom.

"We live on the equator," one of the kids tells me. "The water on the northern hemisphere goes clockwise, but when you go to the southern hemisphere, the magnetic pull makes the water go counterclockwise."

"What are you talking about?" I ask.

There's an impish glee about the children as they encircle the two buckets to watch the demonstration. One child plugs the hole on the bottom of the second bucket, then pours half the water from the first bucket into the plugged bucket, placing a few blades of grass on top so the swirl can be seen moving clockwise as it drains out the bottom hole.

Next, we walk two hundred yards, into the southern hemisphere and they repeat the demonstration. This time the water swirls counterclockwise as it exits the bucket. With wide eyes, I'm amazed.

On our way home, I notice the children busily collecting sticks, so I bend down and join in the collection.

"Why are we collecting sticks?" I ask.

"Oh, for the fire," one of them replies. "We have to have sticks for the fire tonight."

As they skip along the road, they start to sing. They also pick some small leaves from the nearby trees.

"What are these leaves we're collecting?"

They laugh. "For the air freshener. They're eucalyptus leaves. When we have the fire tonight, we'll tell you when you can put them in. It'll make the whole place smell like eucalyptus."

I don't know what that is, but it sounds exotic.

Back at the house, Jim's chopping logs to build a fire. There's a team here from America and they've brought marshmallows, so after dinner we roast marshmallows late into the night.

In the silence of the evening, the crackle of the fire is all that can be heard. Our mesmerized eyes watch the flames lick the wood as the glowing sparks dance to the rhythmic cracks of the fire, the smoke carrying away the day's worries. When the children sprinkle the eucalyptus leaves on the fire, a fresh lemony pine scent wafts in the air.

    The corner of my mouth lifts; I'm not entirely sure if the warmth inside comes from the fire or the love emanating from within. This is the Kenya I fell in love with three years ago and which I'm falling in love with again. God's showing me the desires of my heart.

CHAPTER TWENTY-ONE
THE CLASHES

I will not leave you as orphans; I will come to you.
(John 14:18, NIV)

KENYA IS THE MOST STABLE COUNTRY IN EAST AFRICA AND THE REGION LOOKS TO IT for security, politically and economically. Through Mombasa on Kenya's east coast, shipments safely move inland to Somalia, Ethiopia, South Sudan, Uganda, Rwanda, Burundi, and the Democratic Republic of Congo. It's not a stretch to say that Kenya is the center of the region's collective universe.

During the time that I'm here, an election has been scheduled for December 27, 2007. There's a buzz in the air between the supporters of the two main presidential candidates, representing the two largest tribes in Kenya: Odinga, a Luo, and the incumbent Kibaki, a Kikuyu. I keep hearing about how important this election is both to Kenya and the outlying region. Though all elections are important, this one seems to carry with it a certain uneasiness.

In Kenya, each tribe has its own rites of passage for their young men. In the Kikuyu tribe, thirteen-year-old boys are circumcised late at night, after submerging themselves in cold water to numb themselves. Traditionally, they stay in the place where they were circumcised for about two weeks to heal; however, these days the cut is done by a doctor. After the procedure, they become "men," meaning they can no longer sleep in their mothers' house. So when they return, a shed is built for them outside the home. Traditionally, the Luo remove six of the lower teeth, instead of circumcision, though that tradition has largely fallen out of practice.

I got to know Irungu quite well when I was at PACE in 2003, and it's been good to catch up with him again. I remember Irungu once telling me that it drives the Kikuyus nuts that the Luos don't circumcise their boys; in the minds of the Kikuyus, an uncircumcised boy can never become a man. Irungu has three boys and can't imagine not following this tradition.

Evidently, PACE follows this Kikuyu tradition as well, which horrifies me. When I tell Irungu that we circumcise babies in North America, not thirteen-year-olds, his response is emphatic: "How can you cut a baby?" Mind you, he also thinks that it's barbaric to allow a baby to self-soothe. Kenyans don't let a baby cry. That's when I started to really understand that the differences between cultures aren't necessarily right or wrong. It'll continue to be a huge learning process while I'm here in Kenya.

I'm both elated from having met the Roland family at PACE and disappointed at having to return to Machakos, just outside the capital of Nairobi. I've decided to follow the desires of my heart, to follow God's leading: I'll finish off the school year at Machakos, then move to PACE for the following year.

But for now it's Christmas, and though our celebrations differ, it's still a celebration of my Savior's birth. I have so much to celebrate.

A few members of the staff have stayed, and after a few days of celebration I need to run into town to pick up some last-minute groceries.

When I open the front door, I find Peter standing there.

"What are you doing here?" I ask. I almost bowled him over in my rush to leave. "How did you get here?"

"You give me money to come." He smiles. "I come."

"Okay, really glad to see you, but I wasn't expecting this." I glance back and forth between Peter and my home. "Why didn't you call?"

As soon as I ask the question, I know full well that he didn't call because he doesn't have a phone.

He tilts his head and looks at me, confused. I take a deep breath. How can I turn this boy away? So I invite him in. This is Africa, where hospitality is of the utmost importance, even if you have nothing. I saw this from Peter's grandmother.

"Come on in, and drop your things in the spare room," I tell him. "I was just on my way out to pick up some groceries. Why don't you come along with me and pick out what you'd like to eat?"

"No problem. I cook for myself. I cook for you," he offers eagerly.

Now that I have this Kenyan in my home, my biggest concern is food, because they really eat so differently. I've come to realize I'm somewhat of a picky eater.

We go to the supermarket and get the ingredients for ugali, which is basically the recipe I used as a kid to make a volcano in science class: flour, water, and salt, minus the salt. Later in the evening, a strange look overcomes me as I try his ugali; the look on his face is just as repulsed as he eats my spaghetti.

There's a big dining room table in the Bonels' house where I'm staying.

"See this line on the table?" I use my finger to draw an imaginary line across the tabletop. "Kenyan food on that side, and American food here. You're welcome to have mine whenever you want, but I don't expect you to try mine, and you don't expect me to have yours. Deal?"

Peter's voice is changing, so it cracks a bit as he laughs. His shoulders bounce rhythmically.

Peter arrived here on December 26 and school will start on January 5, so we'll have a few days to enjoy before he goes back home. Mbulu, my Kikuyu house lady, is so excited to see Peter. The two of them chatter away as she leads him off to the kitchen.

I'm honored when Mbulu invites us up to her home in the mountains. Peter and I keep climbing past Mbulu's place, all the way to the top of the mountain. It's winter and the sights are so fresh and vivid. With the rainy season over, corn stocks and banana trees pop up along the hills. Vibrant emerald and jade gardens have been planted in the red earth, tiered into the hillside.

Along the path, we pass large white rocks riddled with pits and crevasses from centuries of rainwater flowing down to the valley floor. Bright yellow flowers dot the pathway as well. Intermittent red, yellow, and green leaves stand out against the soft blue sky, full of energy.

I pause at the top a little longer than Peter. Is it because my aching bones need a rest, or do I just want to gaze out to the valley below and take it all in? It's a stunning sight to behold for sure, but not stunning enough to ever make another attempt up this hill.

When we return from our trip to Mbulu's home, it's December 28 and everyone is glued to their TV sets to learn the results of the election. Initially Odinga appears to have a strong lead, but Kibaka is declared the winner. Though there's a lot of controversy about the results, as well as claims of ballot box stuffing, Kibaka takes the oath under the shade of darkness at 11:00 p.m. on December 30, instead of waiting for all the ballots to be counted.

Suddenly, the TV stations go down, the radio stations go quiet, and all information stops. A dark cloud looms over me. Fear sets in. In America, we have freedom of the press. Here, they don't. Boulders are dropped onto highways to serve as roadblocks. The matatus can't circumvent the boulders.

There are about forty-two different Kenyan tribes settled in different areas of the country, whereas Nairobi and some other cities are more diverse. Tribal clashes have now begun around the country. We get word that people are being stopped in the street and checked for ID. In Kikuyu areas, the Luo are immediately circumcised because they otherwise aren't recognized as being real men. I hear there are cases where Kikuyu in the Luo areas have been killed.

Eldorat, a major city along the Rift Valley in West Kenya, has a mix of Kikuyu and Luo, and we hear news today that a group of Kikuyu women and children took refuge in a church. We also hear that the Luo surrounded the church and set it on fire. It's being reported that one grandma threw a two-year-old baby out the window to save its life, and then a Luo outside took that baby and threw it back into the burning building. The tribes blame each other, but I look at the whole situation and see that both sides have done things; it's people hurting people, and that is not what God calls us to do. We're supposed to love who He loves—and He loves the whole world.

I'm convinced that the Kikuyu couple who work at the school will have the best advice regarding what to do about Peter. They agree that in this political climate, I can't send him back. It's far too dangerous for anyone to travel, let alone travel alone, so Peter will stay with me. He becomes my sidekick at school, going to classes and helping me prepare.

"Mom, can I go play?" Peter asks, peering through the window of my classroom at the end of the day.

I'm stopped in my tracks. He called me Mom. I really love this child. It's like I've found the child I lost, like Jesus brought him to me as a gift.

I realize that Brian would be thirty-two by now. It's just crazy that he'd be that old. My second child would be about seven. I feel she'd have been a girl. I've dreamed of brushing her hair and putting it up in braids and bows.

But now I have Peter. I stand close and wrap my arms around him, holding him tightly.

"Yes," I tell him. "Go play with the other children."

For the first time in his life, he's able to be a kid and just play with the other kids.

The tribal clashes continue for three weeks, with the tension continuing to build. One day, a meeting is held on campus for all of the agency missionaries. I haven't been invited, since I'm not part of the mission agency; I've come to Africa through another agency.

Fortunately, one of the missionaries updates me on the situation when the meeting is over.

"The agency has airplanes and helicopters at their disposal and they're planning to airlift us out of here," he explains.

"Are you kidding me? These nationals can't get out of here." I grab his sleeve, his words becoming a blur. My pulse pounds in my ear. I'm having a hard time breathing.

"Joanie." He holds my face in his hands. "You're not an agency missionary, so you should make plans to leave the compound immediately and find a safe place to hide. Once we're gone, this compound won't be secure anymore. Where can you go?"

"Go? I don't know. I guess I could go with Peter to the hills, but I need insulin medication for my diabetes… it needs to be refrigerated. They don't have fridges outside the compound."

My head is spinning. There are too many moving pieces.

"You should make plans for Peter to get home and find a way out of here for yourself," he says again. "It's not safe, Joanie. It's not safe."

But I can't send Peter home through Nairobi and Eldorat. And he can't stay here any longer either.

"I'm not leaving them here," I call after him as he leaves. "It's not safe for them either! How can you leave?"

"Joanie, call somebody and get out," he calls over his shoulder. With that, he runs into his house.

Left alone, I close my eyes and pray: "Jesus, what should I do? Where should I go?"

With no one here to help me plan, a verse comes to mind. Proverbs 11:14 says, *"A nation falls where there is no wise leading, but it is safe where there are many wise men who know what to do"* (NLV). I'll call the wisest men I know. Kenya should take this advice.

I run to my house and call my trusted church elders and Pastor Lara. Though I'm not as familiar with Judson's new pastor, I do have full confidence in the council of the elders who have guided me for years. Their advice is that because the clashes are intensifying, they'll make arrangements for me to leave.

Oh my gosh, I'm no better than these missionaries, I realize when the conversation is over.

I feel nauseous, and my stomach drops.

Reluctantly, I put Peter on a matatu. I can't even watch as he drives off.

Three days later, I'm on a plane heading home. Jesus, why did you send me to Africa only to bring me home? I don't understand.

• • •

I'm safe at home, but still worry about my friends. Wachira has let me know that Peter's okay and is safely back with his grandmother. I thank God for his safe return and ask for forgiveness in letting him travel alone. Nyahururu is primarily Kikuyu, so he'll be safe now with his people.

There must be a reason I'm back home. I need to listen and figure it out.

In order to get a teaching license in the U.S., I must expunge my outstanding 1990 drug felony; there's a pending deadline, so I have to act fast. One of Judson's elders is a lawyer, and he encourages me to work on it with his help.

I do enjoy being home, feasting on Chicago deep dish pizza, Ma-J's collard greens, and catching up with her children and grandchildren. She's a mother to me, too, which brings us one day to the subject of my own mother. This isn't a subject I'm fond of talking about.

"Joanie, you should consider making things right with your mother," Ma-J says one day while we sit together at her kitchen table. "You need to let her know that with God's grace and power you've let it all go, and you've come through the other side. You can honor your parents by being a witness to what Jesus has done for you. He will use it."

My sullen face droops further. How could God ask me to honor them?

Ma-J cocks an eyebrow. "It's not about you anymore, you know. It's all about God and the grace He's given you. As Romans 5:8 says, *'But God showed his great love for us by sending Christ to die for us while we were still sinners.'* He loves us at our darkest."

"I can't imagine how He could use it." I mutter, my head dropping.

I think about my life before Christ. It was dark, ugly, sick, gross, horrible, and every other word you could think of. My hand begins to shake a little as I realize that Ma-J's right. I'm still holding on to some anger toward my mother.

"He already has," Ma-J says. "You've found joy in your life. That's your testimony. It's not what happened to you. It's how through Him you respond and give glory to Him. You need to let go and set both of you free from it."

"I really am happy. He really was able to take all this stuff away from me. I don't think about all this junk like I used to anymore."

Her eyebrow raises over her glasses. "And your mom?"

"I guess I haven't quite let that go yet," I admit sheepishly.

"He has brought you through all this junk in your life for His glory. You know Holy Spirit is working in you, even now. You are changing and growing. You can do this, too."

"The more I got to know the Lord, the more I wanted to make sure I didn't hurt Holy Spirit inside me. You know, it's been five years since I've thought about killing myself. I used to think about it every day. Dr. Childers said this day would come and I just couldn't believe it, but now it's here."

She reaches over and holds my hand, her black eyes piercing my soul. "He has so many plans for you, Joanie, you just can't imagine. Your life will have such significance."

"You're right. I can't imagine." I throw my hands up in surrender and roll my eyes. "I thought I was supposed to be in Africa, but now that's gone."

"It's not gone. He has a reason for bringing you back. You have unfinished business, business with the law… business with your mother. He's already working on that legal stuff for you and He can take away that pain you're holding inside yourself against your mother, too." Her tone intensifies. "Let it go, Joanie. Lay it at the foot of the cross. Give it to Jesus. Let her know you're okay and you forgive them." She pauses and smiles. "Then you can go back to the Kingdom work He has for you to do."

I close my eyes and nod. I know she's right.

Wanting to meet in a neutral zone, Ma-J drives me to a bunch of local department stores in the Wheaton area. I know my mother works at one of them, and I hope I'll find her. I pray for courage and strength before getting out of the car at each store, my hands trembling so hard that I'm barely able to grasp the door handle.

But after checking each store, I return empty-handed. No Alice Brusseau. I feel regret that I've not been able to release my mom. I haven't seen her in so many years that I'm not sure how either of us would've reacted anyway. I'm satisfied I've made my best effort, and can let it go.

A long sigh escapes my lungs, my heart returns to a more regular rhythm.

• • •

It's my final visit to the DuPage Courthouse. Today my felony will be expunged. I skip in, happy to have this behind me, until I'm notified that I'll have to pay a $250 fee—and they'll only accept a cashier's cheque, which I don't have. I'm directed to a currency exchange nearby that can help.

Driving up, I see there's a department store there that I didn't know existed. As the cashier's check is being cut, my attention is drawn across the street.

The billowing grey clouds above have been threatening rain all day. My fingers tap the steering wheel anxiously as I stop in the parking lot, my heart beating in my throat, eyes laser-focused at the store entrance… watching, waiting for I don't know what.

Suddenly the heavy clouds let go and rain drops bead onto the windshield, at first slowly, like teardrops, matching the tears falling from my cloudy eyes.

With a deep breath, I muster some courage, wipe my eyes, pull the hood over my head, and dash through the now torrential rain to the entrance. My hair's stuck to my face, my clothes cling to my body, and I'm soaked as I scurry around the ladies department. Like a gopher, my head periodically pops up between the clothing racks, but I don't see her anywhere.

"By any chance does Alice Brusseau work here?" I ask a kind customer service employee.

"Oh, I'm sorry, she's sick today. Is there something I can help you with?"

I leave for Kenya in three days, so I won't be able to try again. It was a big step for me to make *this* attempt.

"No thank you," I say, smiling. "I heard she worked here and was just hoping to run into her."

I turn, put my hand to my heart, and whisper, "I forgive you, Mom." A single tear runs down my glowing cheek.

In my heart, I have finally forgiven her, but somehow I still need to let her know. I purchase a Mother's Day card, write a note on it explaining how much I love her and have forgiveness in my heart for her and Dad for everything that happened, and mail it.

That night, I cry inconsolably in the shower, sliding down to the floor, my tears washing down the drain, mourning the fact that I wasn't able to let my father know before he died.

I am at peace. Now I know why I had to return home.

CHAPTER TWENTY-TWO
BLACK AND WHITE

For now we are all children of God through faith in Jesus Christ…
We are no longer Jews or Greeks or slaves or free men or
even merely men or women, but we are all the same
—we are Christians; we are one in Christ Jesus.
(Galatians 3:26, 28, TLB)

IT'S HARD FOR ME TO CONTAIN MY EXCITEMENT AS I DESCEND THE FAMILIAR STEPS of the Jomo Kenyatta International Airport. Irungu will be picking me up and taking me back to Nyahururu. I wiggle, like I have ants in my pants, while security checks my luggage, and oh do I have luggage! I'm planning to stay this time.

When the doors open and I step outside, Irungu's the first person I see, wearing a button-down shirt and slacks. His whole face beams when he sees me, dark eyes twinkling from under his signature baseball cap. Are those crows feet at the corner of his eyes? Huh. He's matured in the five years since I first met him in 2003.

He removes his cap and nods hello. His hair is clipped close to his head. A perfect smile emerges from under his distinguishable Nubian nose. Irungu is about Brian's age, and as dear to me as Brian.

In Nyahururu, Irungu points out the children begging in the streets. My chin trembles uncomfortably and I lower my head, remembering what it's like to be invisible on the street. I feel the shame of realizing they've already become an invisible part of the landscape to me.

"They beg for food and education," Irungu says.

"What do you mean? I thought the public schools are free now."

"Yes, public schools are free, but they still need to buy their books, pencils, and uniforms. Private schools, like PACE Academy, have tuition. The children take a form home telling how much they need to pay for the child to come back to school. If the child knows their parents don't have enough money, they'll take to the streets, begging for money to get back to school."

My heart breaks to see how desperate they are and how happy they'd be to get back to school. It kills me.

"They'll be so sad to have missed three days of school, especially the older children," he says. "Everything is based on the test scores. Their test scores decide if they go to high school or not. If they don't do well, it doesn't matter if their parents can pay. University, too. It's all about those test scores. It's extremely important. I tell my boys they need to study hard." Irungu has two boys at PACE, Simon and James, and his wife Njoki, also known to me as Mama Simon, is pregnant with another. It's difficult for them to pay the fees.

We turn off the main road and I chuckle as we weave around the potholes and an unaccompanied donkey walking down the laneway.

My heart quickens as we arrive at the gates of PACE Academy. Soldier waves at us, an ever-present smile on his face. In Kenya, all security guards are named Soldier. My excitement is hard to contain, but I'll have to wait a few moments before seeing the school again. First we head to my new house, which is only a short walk away. Wachira's found a place that's close to the school so I can even make it with my bum foot. Maina YM is there waiting to help move me in. I feel at home immediately.

As I unpack my things, I feel a bit disappointed by Wachira's news that I won't be teaching. But as I consider how the classes are run, which is nothing like our schools in America, I can see why. The students need to prepare to write the national exams in the learning method their exams are written for, by rote learning rather than by critical thinking. In the U.S., students have a sense of entitlement you don't see here in Kenya. Here, education is their way out of poverty; it's more than just being able to access that education, it's about doing well.

So I won't be teaching. Instead I'll be Wachira's assistant, working with visiting teams and updating donors on what's happening here, trusting that God will use me for His glory and purposes, not my own. As John 3:30 tells us, *"Jesus must become more important, while I become less important"* (CEV).

• • •

In the US, Obama has been elected president. The Kenyans are excited, because his father is Kenyan. Somehow they feel that since Obama's become president, he'll help their country. A public holiday is declared and school is out all over Kenya, but the kids aren't as excited as you'd expect, because there's nothing for them to do in this sleepy little town when they have a day off. There are no libraries to borrow books, no video stores to get movies. They may have a ball made of old rags tied together to play football, but that's only if they're lucky.

When the holiday is declared, I approach the teachers about having a special dinner for the children at my house. I know it's a good idea, and I have money for supplies, but I have no clue how to cook, let alone host so many people. The teachers have my back, though. A goat is slaughtered, a fire is built, and food is cooked… all things I don't know how to do.

About twenty kids and their teachers show up. There's plenty of food and they all eat to their fill. I'm happy to see Wachira pop in, too.

Everyone stands up to say what they're thankful for, specifically what Obama's win means for them. An eighth grader stands, holds his head high, and proclaims, "If a black man can become the leader of the most powerful country in the world, then what does that say for me?" There's a glimmer of hope in his eye; Obama's only one generation away from Kenyan, meaning that they, too, can do something great.

From what I can see, these kids think about the U.S. as being all-white. They don't learn about their people having been taken from their continent in boats against their will. They don't know about slavery or what the Blacks have had to overcome in the U.S. To them, Obama and any other potential Blacks in the U.S., have recently escaped Africa and made it in America where the streets are paved with gold for everyone.

• • •

In addition to the mission teams that come to PACE, Wachira has a heart for the needy in Africa. He's involved in so many ministries. There's the PACE Academy and High School, which now have more than two hundred students, including eighty refugees who were displaced from the 2007 election clashes, and kids from the other countries in the region. James and Dorris have been hired to support local leaders through college and seminary programs. Wachira also plans mission trips within Africa. He holds a weekly prayer meeting at the city hall and mentors some local pastors known as the Caleb Pastors, each of whom he requires to host a ministry outside their pastoral duties. Like all visionaries, he is very busy.

When we build a church or pastor's home, the community needs to bring something to the table. Wachira believes it's important for them to have skin in the game, and participate however they can, so they have ownership in it. Some provide money, or supply the posts for the structure. It's so interesting to see how different people participate. In some tribes, the women do all the work, including the heavy-lifting. They carry huge tree trunks and beams while the men walk behind, or sit in the shade calling out instructions. It makes no sense to me, but this is Kenya. It's a different culture.

Wachira often uses the phrase "my people" when speaking about Kenyans: "My people have a tendency. When you say you're going to do something, they're expecting you will do it all by yourself, because you come from the land of milk and honey where the streets are paved with gold." He knows he can help more people if he meets them somewhere in the middle, stressing that "my people" must learn to help each other and not rely on the white savior to rescue them. Western teams don't go out alone on mission trips to the rural areas; they work together with local Kenyan teams.

We have seven mission trips planned for this upcoming year, and though I'm not in charge of them, I do play a huge part in planning the trips, from scouting out the destinations, which could be as far as six hours away, to finding a local contact who will be in charge. I also help find places for teams to sleep and eat. Irungu and Maina YM, who's now just called YM, are my constant companions on these scouting adventures. I lean on their expertise with the culture, language, and logistically navigating our way to the locations.

"YM, why do they call you YM?" I ask on the drive out to one of these remote communities.

"There are so many Mainas," he responds succinctly. He is a man of few words.

Already having met Maina the cook, Maina the mechanic, Maina the driver, and Maina YM, I concede that there are indeed many Mainas.

"But why *YM*? I ask, still confused. "What does it mean?"

He grasps the brim of his YMCA hat and nods.

"Oh!" I chuckle. "But what happened to the CA?"

"Too long," he responds simply.

Today we're traveling off-road—off the regular dirt roads, that is—using trees, large stones, and shacks as our compass. I watch the camels to my left, and the trees moving ahead, evidence of elephants roaming in the brush.

"How are we going to find where we need to go?" I wonder, the breeze flowing through my hair from the cloud of dust we're kicking up.

"Oh, Joanie, we can find it."

I trust in Jesus, but sometimes it's challenging. I start squirming in my seat.

"I need to help myself," I say. That's Kenyan code for *I need to pee*. "We need to find a good place."

YM stops the car. "This is a good place."

"Here? It's the middle of nowhere!" I throw my hands up.

He squints at me. "Where's the middle of nowhere?"

"This…" I do my best Vanna White impression. "This is the middle of nowhere! There is nothing out here."

"I want to find where nowhere is," Irungu says, chuckling sarcastically.

I struggle to get out of the car; after three hours in an old jeep, I need to stretch. I hobble around to the back, hanging onto the side so I don't fall. Unable to squat, I'll need to hold onto the bumper.

Just then, an inquisitive toddler approaches the car—and as soon as she lays eyes on me, she wails, "AAAAAAAAAAH!"

"What's wrong, what's wrong?" My head swivels around, looking for a charging elephant. Then I start screaming along with her and pull up my pants.

Irungu jumps out of the vehicle, runs to the child, and speaks to her in the local language. He holds her hand and brings her over to me, lifting the bottom of my trousers.

"She thinks you're a ghost," he explains. "She's never seen a white person before, so I'm explaining who you are and I'm showing her the problem goes all the way down to your feet."

I pull a sweet stick from my pocket and hold it out for her. She peeks shyly out from behind Irungu's leg and cautiously inches her hand toward the candy treat. She quickly snaps it up in her fingers and scurries away to a safer distance, her shrills cries continuing.

It's not until I'm secured in the car again that her crying stops. Holding my knees together, I'm resigned to help myself in the middle of some other nowhere.

• • •

On another trip out to a remote village, we travel on a bus with a team of fourteen African Americans. When they first arrive at PACE, though, I can tell they don't like me. Irungu can tell as well.

"Why aren't they greeting you?" Irungu asks.

"Don't blame them," I say. "Things are difficult between them and whites back home."

I lower my head and stand back. How do I explain everything that's happened between Blacks and Whites in America—from the passage across the Atlantic, to slavery, and their clawing to gain equality when the only difference is that the color of my skin, or lack of it, gives me more opportunity?

"But we are all Christian," he says. "Don't they know the love of Jesus covers all of us, Black and White?"

I shrug and offer a little nod. Irungu must know something about this. They've lived under imperialism.

Shaking my head, I make my way to Wachira's office. There's nothing I can say. I can't fix all these problems right now; we have a mission trip to conduct.

"Wachira, please don't send me with them," I say, sitting down in the chair opposite his desk. "If you send me to the remote areas to do a mission trip with them…" I pause to get his attention. "You know it's different."

Wachira's looking at one of his phones, and Dorris is working beside him.

I raise my voice a bit and continue. "When they get off the bus in these places, even if they're light skinned, nothing will happen." I think back on my experience with the little girl. "But when I get off, you know the children will be screaming and calling out, 'Mzungu! Mzungu!'"

The older people in Kenya have a better understanding of what mzungus—white people—can bring. White people have money. Irungu has explained that Kenyans believe there's a limited amount of good in the world, and so they have to seize opportunities when they arise. As he says, "If you have the good, then there's not enough for me, so I have to get in on the good you have." Dorris should understand this, too. She's an African American who came to PACE from Atlanta shortly after Wachira and Glenda began the ministry.

"That's the last thing an African American needs to hear when they're going to the mother continent, to a place where they're going to see people like themselves," I point out. "It's not good for the white person to get all the adulation."

My eyes are trained on Dorris, looking for confirmation.

"I beg to differ, Joanie," she interjects. "They need to see we can work together."

Wachira looks up from his phone. "I need you to go with them. I need you there. But thanks for bringing this to my attention. You will stay in the bus and be the last to get off."

I let out a big sigh, nod, and make arrangements to go.

"Jesus, let my presence here honor You," I whisper under my breath.

CHAPTER TWENTY-THREE
GROWING IN HIS GRACE

And I am sure that God who began the good work within you will keep right on helping you grow in his grace until his task within you is finally finished on that day when Jesus Christ returns.
(Philippians 1:6, TLB)

AT FIRST IT'S HARD FOR ME TO SEE HOW GOD CAN USE ME HERE, BUT AS THE YEARS pass I see how the small things I do are making a difference in bringing attention to special needs kids, kids with AIDS, and kids who live on the street. I'm learning how to use the difficult times in my life to speak to people and be a witness to what God has done in me.

The Caleb 8 are an interdenominational group of pastors who Wachira mentors. They work together to build the Kingdom of God in Nyahururu and beyond. Each pastor leads a church and also works in another ministry within the community. I'm amazed at how God has used my presence here to fulfill His greater purpose through the work of some of these men.

Pastor Macharia and his wife Faith work with the elderly at two locations in the greater Nyahururu area, the first being about a half-hour out of town and the other about an hour and a half away. As in many areas, the youth are leaving rural areas for the city to find work. The elders, who have traditionally been held in high esteem, are suffering the same isolation in remote Kenya as they are in America, but here they don't have access to as many opportunities.

We drive out to the farthest location. With the many potholes, the main roads more closely resemble swiss cheese than a thoroughfare. When we leave the paved roads, we land on dirt roads, barely faint tracks in the dust. Today we're lucky there's no rain and the roads are dry, or we'd be pushing the vehicle through mud fields.

We approach the small house, no more than a tin roof raised on four large branches covering a couple of benches. Here, two elderly parents are raising their adult son who suffers cognitively from having been dropped on his head as a child.

There's a power outage today, a frequent occurrence in Kenya and one I've become quite familiar with. Irungu is not only familiar with it, he's also prepared. He sets up the generator while I hook up my computer. The locals mill about, some poking their heads in front of the screen while others follow the wires. They are so amazed by this unusual technology that they've forgotten the table of food waiting for them.

My plan is to show *The First Grader*, a movie that follows the true story of the crippled eighty-four-year-old Kimani Ng'ang'a Maruge, who enrolled in school in 2003 after the Kenyan government announced free education for all, because he wanted to learn to read the Bible. His story became so well known that he was invited to speak at the United Nations on the importance of free education, but during the 2007–2008 election clashes he lost his property and was forced to live in a refugee camp.

Like Maruge, many of these elders weren't entitled to an education in their youth. I'm not entirely sure they understand what's going on in the movie, but observing their attentiveness as they watch with bugged-out eyes and gaping mouth is phenomenal. They're on the edge of their seats, watching a moving picture projected on an old sheet for the first time in their lives.

Pastor Macharia periodically asks me to pause the movie so he can translate for them what's going on in their native tongue.

"Most of these old people don't even know Kiswahili," Irungu leans over to whisper in my ear. "Kiswahili and English are taught in school for commerce. These older people only know their mother tongue. If a Konga marries a Kikuyu, they speak Kiswahili to each other in the house, but their parents would not understand. These grandparents don't understand the language their grandchildren speak at all. It's pretty significant out here."

These elderly folk walk two or three kilometers just to spend time with other people. It's so good for them to have this community, to hug each other and have uggi, a drinkable oatmeal. When a team like ours comes, we bring some sweets as well. Pastor Macharia brings the Word of God and together they fellowship.

At the other location, the old people sit down on the grass in a field owned by the church. It starts to rain, and the visiting missionary team notices that nobody has umbrellas, which are unaffordable and unnecessary; Kenyans concern themselves only with necessities. As a temporary solution, the team decides to purchase a polyurethane tarp so the elders can have cover. Concerned for the long-term, they also offer $1,000 to build a more permanent shelter, basically four posts and a corrugated roof.

Wachira turns to me. "It's your job to secure the funds once they come in, then purchase the supplies, hire the workers, and update the team on the progress once they return home," he says. "With so much corruption in Africa, they need to see the work is being done, that the money is going where it should be going."

Over the next two years, more teams come and improve the structure, building walls and providing chairs, a stage, and a podium. With every improvement, I'm fortunate to receive the gratitude of these grandparents—the hugs, the love… I know God is using me here.

• • •

When a large Canadian team arrives, we see that there won't be enough room for them in one location, so we split them into two groups. As the project coordinator, I take three teenagers with me in my house and get to know them quite well, especially a young man named Jon.

Today we're going to visit Pastor Francis and his wife Beth, who run Victory School, the only preschool in the slum town of Maina just outside of Nyahururu. Ten thousand people live in shacks covering about six square kilometers. Ninety-three children between the ages of two and five come to Victory School, a private school. Some never pay, because their parents just can't afford anything. Others can afford a dollar a month.

Francis lines the children up along a fence and they sing Kikuyu songs—songs about AIDS and hygiene, two things that are important to their survival. While most children are barefoot, one child has cut the toes off her shoes so her feet can continue to grow.

"The children don't have breakfast," Francis explains. "Some don't come back after lunch, because they are so hungry and too tired to learn."

Francis looks a bit like a Black John Lennon, peering over his stylish round, rose-colored glasses. They were clearly a gift from a previous team.

"Let's go into the classrooms and see how they learn," he adds, directing us to the two lean-tos next to the rustic house on his property.

Beth has painstakingly stitched numbers and letters onto old polypropylene bags, and the children sit on tiny wooden chairs, repeating the letters by rote. Most kids are wide-eyed, eager to show off for the westerners. A few teetering, malnourished heads flop on their desks in exhaustion.

A tear rolls down Jon's face, and then he quietly leaves the group to walk down the streets. I excuse myself and follow after him.

"How can you do this, Joanie?" Jon gasps for a breath, unable to fight back his tears. "How do you see that and not be able to help?"

I put my arm around his heaving shoulder, and take a deep breath. "It's hard. It's hard not to be able to help, knowing those kids are going to bed hungry, but the only thing we can do right now is to pray for them."

"No, I can do more than that." His shoulders square as he rises up, face resolute and determined. The gears are moving in his head as he tries to work through the problem and find a solution. "I want to do something, to bring them milk and bread every day."

"Wachira is all about sustainability," I tell him. "He's always concerned about starting something that can't be continued long-term. Personally I'm not sure… I think providing milk and bread for six weeks is better than not providing any at all, but I'm just letting you know that you should think long-term. A team came once and gave them goats, then another team came and built a pen for the goats, so when the goats got pregnant they'd have milk for the babies and the kids. But it was never enough." I sigh. "There are so many children."

"How much would it cost?" John asks. There's a youthful determination about him.

In my head, I do a rough calculation. I figure out what it would cost to provide a loaf of bread, estimating slices in each loaf, then costing out cartons of milk for each kid. My head's spinning. I purse my lips and come up with a value.

"I can do that!" he says. "All I need is ten people to give ten dollars a month. There's no excuse for people on my side of the pond not to be able to do that, in order to provide nutrition for kids so they can stay awake in class."

Back in Canada, he does it. Jon figures out a way and God brings it all to fruition.

In Kenya, things move very slowly, but with Irungu's support I'm able to secure the right price for the bread and milk. With Jon's financial support, I secure the milk and bread and also get crates to transport it back and forth each week.

I'm blessed to be the one who brings lunch to the children. Bringing my camera, I take lots of photos of the tiny little hands, full of dirt and dust, clutching four or five pieces of bread and a triangle carton of milk. I stumble as I balance the camera in one hand and cut open a corner of the milk carton with the other. If only I could transport Jon here to hear the screams of delight and feel their tiny arms wrap around his legs as they express their thanks.

● ● ●

Pastor Mugo and his wife, also named Faith, came to Nyahururu with their three daughters from Kisumu near Eldoret in 2007 during the election clashes. He's Kikuyu and had lived in Luo territory as a missionary for years. They had a shop and a house, and he'd built a church among the Luo.

A team from Detroit is now going to Kisumu county with him as he returns to rebuild the church that was destroyed during the clashes.

As we take out seats on the bus, Mugo begins to speak. On any given Sunday, Mugo's powerful Pentecostal voice booms like thunder in the sky, but today he is quiet and reflective. We're on the edge of our seats listening to Mugo as he explains why they left.

"Faith and I were in our home on December 26 at about 1:15 a.m. when terror struck," he says. "It is a day that remains memorable in my life—when friends turn foe, when your brothers become your enemies, and when people you trust turn against you. I heard a bang in the house and suddenly all the windows were broken, smashed by rocks, and I stood helpless to defend even my wife. They came with burning torches in hand. I had helped birth one of their children, and found a job for another, and here they were at my house with evil intentions. But even in this time, God had created a corner in my home, a corner I didn't even know existed, and this is where we hid and I held the hand of my wife. With bated breath we prayed, asking God for protection. I managed to get on my phone and call my brother-in-law. In a whispered voice, I told him this seemed to be our last night, but if there was anything he could do, please help us. He called the police, who came, but there were killers all about in the night and there was nothing they could do. So they told us to go back into the house and close the doors. All night we remained awake, trembling, and in the morning we got into our car and drove east, not stopping until we reached Nakuru where my brother-in-law lived, and we stayed there for three days."

We are all riveted by Mugo's story. His voice quavers as the story continues.

"On December 30, at 11:00 a.m., the story of Job became a reality to me and my family. I received a call saying that the church we had labored to build was up in flames. Thirty minutes later, we received another call saying our house had been broken into and raiders had taken everything. As difficult as that was, we received yet another call an hour later. The shop we owned had been broken into and our business was gone, and the sugar cane fields equally gone. Like someone groping in the dark, I went outside and saw some stones by a tree and sat down under that tree. Then the Lord spoke, because the Lord of second chances still speaks, from Micah 7:7–8: 'But as for me, I watch in hope for the Lord, I wait for God my Savior; my God will hear me. Do not gloat over me, my enemy! Though I have fallen, I will rise. Though I sit in darkness, the Lord will be my light.'" Mugo stands, raising his hands. "And with tears running down my face, I rose and began to thank God that the Lord of my salvation would hear me and give me another chance. As I entered the home, seeing everyone heartbroken, I reminded them of what God had told me, and we prayed together.

"Though the enemy is laughing that we have fallen, left with nothing, yet we shall arise. I know it is easier said than done, and the Bible says it is not possible without faith. So Faith and I bought a mattress and two blankets and drove to Nyahururu with our three girls, broken refugees, thinking we would only stay awhile. Six months later, God told me to plant a church there, and we have. Now a year later, I am blessed to have you join me as I return to help rebuild the church that was destroyed. Regardless of what we've been through, He will always come to our rescue and give us a second chance. He will bring in new people, take you to new places, and use you in ways you would not have known, by God's grace. Let the world take everything, but I believe in Him and trust Him in His faithfulness to give me a second chance."

Mugo takes his seat. There is not a dry eye on the bus. None of us can imagine the faith and courage it takes for him to go back and rebuild that church for the congregation who took everything from him.

When we arrive, we take the sheet metal and wood and rebuild the church. This is a kind of forgiveness I have never before seen on earth.

While we're building, one of the team members asks Mugo why he went back and how he can love these people so much.

"That's what God calls us to do," Mugo says. "Because He has done the same thing for us."

• • •

Faith couldn't go back to Kisumu. It was just too hard, and I totally understand; it's hard to face those demons lurking in the past.

Shortly after we return from our trip to Kisumu, Faith's hands are shaking. She appears to be anxious and nervous, which is totally understandable since Mugo has just returned from the place where they'd been attacked and where she felt so unsafe.

But something is off. Faith bumps into a table and tries to brush it off as clumsiness. Then she falls down, mumbling and slurring.

Panicked, Mugo runs to her side as a seizure takes hold.

"Stroke!" others begin to yell. "Stroke! She's having a stroke!"

Being diabetic, I recognize the signs. Faith's stroke is a result of diabetes, and she's about to go into a coma. Her blood pressure is sky high. I use my own test kit to measure her sugar levels—and they are extremely high.

"Wachira, she needs to get to a hospital in Nairobi," I explain. "She's having a stroke. The hospitals here just aren't equipped to handle this."

Things are not as simple here as they are in America. Transporting someone to Nairobi is not an easy decision; it requires about $50 in gas, overnight stays, and food. About $150 later, it's a crippling expense for a community like this where the school principal makes $2.80 a day.

Wachira looks at me with concern in his eyes. With a commanding voice, he declares, "Go!"

Irungu darts out for the car, and as quickly as we can we get the forty-three-year-old Faith and Mugo to Nairobi where she's taken care of. She's given meds for her blood pressure and insulin to lower her blood sugar levels. She's provided diabetic education and is scheduled to undergo physiotherapy in Nyahururu. Though she may never physically be quite the same again, her mind is sharp and she's able to return to her family.

"I don't know where we'd be without you," Mugo says, taking my hand and looking into my eyes. "You're such a Godsend to us."

"Thank you for saving my life," Faith chimes in, surrounded by her three girls.

"I didn't do anything," I insist. "Everything I did was after the fact."

The way they look at me overwhelms me. As Esther 4:14 tells us, *"And who knows whether you have not come to the kingdom for such a time as this?"* (ESV) There's a twinkle in my eye.

"Jesus is the one who did this for you," I say. "Because let me tell you, if I wasn't diabetic, I wouldn't have known the signs. And if it wasn't for Him, I wouldn't even be here. The only reason I'm here is because of Him, and the only reason I'm doing what I do is because of the people back home who are supporting me. Praise Jesus."

"Yes, it is God's faithfulness once again." Mugo's face breaks out into one of those smiles where no part of his face is left out.

For such a time as this. I'm reminded of the people Jesus put in my path when I didn't even know who He was.

"Thank You, Jesus," I whisper.

• • •

Pastor Peter Njihia and his wife Joyce have a heart for Rwanda and each year he takes a team out to help build churches and train pastors there. The election clashes here are all too familiar to the stories I've heard about the Rwandan genocide in 1994. How easily disagreements can escalate! In three months, somewhere between five hundred thousand and a million people were killed in tribal warfare, killed with machetes. Rivers ran red, filled with bodies, and the stench in the air lasted for years. I think about John 3:16—*"For God so loved the world that he gave his one and only Son, that whoever believes in him shall not perish but have eternal life"* (NIV). He loves the whole world—everyone. That's the love we are supposed to share.

There are seven of us on this trip: Pastor Peter, Pastor Mugo, Pastor Wachira, Irungu, myself, and two others. Again, I'm there to record what is happening and update the western churches who are supporting the effort.

Irungu has been there before and tells me what to expect. "It's a twenty-five-hour bus ride, Joanie, on the roads of East Africa. Are you sure you're up for this?"

"I can do this. Jesus will be with me," I assure him as we enter the public transit bus that will take us to Rwanda. Seeing that the back of the bus is empty, I think we've just hit the jackpot. "Hey look, we can lay down on the seats back there. Nobody's there."

A few hours into the journey, visions of my childhood bus rides bounce into my head as our bottoms are airlifted up off the seats.

"We've gotta get up to the front of the bus, Irungu!" I realize.

We stop every few hours. All the women go to one restroom, and for 10 KSh we get four or five squares of toilet paper. Once again I'm faced with the Kenyan squatty-potty-hole-in-the-floor toilet. I can't squat, and there is nothing to hold on to. Irungu insists I should help myself, but I decide that I'll be fine if I just don't drink anything for the remainder of the trip.

At one particular stop, Irungu comes back onto the bus with plantains and rice for dinner. It's 10:00 at night. I can't even think about eating them, knowing what they'll do to me.

At about 12:30 or 1:00, we're in Uganda and I'm buckled over, desperate to go pee. I don't think the driver's going to stop until we need gas. He's going to drive right through the night.

Irungu sees me bouncing. "I told you to help yourself," he says, smirking.

"I know what you told me," I retort, gritting my teeth. "We just have to deal with what's happening. I have to go *now*."

Irungu strides to the front of the bus to wake Wachira, whispering in his ear. Embarrassed, I sink down into my seat, my face turning multiple shades of red as Irungu informs the driver.

They call this the dark continent for a reason… it's pitch-black outside. There's absolutely no light pollution here. With no moon or stars out, you can't see your hand in front of you. Tonight it's cloudy and not a single star twinkles in the sky. It's late and we haven't seen traffic in hours, not even the sporadic boda boda motorcycle or matatu.

The bus stops and Irungu follows me outside with a few pieces of tissue. He knows about my leg issues and instructs me to hold on to the back bumper as he stands to the side of the bus.

A faint rumble from off in the distance quickly becomes a full throttle vibration. I can almost feel it. When Kenyans help themselves, they just walk away from the road into the bushes, but I can't because I need to hold onto the bumper.

I can only imagine the fright of the boda boda driver as his headlights light up my glowing white behind. So what does he do? This boda boda driver pulls up behind me and turns off the lights. I'm midstream, and I can't decide if I want to yell at this guy for not continuing down the road, or yell at Irungu for walking over to him, albeit very careful to keep his back to me, to talk to the guy! I don't know what the chatter's about, but eventually the guy turns on his boda boda. The lights flicker on, the engine revs, and he's outta there as I'm pulling my pants back up.

Now *there's* a way to shine your light! Irungu and I laugh hysterically as we climb back onto the bus and continue on to Rwanda.

● ● ●

School's almost out for the December holidays and I'm anxious. My friend Denise usually orders my meds online and ships them to me from Chicago, but there's a shortage of my bipolar meds and she can't get them. I'll run out by December 10 and I don't know what to do.

A team will soon be coming from Detroit, so I contact them to see if they can get the meds to me sooner, but they can't get it either.

Because of the stigma around mental illness, I haven't shared all my medical issues with Wachira. I've been trying to act as normal as I can, which for me is difficult on a good day, but Wachira has noticed a change in my behavior. He believes it's due to stress and offers me a few weeks off. This is huge. Things at PACE never stop, even when school's out, and I'm so grateful for God's most timely provision of time.

On Christmas Eve, Irungu takes me to the post office—and it's there! A week later, the drugs catch up to me and I get back to normal, just in time to return to work. Every day I learn to trust Him. God is good!

CHAPTER TWENTY-FOUR
BLESSED TO BE A BLESSING

We are confident that God is able to orchestrate everything to work toward something good and beautiful when we love Him and accept His invitation to live according to His plan.
(Romans 8:28, Voice)

OVER THE YEARS, I'VE JOINED MANY TRAVELING MISSION TEAMS ON SAFARI AND SEEN so much of God's beautiful creation here in Kenya. Today I also see the darkness of nature.

We approach a pride of lions. Two males, visibly agitated, pace around each other, deep-throated snarls emanating from them as they bark at each other, the younger challenging the elder to a duel. With panting groans, the lionesses and cubs move back, creating a wider circle, allowing this fight for dominance to proceed.

The patriarch runs forward, defending the supremacy of his pride. Projecting an aggressive grunt, the elder bares his teeth and reaches for the younger's neck, but he is disoriented by the agility of his challenger, whose enormous outstretched paw extends to the buttock of the elder; his claws catch the elder's flank, flipping him over. The king's dark mane kicks up the dust as his opponent, lurching forward, swipes at his face. The king lets out a loud, tormented roar that resonates over the savannah.

Face to face, they engage in a war dance, paws striking and clawing, each shredding the other's thick skin. Blood pumping, saliva dripping, their massive jaws intertwine. Their swatting tufted tails brush the ground, a compass for balance between their muscular hindlegs. Their deep, intense roars reverberate inside our vehicle, pulsating in my chest.

The vicious fight continues back and forth, with the senior crouching down, protecting his hindlegs and circling to avoid being caught in the throat. The junior pulls and tears until the bloody senior, weary and beaten, bows to the successor and limps away, relinquishing the throne and giving up his pride.

The newly crowned king approaches his new pride, the lionesses grunting and snorting helplessly. He approaches their young cubs, who try to defend themselves with high-pitched growls. One at a time, he grabs them by their necks in his relentless jaws, viciously shaking them and dropping their bloodied bodies to ensure their demise. The submissive lionesses are now under his sole control.

This is the way of nature. There's a need for domination, a natural bloodline. But his reign will be short, for in a few short years he will be challenged and succumb to one stronger than himself.

As I watch, I'm reminded of my father, fighting the forces of his own nature, eventually breaking and killing a part of me as my submissive mother sat by, forced to choose between her mate and her baby. I think about my own battles with nature, finally choosing to let go of my babies, believing there to be no other way. I've fought and lost many battles, with my family and with those many men with whom I sought to fill the void in my life.

But Jesus, the Lion of Judah, has brought another force into my life—not of flawed nature but unconditional, unrelenting, unmistakable, and powerful love. It's a supernatural love.

I see now how my Father's hand has been over me, through the saints He surrounded me with, before I even knew Him. I think of how His Son, the Lion of Judah, fought for me and won, and how He gave his Spirit to comfort, protect, and equip me for this. I can't help but be amazed by this love, a love unmatched here on earth.

As Joseph said to his brother in Genesis 50:19–20,

Don't be afraid of me. Am I God, to judge and punish you? As far as I am concerned, God turned into good what you meant for evil, for he brought me to this high position I have today so that I could save the lives of many people. (TLB)

I'm still working out the kinks after having been forgiven. I'm not sure I'm in a high position, like Joseph's or saving lives, but I do know that I'm making a difference.

God has taken me to so many tribes among the Kenyan people, including the Samburu, Maasai, Turkana, Kamba and others. I've built multipurpose schools and church buildings in the most remote parts of the country. Many tribes will bestow a tribal name on their guests. In Samburu I'm Kayla, which means peace. The Kikuyu call me Gakenya, meaning one who smiles a lot. And the Kamba have given me the same name. My smile stretches from ear to ear as I contemplate the joy and peace I have in being where God wants me.

• • •

There are several wooden buildings on the PACE campus that were mixed dorms when I first got here, but now they're reserved just for the boys. A new stone building has been erected to house the kitchen and dining room on the ground floor, offices on the second, and most recently, the girls dormitories on the third.

During the week, the children gather in the dining room for assemblies and on weekends for chapel and movie nights. I love movie nights, but I love chapel more. I share the testimony of what God's done for me whenever I can, and today at chapel is one of those times. Rows of academy children in their red sweaters, and high school students in their orange sweaters, wait quietly to hear my story.

My car accident has left me with my most noticeable scars, so that's a good place to start. I limp to the front of the room, the dust kicked up from the dirt floor dancing in the sunlight that streams through the windows into the darkness of the room. I run my finger along the scar on my jaw.

"One tiny bolt that was supposed to keep me safe in the accident was faulty, defective," I say. "My foot was crushed, my face slashed, my lungs punctured. That tiny defective bolt should have cost me my life, but Jesus saved me, just like He saves me from every sin, even the tiny, insignificant ones that should cost me my life."

I explain how being homeless brought me to a Christian counsellor who changed my life.

"This woman of faith was kind and helped me remember about my son Brian." A tear runs down my face as I talk about Brian and the pain of losing him. "My father is his father, too."

I then lift my sleeves to expose the physical scars from the self-harm I inflicted on myself.

"I cut and burned myself because I was dead inside. I needed to feel pain to know I was alive." Suddenly, my face lights up. "But now Holy Spirit lives inside me. I'm alive and well, with a good Father who loves me. Through all these challenges, He had His hand over me and brought people into my life who would help me even when I was blind to see it."

Then the inevitable question surfaces from one of the children: "How can you be so happy? I would never have guessed these things could have happened to you because you're just so happy."

"Yeah, I really am happy," I reply. "God has been able to take this pain away from me. I don't think about all the junk anymore. He has so much good planned for me."

Matron is the house mom to about one hundred girls who live at PACE, and she follows me outside after the service. In Kenya, handshaking lasts an excruciatingly long time, and my hand is so tired and sore before she finally gets to the point.

Her voice softens, her toothy smile disappears, and her eyes dart around to ensure we aren't being overheard.

"There is a thirteen-year-old girl who has just come to us from one of the remote areas outside of town," Matron says. "She is pregnant. I'm not sure if it's the father's or the grandfather's, but it's somebody in the house. She's afraid to go home for…"

Most Kenyan children board with us during the three-month school semester and then return home during the one-month break between semesters.

"I'll take her. She can stay with me at my house." The words spill out of my mouth before she can finish her thought.

Tears well up in my eyes. This is a really hard part of the culture for me. In America, this child would be removed from the home, but here the child has to go home because that's where her family lives.

The girl, Muchina, stays with me through the upcoming one-month break. She has a lot of questions for me. Well, a lot by Kenyan standards. They don't ask a lot of questions, especially about pregnancy. I would never know a woman was pregnant before the seventh month, and even then it's not really talked about it. I'm always sarcastic, like, "Oh, okay, so we're just going to ignore the fact that this mother's going to have a baby?" They're not open about private things.

"Did you really have your daddy's baby?" Muchina asks me. "Your baba's baby?"

"I did."

I don't ask her about who the father is, but I tactfully ask how she feels about going home, about what that's going to be like for her. I know in this culture that a lot of things aren't fair… aren't right. There's nothing else I can do but pray, confident that the same God who was with me through the birth of Brian will be with her through this dark time.

Eventually, Muchina starts showing and goes home to have the baby. A year or so later, she returns to PACE with the baby for a visit.

"Wachira, let her stay," I plead, grabbing his suit jacket. "I will pay for her school."

"It's not about the money." There's a look of concern in his eyes. Having lived many years in the U.S. and being married to an American wife, I know that he shares some of my struggles with the culture. "We have many students who can't pay. She could come, and we would waive the fees, but her parents won't let her come back. She's worth more to them by working than she is getting an education."

The baby's really cute. Muchina is doing a fantastic job as a fourteen-year-old mom. Her grandfather has passed now, so she and the baby are living with her grandmother. They seem to be doing well. Reluctantly, I concede to Wachira that she's caring for and supporting her grandmother while her grandmother tends to the child. This is life in Africa.

Muchina stays with me while she's in town. We watch movies and have popcorn while I paint her nails. She does my hair; Kenyans love trying to braid my much straighter, thin red hair. In the evenings we play UNO, do puzzles, and read the Bible.

Before she leaves, I give her a Bible so she can keep reading at home, and I encourage her to memorize scripture. I know how important that's been for me.

As the car drives off, I hold my hand to my chest and look up in silent prayer: *Be near her, God.* I'd love to have her stay with me and continue school, but it's just not possible. She's needed at home.

• • •

"You mzungus share so much of who you are," Irungu always says. "We are much more private and traditional."

The Kikuyu have a definite naming pattern than we do for their children. The firstborn takes on the father's name, reversed, so that Irungu Geshinga's first son is named Geshinga Irungu. The second son follows the mother's father, and this continues down the family tree with each subsequent child so that there's no question about what a child will be named.

With colonization, the option of a Christian name has been added to each person's birth certificate—at a cost, of course—in an effort to "civilize" the "primitives."

After hearing the story about my baby, Irungu does such an amazing thing. He names his newborn son Brian Michael Mwangi. I'm overwhelmed by the gesture of my best friend.

• • •

When the teachers at PACE ask me about various holidays in America, they are intrigued by the concept of Mother's Day.

"It's just a day in May where we thank our mothers for how much they do," I explain.

"We want to do that," they say. "We want to have a Mother's Day."

The nine teachers pick an upcoming Saturday and invite their moms to my place. Some of these teachers have been at PACE for two or three years, but their moms have never been out to see what they do.

Nguku's mom makes a six-hour trek, by foot and matatu, over the hill and far away, and when she arrives she looks as pristine as ever. The Kenyans' ability to look well-pressed regardless of the events of the day never ceases to amaze me. I think back to all the primping and preening I've done in the past, and I never looked as polished.

The teachers have prepared a feast and set up the tables from PACE out in the yard. The schoolchildren helped decorate. The corn is husked, the goat is slaughtered, the chapati is made. For refreshments, chai tea and a case of soda. It's all so exciting.

Each teacher has prepared a slideshow presentation to be projected against the wall of my house, with pictures I'd taken of them teaching. The mothers are presented with scarves. These mothers sit straight up in their seats, chins held high, their plump ebony cheeks glowing; they demonstrate no less pride than any parent I've seen at an American university graduation. They don't have much, but at this moment they are richer than most.

After everything is done, the teachers whisper in a corner. I'm then called up to sit on a chair placed in the center of the group and presented with a lovely lace top and straw handbag. They celebrate my motherhood as well. I'm touched by the generosity of these teachers who are about my Brian's age.

It's not until Wachira walks by with a pastor friend and takes a photo of the group that I realize I haven't consulted him.

"Should I have asked your permission?" I ask.

"No, no. Not when you are doing work like this." The delight on his face reflects that in his heart he wishes he could have done this for his teachers. With limited time and finances, there's just so much he can do.

I feel content that God has brought me here to do even this little thing.

• • •

I mother so many here in Kenya.

So many of the children at PACE suffer from bedwetting, but only about five percent of them are girls; the majority are boys. There are no western conveniences available, no plastic sheets or pull-ups, so the urine just goes through the thick mattress. The reek of ammonia fills the dorm.

The children have to do their own laundry, so this becomes embarrassing as they get older. It's just so hard for them as they drag their mattresses outside to air out.

Ash is one of the students who talked about the importance of Barack Obama in his life as a Kenyan boy, and he has a bedwetting problem. I first try to help him through the use of medication, which is stupid, because the pills are expensive and unsustainable, as Wachira often reminds me. But being western, that's where I go first.

The medication must be taken at the same time each day. I solicit Soldier, one of two security guards who works twelve-hour shifts seven days a week, to monitor Ash's medication and liquid intake after the 6:30 tea time. He is to wake him to urinate at midnight.

The problem does get somewhat better, but it's not fixed. I want to help so much more than I can.

• • •

Little Brian, now three, comes to visit me every couple of weeks to practice spending a night away from home. I'm *cucu*, his grandmother.

My friend Toni from back in Chicago bought some pull-ups for Brian, and she has sent them to me through Denise, a friend who's travelled from Judson on a mission trip.

Brian's coming along on our safari so he can see the animals of his country that most Kenyans don't get to see. Aside from our practice overnights, it'll be the first time Brian is away from his parents for any extended period of time.

Irungu's worried. "I don't think he's going to do it, Joanie. I think he's going to panic."

When Irungu comes to get Brian the next day, the boy is lying on my couch wrapped in a blanket all cozy with juice and popcorn, watching cartoons. Irungu walks in and knocks on the wall, fully expecting Brian to be excited to see him and rush over into his arms. But Brian doesn't move.

He knocks again, and Brian waves him off. When Irungu comes over and speaks to him in Kikuyu, Brian just turns around with a look I've seen on many an American kid; I can't speak his language, but I can tell the answer is an emphatic *No*. That's when we know that Brian will be okay on the safari.

Brian doesn't speak or understand English, but the Kenyan safari driver knows English and Kikuyu, so we're good. Anyway, there are some things you just don't have to say—you just get them—and one of them is love.

We spend the day on the game reserve. It's the bomb. Brian's eyebrows dance as he gazes wonderstruck out the window. Giggles bubble up through his lips as he listens to the roar of the lions. He watches intently as the giraffes gracefully move across the Serengeti like ships on the ocean. He squeals in delight at the cavorting baboons circling around us, scouting for unattended goodies while we lunch on the fallen logs.

In the evening, we return to camp for a Maasai dinner before retiring for the night.

I'm convinced the exhausted toddler will fall asleep quickly, but he has other ideas. Denise's daughters, Anna and Rachael, have come over and they quietly play music on my computer when Brian starts dancing. He's wearing the little outfit Toni sent, switching the baseball cap backwards and forward and posing, just like his dad. Of course, the more he dances, the more we laugh, and the more we laugh, the more he dances. It's just hysterical.

After about an hour, we shut things down. It's time for Brian to go to bed. The girls leave for their tent, Brian washes up, we sing songs together, and I tuck him into the bed next to mine. He's all smiles.

As soon as I crawl into my bed, his big black saucer eyes gush with tears, his chest heaving uncontrollably. I shoot him "the look," convinced he's just upset that the party's ended, but that's the extent of our ability to communicate.

"Brian," I whisper, not knowing what to do.

He sobs harder.

I crawl out of bed, but before I can even get to his bed he pops out of the blanket, grabs my leg, and holds on as tight as he can, wrapping his little legs around me. Scooping him up in my arms, I bring him into my bed. His smile says it all: *Okay, she figured it out.* It's so sweet that my heart melts. I wrap my arms around him and hold him tight. I love this boy.

Then it strikes me: this boy has never slept alone. Most Kenyan homes have three rooms: two bedrooms and a living space. The parents sleep in one room with unweaned children, and all the other children sleep together in a bed or on the floor in the second room, across the living space. Brian slept with his parents until he was weaned and then slept with his brothers Jimmy and Simon after that.

I hold onto him tightly, better understanding our cultural differences.

I often think about my Brian, convinced that it's a good thing I gave him up, so he wouldn't have to go through all the crap I went through. Today, as I look down at little Brian sleeping soundly in my arms, I wonder how my life may have changed if I'd kept him. It could have taken me on such a different road, of growing up and being responsible.

I think the same thing about the child I aborted. I dream she was a girl. If there's one regret I have in my life, it's that I don't have a child of my own. God puts something inside of us that makes us want to have a child.

I'm aware that I must live with the decisions I've made in life, as well as those of the people around me, like my dad and my mom. My decisions weren't all good, and certainly not what God would have wanted for me. Yet in spite of them, God has blessed me to be a blessing to others. He has given me a purpose. He has given me my heart's desires. In Christ I have a mother, brothers, and sisters. He's also given me a son, a grandson, and the greatest Father of all.

Like Joseph, God has been with me throughout my life, and like Joseph, as horrible as some of those days were, He used those difficult days for His good. He put me in the right place at the right time so my story could glorify God—not perfectly, but as a small reflection of the love He has for me.

CHAPTER TWENTY-FIVE
BE STILL MY HEART

He says, "Be still, and know that I am God; I will be exalted among the nations, I will be exalted in the earth."
(Psalm 46:10, NIV)

AS DIRECTOR OF PACE MINISTRIES, WACHIRA IS UNDER A LOT OF PRESSURE. JIM AND Heidi have gone back to America, and it's not unusual for both chairs in front of Wachira's desk to be filled with people seeking direction while he's calling out to someone in the hall and answering both of his phones at the same time. A godly man, he is sought-after for his wise, sound advice; small in stature, he carries a heavy load.

I've discovered a blood pressure cuff and stethoscope in a storage room. With it, I decide to go into Wachira's office early in the morning and check his vitals, convinced that they'll be elevated. To my surprise, his blood pressure is a normal 120 over 80. Unconvinced, I check again. It's still normal. I scratch my head but shouldn't be surprised. I'm a type-2 diabetic on less medication here because of my diet; there are no processed foods to be had. I've been forced into a healthier lifestyle.

Wachira is busy and tired of my medical interventions, so I respectfully leave, having things to do as well.

Mathenge, the principal of the Academy, lives on the campus with his wife and daughter, who's about the same age as little Brian. Mathenge's sister-in-law has had two or three miscarriages, but now she's finally carried a child to term and he's asked me to pick her up from a private hospital outside Nairobi, saving them a difficult trip on the matatu. Kenyan roads are difficult to navigate and require a firm hold of the steering wheel to navigate around the enormous and countless potholes.

It's a twelve-hour return trip from 6:00 a.m. to 6:00 p.m., and when I get back I'm exhausted and my arms are sore. Afterward I lie down on the couch with Pacey, my cat, to watch a movie before bed. Pacey loves to lie on my chest, but today I'm just not feeling it and brush her off. I hold my chest and notice that it feels a bit tight. I'm also short of breath.

It must be nerves. I'm giving the message at the 2009 Easter service the next day, and though it's only a fifteen-minute walk, I'll need to leave early to get to the church in time.

I retire for the night.

But I toss and turn, unable to get comfortable. The tightness in my chest is still there, and I can feel more pressure now radiating to my arms. The twelve-hour drive must have been too much for me. I figure that my grip on the steering wheel was too hard on this old body.

I need to sleep. Perturbed, I punch my pillow and struggle to get comfortable. My stomach turns quickly, and I run to the bathroom to throw up. Shoot. It's the flu. I'm glad to at least be clinging to the sides of my western toilet.

Pacey then jumps up into bed with me, snuggling on my chest. My left arm is stiff and sore, and I brush her off again.

At about 5:00 in the morning, I've resigned myself to the fact that I'll not be getting any sleep at all. I find my Bible and prepare for the morning service.

With worship music playing in the background, I sit on the couch in the living room, gasping for air. Suddenly I can't move. Unable to breathe, I'm thankful that cellphones are so prevalent here. I reach over to call Wachira and Glenda, and in the meantime Holy Spirit is keeping me alive.

Wachira shows up at the door in no time. With one look, even before he opens his mouth, I know things are bad.

"Joanie, you don't look very good," he growls in his deep guttural voice.

Quickly moving everything out of the way, he helps me up and walks me to the car. By this time, Glenda's rushed out of the car to open the back door and help me into the back seat.

The tires spin as the car moves out of my driveway. Wachira's not even taking the time to close the compound gate. We're about to leave the dirt road for the paved road when Wachira stops the car, gets out, and whistles, making grandiose hand gestures in the dark.

"What is he doing?" I wheeze.

"He's calling Irungu," Glenda says, forcing a smile on her face.

Wachira knows Irungu is my best friend, my work husband. When I need a fire, he builds it. When I need water in the tank, he fills it. When my car breaks down, he fixes it.

In no time, Irungu appears, running up the road with his shirt flapping behind him. He climbs into the car and puts his arm around me. In all the years I've known Irungu, I've never known him to do anything like that. Kenyans are a private people. I rest my head on his shoulder and gasp for breath.

In fifteen minutes, we arrive at the hospital. There's no stretcher, no wheelchair, no anything.

Irungu helps get me to the triage area, where they check my blood pressure. It comes up as 217 over 156. I'm whisked to another room down the hall and hooked up to all kinds of electric monitors, IV drips, and diagnosed with a myocardial infarction. Evidently there's little they can do for me there, so when my blood pressure comes down to about 150 over 100, I'm released and told to go to Nairobi. I'm driven home until we can assess the situation.

Esther is an African American friend of Dorris's who is visiting from Nairobi. She sits herself down across from me and looks directly into my eyes: "You've had a heart attack. You need to go to Nairobi and then go home."

By home, I know she means America.

"Home?" I say, coughing laboriously. "No way. They just said I need to rest for a few days. I'm okay. I'll be back at work soon."

Wachira hears Esther's assessment and gets on it. I'm not to be left in my house alone. It's just not safe. With the locked compound and bars on the windows and doors, there's no way to get into the house if I run into a problem. A number of people are assigned to stay with me throughout the day and night.

"You're not getting it," Esther insists. "I'm looking at you and your face is ashen. Blood isn't circulating through your body. You're not in good shape. You need a doctor."

I start realizing how precarious my situation is. It's Easter Sunday, the day my Lord and Savior rose from the dead, so I figure that maybe it's a good day to go.

On Monday morning, Irungu calls some doctors in Nairobi, speaking in Kikuyu and Kiswahili. He gets in touch with two different hospitals.

They can see me in three weeks.

"I'm coming over," Wachira tells me when I give him the news. His voice carries authority. "I'll talk to the doctors. They'll find out they need to see you tomorrow."

"It just doesn't seem right," I protest. With no other options, Kenyans would just stay home.

On Tuesday, Irungu gets a hold of Dr. Charles Kariuki, a Kikuyu. When all the Kikuyu on campus hear his name, they have the same reaction: "Oh, Dr. Kariuki. That's good. You are going to be okay. He's Kikuyu."

I just close my eyes and rest. His tribe doesn't have anything to do with anything, but I'm glad they're so confident. I provide Dr. Kariuki with the details of my medical records, sent over from the hospital in Nyahururu, and he has agreed to see me on Thursday, the next time he's back in Nairobi. He gives careful instruction to Irungu, who will be the one driving me to the appointment, about what to watch for.

When Thursday comes, Irungu and I talk along the way. I feel calm and relaxed knowing that I'm in God's good hands. As I drift off, I feel the gentle touch of Irungu's hands checking for a response. He's hoping I haven't passed.

"Irungu, we all have to die some time," I say. "When it's time for me to go, I'll go."

His face is tight with worry. "Don't die now!"

"Okay, I'll try not to."

"No, I'm serious. Don't do it now. You have to wait until we get to the doctor." He reaches over to tap my shoulder again.

As soon as I get onto the exam table, my feet don't touch the floor again. Unlike the hospital in Nyahururu, this is a state-of-the-art facility with modern equipment. Dr. Kariuki starts checking monitors and spews a whole monologue in medicalese.

"This is serious," he says, tapping the chart with a pen.

"How serious?"

"Well, I can tell from looking at this that you've had a heart attack." Evidently there's a chemical in the blood that proves it.

I begin to bargain. I'm good at that, always have been. There's a mission trip I've been planning, and I desperately want to go. But with Dr. Kariuki, there's no bargaining.

As quick as lightning, I'm on my way to the hospital ward; there are no separate rooms, but it's clean and curtains separate the patients. There's good food and I have ice for my water every day. In Nyahururu, nine women in labor have been known to share the same bed, waiting for the babies to come.

The doctors determine that I need a cardiac catheterization to find out where the blockage is. I'll be there for at least five days, unable to move, not even to go to the washroom.

Irungu has the saddest puppy dog eyes I've ever seen as he says goodbye and leaves to return home. Walking backwards through the room, he almost runs into the door. I know his heart breaks at having to leave me there.

I have $25 in my bank account, but the hospital bill is $1,500—and then I'll need another $1,500 for the flight home. My first call is to Jim and Heidi, then Roy and Toni. Soon all of Judson knows. Within an hour, the hospital bill is paid and I have a paid ticket to return home.

The following week, Irungu picks me up and takes me to a guest house in Nairobi. I rest there a few more days before going back to Nyahururu. Evidently, as a heart patient, the airlines are reluctant to have me as a guest until at least two weeks after a heart attack. So I wait.

The airline requires a note from Dr. Kariuki stating that I'm clear to fly. In order to get that note, I'll need to successfully complete a stress test, which I do.

Throughout the process of entering the plane, I'm greeted by kind attendants who assure me that everyone on the plane is aware of my situation, even the pilot. Should I need any assistance, they are there to help. In my opinion, it's a bit of overkill, but it's comforting to know.

Five hours into the eight-hour flight to London, we've eaten and it's dark outside. People around me are sleeping or quietly reading.

I raise my hand for the flight attendant. He leans in and turns on the light.

"You don't look good," he says. He has the same look on his face that Wachira had on the morning of Easter Sunday.

"I don't feel good," I admit. The air passes slowly through my lips.

"Come with me." The attendant helps me up and takes me to an empty seat at the back of the plane. "Do you have nitro?"

I sigh. "No, I don't."

He quickly gets on the phone with the pilot. I can only hear one side of the conversation, but I rapidly get the drift. They're in contact with a doctor on the ground and are considering landing the plane in Egypt. Evidently, they don't like people dying on their planes either.

"Oh no, it's not that bad," I insist. "I'm just a little out of breath. I'll be fine."

They totally ignore me. A decision is made; there is some nitroglycerine on the plane and so we'll carry on with the flight.

I place the pill under my tongue, and as it dissolves I immediately feel relief. I'm moved to first class, which is exciting; I've never been in first class before. I lay down in the bed and get comfortable. Every fifteen minutes, a flash of light crosses over me and I turn my head to shield my eyes from the intrusive light. The attendants are checking to see if I'm still alive.

I feel a tightening at my waist and realize that a grinning flight attendant has buckled me in for our descent. I drowsily return an acknowledgement and rest until we've landed.

"This is your pilot speaking," I hear over the intercom. "We are going to ask you all to stay in your seats. We've had an emergency on board and we need to have this passenger released before we allow you to exit the plane. Thank you for your patience."

I sit straight up in my seat and begin looking around the plane. "Oh, did someone get sick?" I glance at the attendant beside me, "What's the emergency?"

"You are the emergency," he snaps incredulously, almost rudely laughing as he unbuckles me and helps maneuver the special wheelchair down the aisle.

I've always disembarked to the left, so this is the first time I've even noticed that there's a door to the right. I'm lowered to a waiting ambulance outside. I strain for every breath, my hands moist and clammy. It's not the onset of another heart attack, but the realization that I'll be missing my next flight. I won't be making it home tonight.

This is not how I pictured this day going.

"I can't go to the hospital," I say. "The nitroglycerin worked. I have a flight to catch."

"You're not flying anywhere," the first EMT announces as they lift me into the ambulance.

I try to claw my way off the gurney. "Please don't get me upset. I'm a heart patient."

"I'll let the ER doctors know," the second attendant assures me as he tightens the strap, forcing me back.

At 8:00 a.m., I'm at the hospital in London, being hooked up to the EKG. This confirms my fears; I'm not going to catch my next flight. And not being British, I'd have to pay for a room at this hospital. But with the state-funded program, at least the emergency area is free. They place me on a gurney in the ER hallway with no TV or anything. I'm filled with thoughts of loneliness and abandonment. It's the May Day holiday and the hospital is short-staffed. The cardiologist who could write me off isn't working.

A missionary has come to visit and brings flowers, but there isn't a vase to put them in or a table to place them on. There's not even a chair for her to sit on. My face warms as I get emotional. I'm losing control.

"C'mon, this is the developed world," I shout to a passing nurse, feeling erratic and disagreeable. "Can't I get a room? Why can't you find a cardiologist to get me out of here? What's the problem?"

"Joanie, if you don't calm down, we're going to have to get someone down here from psych," the nurse retorts as she hurries by.

That shuts me up right away. A flood of memories invade my weakened mind. My medication! Sorting through the bottles, I see that I've only been given blood thinners and insulin. My anxiety builds as I realize that my bipolar medication isn't listed.

I call Roy and Toni. It's 2:00 on Sunday morning there, but Roy answers. Roy's a doctor and agrees with the decisions being made by the medical staff in London, but he'll have all of Judson praying when they get to church.

A huge sigh of relief escapes me. The weight of my body conforms to the bed. I know I'm in good hands now.

On Monday, the cardiologist shakes his head as he checks my chart. "Let me explain this to you. It could cost upwards of $50,000 if you fly and they have to make an unexpected landing. We okayed someone recently and the guy died on the plane. I just can't take the risk."

"But we all have to die sometime," I argue. "I really feel okay. I need to get home."

"I just can't do it. I'm not going to okay the flight."

Dr. Roy is on speakerphone, and he quickly speaks up with another option. "Will you be willing to do a hand-to-hand trade-off? I'll come to England and pick her up. You can just release her to me."

The doctor's face wrinkles. "No, we're not doing that either."

By Thursday I'm in a cardiac ward room. I'm separated from my roommate, Betty, by only a thin curtain. At forty-eight, I'm the youngest on the cardiology floor, but Betty and her husband appear to regain their youthful vigor as they listen with bated breath to the plans I'm making with Toni and Roy.

"Look at what Jesus has done!" I say, pulling back the curtain to their eager gawking faces. "Toni has booked me into a B&B. They'll even come pick me up from the hospital. I'll have to leave against medical advice, but that's okay. Jesus has my back."

I eagerly relay the plans, excited at the prospect of getting home soon.

"They've also booked me a flight on another airline where they don't know about my medical condition," I explain. "I can't tell them about my heart attack. I'll need a wheelchair, so I'll use my foot condition as an excuse for that. Look at what Jesus has done! I have to leave the hospital tonight." I tap the package on the stand next to me. "The hospital has given me some nitro, so I'm good to go."

Confident, I turn my attention back to Toni, who's still on the phone.

"I'm okay," I say to her. "I know Jesus has me."

With that, I hang up.

I look back to Betty and her husband. "Do you know Jesus?" I ask the couple, knowing that this could be the reason Jesus has brought me here.

Betty tilts her head. "Evidently not as well as you do."

I take the Bible from the drawer next to me and write down a few gospel verses so they can get to know my Jesus better. I feel an urgency as I write. They're old, and we're on a cardiac ward. There's not much time left. I ought to know.

Soon after, I'm picked up by a guy in his mid-twenties who'd like to show me around London, but I'm just eager to get to the B&B.

"Maybe tomorrow," I tell him. I'm really not up for sightseeing right now. "Or if there's time, before the flight on Saturday."

The B&B is lovely. The owner has spoken extensively with Toni and couldn't be more gracious.

On Friday, my young chauffeur picks up my bags from the airline and tours me around London. I'm really only interested in seeing the old churches, and we stop by a number of them, but I don't dare to get out.

Lunch is a different thing. We stop at his favorite pub, and I struggle to get out of the car for a burger and a warm beer. It's England, after all.

Clearly God's not ready for me yet, because I'm doing everything in my power to get to heaven, but I'm still here on earth.

CHAPTER TWENTY-SIX
DO YOU KNOW JESUS?

*Quietly trust yourself to Christ your Lord, and if anybody asks why
you believe as you do, be ready to tell him,
and do it in a gentle and respectful way.*
(1 Peter 3:15, TLB)

THERE AREN'T ANY NEW COMPLICATIONS DURING THE FLIGHT, AND WHEN I ARRIVED back home and walk out through the customs doors, I see Toni and Denise and break down. Every emotion I've ever been held back suddenly bursts out in a flood—the fear of the unknown, the anxiety of having flown for six hours with a ticking time bomb inside me, my anger and indignation with God for taking me away from my work in Kenya, my disappointment over leaving family behind and not having the time to say a proper goodbye, my gratitude for the friends who have stepped up to help, my longing for American food, the joy of being home and being welcomed by my friends. In the end, it all points to Jesus.

The attendant who wheels me out stands back, stunned, as my friends envelop me with love. I haven't been home in quite some time.

Once everything else subsides, my longing for American food still remains.

"Can we stop by a restaurant before we go home?" I petition through my tears.

"Let me call your doctor and see what he says." Toni holds her hand to her ear, fingers extended, and pretends to make a call. "He says, 'No, you are not to stop anywhere. You are to come directly to the hospital. Do not pass Go, do not collect $200. Just go to the hospital.'"

The cardiac catheterization procedure was never done in Kenya, not because Dr. Kariuki wasn't competent, and not because of the cost—it would have been much more affordable in Kenya—but because Dr. Roy and the elders at Judson just wanted me home as soon as possible. Trusting my church family, I complied. The cardiac catheterization is performed at the West Suburban Medical Centre. I have a private room so the ladies of Judson can come visit.

Soon after, I'm in surgery again, this time to insert stents. With a ding, the elevator doors open and I see Ma-J and Carol standing down the hall by my room. The walls cave in around me. The air presses in but can't get into my lungs. I can't breathe. It feels like an elephant is sitting on my chest again, squeezing my heart. My jaw is stiff and sore.

In terror, I look up at the doctor, my eyebrows triangulating. There's no question what's happening.

One word fizzles from my mouth: "Heart…"

"Code blue!" The words echo through the hall, and doctors and nurses glide masterfully around me. My bed's pushed into the room trailed by crash carts and machines, an organized mayhem calmed by the words of the Psalmist, spoken by the surgeon holding my hand.

Yea, though I walk through the valley of the shadow of death, I will fear no evil: for thou art with me; thy rod and thy staff they comfort me. Thou preparest a table before me in the presence of mine enemies: thou anointest my head with oil; my cup runneth over. Surely goodness and mercy shall follow me all the days of my life: and I will dwell in the house of the Lord for ever. (Psalm 23:4–6, KJV)

I'm told I shouldn't have remembered these events, but they are crystal clear in my memory. Evidently an artery was nicked during surgery. I'm placed in ICU with a tube running from my groin up into my heart. I can't move.

• • •

Before long, I'm released to Toni with diet and exercise instructions. I'm in constant fear, scared to eat, scared to exercise, and scared to strain myself too much. I sit motionless in the corner of Toni's kitchen like a rag doll.

"I feel left out in the cold," I say, quivering as I share my fears with her.

"Joanie, you're worrying too much. You just need to rest for a while. This will all come together." When her phone rings, she checks it. "I've got to take this."

She holds up her finger, pausing the conversation, and walks out to the front porch. The screen door squeaks as it shuts behind her.

The elephant returns. Short waves of air enter and I gasp for breath. I can't call out; I'm voiceless. There's a spoon and a pot on the table from lunch and I reach for the spoon, my fingers tightening around it like the muscles in my jaw. I begin tapping and increasingly banging on the side of the pot, searching for a glimpse of Toni.

Toni peers in through the screen door to see what the commotion is all about, and in an instant she hangs up.

"Roy, get down here," she cries out in her fiercest voice. "Joanie's having a heart attack!"

She runs to my side, a deathlike pallor coming over her face as she turns to Roy, who's run down to the foot of the stairs.

"Should I call 911?" she asks, her voice cracking. She picks up her cellphone.

"No, I can get her there faster," Roy barks. "Let's put her in the car."

Within minutes we are rushing to the hospital, certainly not following all the regular rules of the road.

At the hospital, the surgeons use videos of past open-heart surgeries to explain to me what is going to be done.

"We're going to break your sternum and pull back your ribs to expose your heart," one of them says.

This is just too freaky for me. I'm a stress eater, so I call Ma-J, who comes to the rescue.

"This is the last time I do this for you," Ma-J whispers as she hands me a bag of fried chicken. "And only because they're going to clear it all out anyway."

How I love Ma-J! I couldn't thank her enough for listening to me.

The surgery itself goes well, but the day after the surgery the nurse informs me that they're going to stop dispensing painkillers.

"Oh no… oh no, no, no, no…" I wag my finger, about to go off on her. But then I pause, take a sip of air, and change my tone. "Can I have the phone?" I ask sweetly.

Pleased with herself for so quickly turning me, she hands me the phone. "Oh, sure."

My eyes twinkle and the corner of my mouth curves up slightly. I then take the phone and, right in front of her, brazenly call the doctor: "She's trying to take me off painkillers! She wants to take them away from me!" I listen to the doctor's response, arch a brow, and hold the phone up. "He wants to talk to you!"

Well aware that I'm a wimp with pain, I pitifully survey my body. There's the reddened scar along my leg, the tubes running in and out of me, and something that pokes me when I move—a proverbial thorn in my side, like the Apostle Paul. But nobody believes me. I need the painkillers. Anyone would. But I'm an addict, an expert manipulator, who's hurting. I'll stop at nothing.

When the next nursing shift comes on, I give them my most helpless look.

"It's just a half-hour early," I said. "Could I have a pill?"

And I do the same thing with the next shift just as I'm just starting to feel the pain come back. I'm pretty sure not all the pills have been recorded, though. Pastor J came for a visit, and I don't even remember him being there. He tells me later that I was a bit loopy. I have so much respect for him that I would have been on my best behavior, had I known.

Pat is my regular nurse, and one day she tries her best to get me to sit and stand up. I'm just in too much pain. I don't understand that everyone around me who's had the same surgery is moving around, but I'm buckled over in pain with this thorny prick in my side, begging her to stop making me move. Seething anger rages inside me, both with her and with myself for not being able to get up.

Seeing my struggle, she comes over to take a look. It turns out that a drainage tube has been missed. She removes it, instantaneously bringing me such relief. Getting right up on my feet, I embrace her, back on the road to recovery with the regular dose of painkillers.

• • •

At Toni's house, I have a bell next to my bed, a bit of insurance that I won't be left to my own devices in case something goes awry.

"You need to get into the shower today," she says, ripping open the curtains.

"Toni, if this is what life's going to be like, I don't want to live anymore." Every bone hurts and I feel like I've been hit by a truck.

"Joanie, you have so much more you have to do for the Lord."

"But the Lord knows how I'm feeling," I say in my best childish whine. "I just don't want to live."

"I just want you to give it a little more time. It's going to get better."

A visiting nurse comes every other day, but otherwise Toni has been screening my visitors. Roy and I fight over the TV, and aside from that things are going well, all in all. I'm even getting outside for a walk once in a while, slowly but surely.

"No pain, no gain," Roy reminds me. "Your heart is a muscle and you need to exercise it!"

The nurse's face wrinkles as she checks my vitals. She tries again, her foot tapping lightly. "How are you feeling?"

"I feel okay."

"These numbers aren't right," she grumbles, calling for Roy. He confirms, then turns and grabs the keys to the car. It's May 25, 2009, and we're on our way to the hospital again.

When we arrived, the ER doctor rushes to my side. "What's this, Joanie? Didn't we just let you go? Why are you back again?"

I point to the sky in despair. "Don't ask me. I don't even know."

"Huh," he reflects, checking the monitor. "Looks like AFib. This often happens after heart surgery. This isn't unusual. We'll give you a drip to take care of that."

He motions to the nurse and soon after I'm released to Toni again.

Not four or five days later, I'm overcome with dizziness while sitting on a flight of steps it's taken me so long to climb. Roy takes one look at me and brings me right back to the hospital.

As the ER doctor rushes to my side once again, I look him straight in the face. "Is there anyone here who doesn't know Jesus? Because evidently that's why the Lord keeps bringing me back here." I sit up and make a general declaration: "Does everybody here know Him? I'm not quite sure why else I keep coming back other than this."

Over the next few days, I feel like the little bird in Dr. Seuss's *Are You My Mother?* I bend every ear that will listen: "Do you know Jesus? Do you know Jesus?" A nurse who has strayed from the Lord comes over, we talk, I invite her to Judson.

"Please come," I beg of her, "or I may have to keep coming back here."

I lay back down, content that my work here is done.

The IV medicine isn't working and I'm put back into the ICU. Perplexed, the cardiologist has no medical answer for my horrible vitals.

"Lord, please give us wisdom," he prays. "Give us answers. Your daughter here, she wants to serve You. Show us what we need to do."

We open our eyes and my numbers start to improve. I know it sounds crazy, and I'm amazed, but that's what happens.

I'm then placed in a regular room where I'll stay another week. I rest quietly, trusting God. He's shown me He's in control.

• • •

It's a hot July and I tug at the sticky heart monitor that's going to be a part of me for the next thirty days. The doctors agreed to let me visit the Rolands, who moved to a farm in Iowa after leaving Kenya. There are two stipulations: they need to have air conditioning and a phone, so my heart can be monitored. The Rolands have both.

Evidently, the information gathered from the monitor I'm wearing can be transmitted to the hospital through a phone line. They really should have been more clear that the phone had to be a landline and work like a fax machine. The Rolands only have a cell phone.

"They just said we needed a phone," I say, fumbling with the monitor and the cell phone, trying to make the two work together. "They didn't specify it needed to be a landline!"

"That's okay, Joanie." Jim's voice could calm the stormy oceans. "We know people with landlines. We'll just take a little drive. You'll love their place."

Jim may be able to calm the oceans, but he can't calm the numbers spewing from the machine. Heidi holds my hand and breathes with me as we drive to the local hospital to fix a small electrical problem with the device.

Relieved to learn the problem isn't a small electrical problem with my heart, I'm able to spend a quiet time of meditation with the Roland family on their farm. We spent the next two wonderful weeks in a home that reminds me so much of Kenya.

I place my hand over my heart and bow my head. My heart desires Kenya. *God, will You give me the desires of my heart?*

•••

"You're stable and you're good to go," the doctor proclaims after the thirty days.

I honestly questioned whether I'd ever hear those words. By now I should have the faith of a mustard seed.

"Like good to go, good to go?" I ask. "I can go back to Kenya?"

He peers over his glasses and closes the file. "Yeah. I'd prefer if you wait three months just to be sure, but yeah, you're good to go."

On January 25, 2010, I'm back on a plane to Kenya. God has such big plans for me. He's not finished with me yet.

CHAPTER TWENTY-SEVEN
IRUNGU

*Don't worry about anything; instead, pray about everything; tell God
your needs, and don't forget to thank him for his answers
…His peace will keep your thoughts and your hearts quiet
and at rest as you trust in Christ Jesus.*
(Philippians 4:6–7, TLB)

ON ONE OF OUR EXPLORATORY EXCURSIONS THROUGH THE ARID, RURAL AREAS of Kenya, about an hour away from Nyahururu, Irungu and I come upon a school. The children run around barefoot. These are areas where the people have never seen a mzungu before and the sight of me causes some distress. I get out of the car, the children stop in their tracks, and some of the little ones scurry to hide behind the older ones, their wide-eyed faces peering between tiny fingers.

I stroll leisurely through the crowd, then suddenly halt, lift my hands, turn to the left, and shout, "Boo!" This ignites shrill screams and winces from the recoiling children. I'm almost apologetic; I try to hide a snicker behind my hand.

"I'm just the same as you," I assure them, waiting for the translation. I lift my hands. "Same hands." I tap my chest. "Same heart." I brush up my arm. "The only difference is that God forgot to put in the color."

I pause as the translator finishes.

"Ahhh." The children nod approvingly.

I turn around and notice Irungu with his pocket knife, kneeling down beside a young whimpering boy.

"What's going on?" I ask.

Irungu's pulling something out of the boy's foot. "This boy has jiggers, and they need to come out."

I wince. "But you're hurting him."

"He was crying before I got here. They are painful and will eat his skin."

"What will eat his skin? What are you pulling out?"

"The fleas. Chigoes sand fleas crawl into the skin to lay eggs, usually under the toenail. The eggs fall to the ground, starting the whole cycle over again. The female jigger flea stays on the person to feed, making holes that are flakey and itchy. The jigger needs to be removed with a special chemical or cut out with a knife. I don't have the chemical… only a knife."

"Why does this happen?"

"It's dry out here. There's not a lot of soap and water for the people to clean."

"How can we get rid of it?"

Irungu pauses and looks at me. "Put shoes and socks on the children."

I used to wonder how people knew God was talking to them, but Kenya has made it easy for me. When you see an injustice, something that would break the heart of God, He's talking to you.

I whisper a prayer: "'Truly I tell you, whatever you did for one of the least of these brothers and sisters of mine, you did for me.'[12] Jesus, help me help these children."

I don't know how He will do it, but after everything He's shown me, I'm confident He will.

• • •

Irungu is the primary driver for PACE, Wachira, and all teams to come on mission trips. If driving is involved, Irungu is there. When teams come, his family may not see him for weeks, since he often crashes at my house after getting home late and before getting back behind the wheel early in the morning.

He's also the general mechanic. He fixes the Land Rover used to haul water, he fixes Wachira's vehicles, he fixes my vehicle, and he fixes the bus. Whatever needs fixing, Irungu fixes it. He knows engines like the back of his hand. It's not unusual to see him on top of a vehicle, dressed in his finest slacks and shirt, straddling an engine. How Mama Simon ever gets his clothes clean, I'll never understand.

PACE secured an old blue school bus to get the local children to and from the Academy. One day, I catch a glimpse of Irungu under the front of the bus doing something with the brakes as I run between the office and the kitchen to take pictures to send to our supporters in the West. Like MacGyver, Kenyans often improvise, using what they have available to concoct something they need, like using branches to build ladders.

Suddenly, the jack he's cobbled together shifts on the uneven ground and a powerful thud can be heard as the bus crashes down on top of him. The inhuman shriek that follows reverberates in the compound, sending chills up my spine. A strange sense of dread hovers over me.

---

[12] Matthew 25:40, NIV.

The thundering roar of four hundred tiny feet, like the galloping hooves of the migrating wildebeests, shifts toward the center of the compound where Irungu is pinned, the weight of the engine resting on his pelvis. The entire campus surrounds the scene. Their shrill chorus cannot outmatch the ear-piercing cry of the man trapped under the bus.

I run to the door and the whole world stops with my gasp, becoming deafeningly silent. The only sound I hear is the beat of my own heart, pumping… throbbing. I feel it expand and contract, brushing up against the ribs inside my chest. I slowly exhale.

As the air escapes, the world again comes to life.

"Jesus, help him," I whisper as I run out to be with Irungu.

Without a thought, adrenaline coursing through their young bodies, the staff and students clammer over each other to desperately grasp onto any part of the bus they can reach. Taking charge, one of them calls out, "On three: one… two… three!" A collective groan is heard and everyone's tiny muscles bulge with superhuman strength, the creaks and grating metal undermining their resilience. The bus momentarily hangs precariously in the air, balanced by dozens of otherwise trivial hands, and Irungu is pulled away from his bloodstained cage, his pain intensifying as the blood now begins to flow more freely. His cries summon the entire neighborhood. His wincing face is almost unrecognizable, charged with excruciating pain.

Wachira has his car waiting, ready to bolt to the hospital, but it's small and there's no way to lay him down flat. The paved road is visible from the PACE gate, but it can be a treacherous trek to get out to it, even for a four-wheel drive vehicle, crossing a floodplain, weaving between the potholes, and spinning tires through the mud and mire, at the best of times.

With every bump, Irungu cries out in agony. Today the vehicle is also running on empty. Being a non-profit, money is always an issue, so gas is only purchased when needed. This drives Irungu crazy. He's always complaining, "It's ruining your car to run so low on gas. It's not good for the vehicle. You're wearing out parts… it's doing damage." But things are what they are, and gas isn't always a priority.

They make it out to the road and the vehicle immediately putters… putters out and stops. It's run out of gas.

I'm told it takes another twenty minutes for someone to grab the jerry can and run out to the gas station down the road. The runner later tells us that he was gasping for breath, having run faster than he ever thought he could in order to get back with the gas and rescue his friend.

By the time I get to the hospital, they've taken X-rays and determine that he has four butterfly fractures, a crushed urethra, and internal bleeding. They need to cut him, make a two-inch incision, and catheterize him to drain the fluids. But there are no pain meds available—no morphine, nothing stronger than Tylenol. Irungu is laying on a gurney, writhing in pain, his eyes closed tightly, teeth clenched and grinding.

I spin Wachira around to look him in the face. "We need to get him to Kijabe."

Kijabe has a mission hospital where people from Europe and America come to do internships, and they do excellent work. If you have money, that's where you go. But the doctors want to keep him here.

"We need… we have to… Kijabe… whatever it takes… doesn't matter… I'll pay…" My mind is racing and I can't articulate my thoughts anymore. I look over to my dear friend. Like a mother bear protecting her cubs, I'm unstoppable.

Wachira agrees and someone calls for an ambulance. I've never seen an ambulance in Nyahururu and have no idea what to expect. What pulls up is a matatu with two seats in the front and two seats in the back so there's room for a gurney. There isn't any medical equipment on board, no blood pressure cuff, no thermometer.

A foley bag hangs off Irungu's gurney with a murky mix of blood and urine, and with that we prepare to go. I pay the doctor $20 and a nurse $10. They agree to escort us to Kijabe.

By now it's dark, and we're all looking at each other, afraid to vocalize what we're thinking. It's the developing world and people here are desperate. You have to be careful while traveling, especially at night, because it's an easier time to be a thief. Carjackings happen all the time. Wachira's been carjacked. Irungu's been carjacked three times. Even Jim Roland was almost carjacked once, three days before he and his family moved back to America.

I never go out after dusk.

Kijabe is two and a half hours away. The roads are brutal when you can see what's in front of you, and tonight there's no moon. Though the driver's doing his best, we're hitting pothole after pothole head-on. With every little bump, Irungu's fracture jolts inside him, sending shockwaves through his body. He can't contain the pain.

And then we hear a mysterious sound—*pu–pu, sssssss*—and the ambulance stops.

"Are you out of gas?" I ask.

"No, I have gas. Look, it's a full tank." The driver pulls himself out of the way so I can see the display. Then he mindlessly starts turning the key, hoping to get another result.

I step out and start yelling to the clouds above. "Are you kidding me? Only in Kenya. What are we supposed to do now…?"

Inside the ambulance, everyone exchanges bewildered glances.

"Who is she talking to?" the driver asks.

"She's talking to Jesus," Irungu replies under his breath. "She's talking to Jesus."

Digging into my pocket, I pull out my phone and call Roy. "Call everyone at church and tell them to start praying. Irungu's been hurt. We're out in the middle of nowhere and the ambulance broke down. I paid $30 for a doctor and nurse and they can't do shit because there's nothing… because they've brought nothing with them… there's not even a stethoscope!"

Of course, having a stethoscope wouldn't have helped at all. It's just the principle of the thing. These kinds of things just shouldn't happen.

Back at the ambulance, they've called for another car, but out here it doesn't mean anything. When someone tells you they're on their way, it could just mean they're rolling out of bed.

The driver opens the hood and looks into the engine. Irungu, diagnosing the trouble from the gurney, gives him instructions to no avail.

By now, Mugo and Dorris, who have taken my car, have caught up to us. I run to them, filled with frustration.

"Joanie, TIA. This is Africa." These are the first words out of Mugo's mouth. "This is just the way it is."

"He could lose his life," I scream hysterically.

He cocks his head, questioning my faith. "He won't lose his life. God is taking care of him."

There's so much faith in Africa because there's such a need for it. As an American, I tend to depend on the systems around me instead of depending on the loving God who created me. This is not my finest moment, for sure. I'm sad and pathetic, not doing a good job for missionaries on the whole. God has shown up for me so often and I should know better, but my human nature explodes out of me.

"Look, I have faith in God," I rant. "What I don't have is faith in Kenya or in the ambulance system. We need to do something."

Forty-five minutes after we pull off the road, another ambulance arrives and we're on our way again. I hold onto Irungu's hand like it will do something, but there's nothing else I can do to help. He's in the capable hands of the Great Physician.

"Just hang on," I reassure him, but I'm speaking to myself as much as to him. "They will have morphine for you. It'll help with the pain."

He manages to raise his left cheek, suggesting a smile.

This last part of the trip requires us to risk the long, windy drive down the steep escarpment of the Great Rift Valley. The spasms in my hands scream as I clutch the armrests of my seat, my toes scrunched in the tip of my shoes as I brace my feet on the floor of the van. The driver rides the brakes all the way down. I can't even imagine the pain Irungu feels in his pelvis with nothing to cling to but Jesus.

When we arrive, I jump out of the vehicle before its wheels have completely stopped and run to the emergency entrance. I grab the nurse who's standing by.

"We have a man from Nyahururu… crushed under a bus… butterfly fracture in his pelvis… all he's had is Tylenol… please, please get some morphine ready for him."

The intern doctor from England makes eye contact with me, a show of understanding and concern. It's an answer to my fervent prayers. He orders the meds and takes over Irungu's case. Before even moving Irungu from the gurney to the table, he gives him an injection of morphine. Irungu's scrunched-up face softens. His clenched teeth relax, his tense lips unlock, and his squeezed-shut eyes loosen and fall open.

"Is it better?" I ask rhetorically.

"Yes," he whispers. "Thank you, Joanie."

I stay with him in emergency overnight. The next morning, a team of doctors and surgeons gather to discuss the next steps. He'll require some minor reconstructive surgery, but as far as his pelvic bone structure goes, it's perfectly aligned and all he needs is bedrest.

The astounded doctor looks at the X-ray, shaking his head. "Unbelievable."

There's a glint in my eye. "I don't think it's unbelievable… I think it's very believable when you know about the power of prayer and who's doing the healing."

"Does he have any children?" the doctor asks, turning his attention to the sleeping Irungu.

"Yes, he has three healthy boys and one on the way. Why?"

"Good, I feel better about that. Because I don't think he's going to have any more children."

Irungu has been the driver for PACE for such a long time that so many people from all over the world know him and appreciate who he is. Through Facebook and email, good wishes and blessings come pouring in, and his medical bills for all ten surgeries are easily covered.

Mama Simon and the boys soon visit. They're so worried for him, and poor little Brian wants desperately to crawl up into bed with him. But he is kept away.

• • •

Irungu had just finished building an additional room to his house, and it now serves as his bedroom. Through many gracious gifts, it's equipped with the best bed and mattress available in Kenya.

God is so good. His full recuperation takes nine months, from bed to walker to walking on his own. His house is in a bit of a valley, and he used to run up the sloped hill. When I had my heart attack, I remember seeing Irungu run up that hill and thinking, *I'm so glad that man is young and is able to do this.* But he can't run anymore. In fact, he'll have to relearn how to walk.

I'm on furlough in America while he recovers. My next trip to Kenya will be my last.

CHAPTER TWENTY-EIGHT
AMAZING GRACE

Oh, what a wonderful God we have! How great are his wisdom and knowledge and riches! How impossible it is for us to understand his decisions and his methods! For who among us can know the mind of the Lord? Who knows enough to be his counselor and guide? And who could ever offer to the Lord enough to induce him to act? For everything comes from God alone. Everything lives by his power, and everything is for his glory. To him be glory evermore.
(Romans 11:33–36, TLB)

PERHAPS BECAUSE I KNOW THIS IS MY LAST TIME IN KENYA, THINGS ARE A BIT different. Perhaps if they weren't, it would be just too hard to leave. Perhaps God is preparing me for what He has planned next.

But even in this short year, He has so much here for me to do in His name.

• • •

Mathenge, whose family I drove back from Nairobi on the night I had my heart attack, is now a principal at another nearby school. He's come to visit.

"Joanie, I hear that you are finding shoes for children with jiggers," he tells me.

"Yes, God is so good. Some friends back home gave me money and encouraged me to start the Shoes for School program so that others could donate, too. Ma-J always tells me to let people help. She's right."

This was such an answer to prayer. I knew God would work it out; I just didn't know how or when.

"Joanie, would it be okay if my Form One students came to help?" Mathenge asks. "It's important for them to learn to help others. This would be a great opportunity for them to see another's struggle and see how they can make a difference."

"Mathenge, could they? That would be the bomb."

Mathenge is from a rural area and knows the need in these communities. He and I first take a trip to speak to the principals of two rural schools and get started. We'll need to figure out how many shoes we'll need to buy, and which sizes.

"How are we going to figure out what sizes of shoes we need for all these children?" I ask, looking out at all the inquisitive faces.

Mathenge smiles, bends down, and proceeds to pick up sticks from under a nearby tree. He glances back at me with a stare that seems to demand, *What are you waiting for?* I quickly join him in collecting sticks.

He calls out in his language, and all the children line up and sit on the dusty ground. Taking the sticks, he measures their feet, breaking sticks to the foot length of every child. The children giggle as the sticks tickle the bottom of their feet. He is so good with the children.

With sticks in hand, we drive to Nairobi's wholesale market and purchase the cleansing solution we'll need. We find a shoe wholesaler, and then Mathenge gives me a handful of sticks. I take a stick and measure it against the sole of each shoe until I find a shoe that matches the stick. Voila!

Shaking his head, Mathenge takes the stick from my hand. "You need to measure the inside, so the foot fits into it." He slips the stick inside the shoe, and I see that it doesn't fit.

With a flushed face, I continue measuring the inside of the shoes with the rest of the sticks, leaving a little room for growing feet. I'm very happy that we have money to spare after purchasing all the shoes, socks, and cleansing solutions we need.

The following Saturday, thirty-two freshman students accompany us up the backroads again, the hills so steep that the vehicles can't make it up with all the weight. Several students get out, singing and dancing as they run up the hill without complaint. As we crest the hill, the young, barefoot children run toward us, excited to see what we have brought.

Mathenge gathers his students together to instruct them on how the day will progress. Separating a group of students he begins: "This group will wash and soak the feet." He points to a cluster of logs set in a circle. "Bring your bowl to one of these logs. The village children will sit on the log and place their feet into the bowl with the cleansing solution. Remember to wear your rubber gloves as you clean the feet."

He then looks to the group of young men standing to the side.

"Who are our carriers?" he asks. The students raise their hands. "Once the children's feet are washed, you will carry them to this area over here where the last group will dry the children's feet."

Finally, Mathenge looks to the last group. "Dryers, hold up your towels."

Half a dozen towels are waved in the air.

Donning rubber gloves, the freshmen sit two children on each log, wash their feet, and soak them in the solution. Once sufficiently soaked, the children are carried to the drying area where their feet are toweled dry and they're fitted with new socks and shiny black shoes with laces.

For most of the children, this is their first pair of shoes. They don't even know how to tie the laces.

Once all the village children's feet have been cleaned, an old man from the village approaches. He sits on the log, stretches out his jigger-scaled feet, and motions to have his feet washed. This sets off a wave of laughter, but all are welcome. The students wash his feet and two young men carry him to the drying area.

Mathenge slips off his own shoes with a smile. I smile back. I'll buy him a new pair when we get back to Nyahururu.

My job is to take photos for the sponsors back home. It's one of the happiest days of my life.

• • •

In Heaven's Eyes is a home for street children who have been either orphaned or left by parents who were unable to care for their older children once younger ones arrived. I understand feeling helpless, succumbing to my greatest fears, and letting go of my children. I also understand the feeling of abandonment. I have lived both sides of this dilemma.

I wish I could bottle the joy expressed by these thirty kids, ranging in age from seven to nineteen, as our van pulls up and we unload our boxes of shoes.

"These shoes have been provided by Jesus Himself," I say, looking directly into two or three of their intoxicated faces. They pause, confused, and tilt their heads, some gazing quizzically up to the sky. "How many of you have been praying for the Lord to provide you with shoes so you could go to school?"

Two-thirds of the children eagerly raise their hands. The younger ones jump up and down, their gleeful faces lighting up. In an effort to prevent the spread of jiggers, many Kenyan schools forbid students to attend unless they are wearing shoes.

"The Lord has heard your prayers and placed it on the hearts of so many people from my home to assist me in purchasing them for you." I put my hand to my ear, then wave my hand to show them it's far away, and finally draw my hands in to pray before spreading them out, palms up, towards the students.

Though there's an interpreter, the gestures are helpful. So many languages are represented here, and these street kids haven't been able to learn English or Kiswahili.

The children nod, beginning to understand that provision doesn't mean shoes will fall from heaven, but rather that God will use people to provide. I'm privileged to be the one who actually brings the shoes, and so thankful for the people at home who have contributed.

I remember Ma-J's wise words: *Some can go, but others can't. Don't block the blessing.* I am so thankful for Ma-J, my church mom, for all her wisdom. In fact, I'm thankful for my entire Judson family. My father was right; I did lose my family, but God has blessed me with an incredible family, His family. He's given me my heart's desire.

• • •

Joan Grace was born to Irungu and Njoki on January 25, 2014. Never having had children of my own, having a child named after me is extremely special. I am *cucu* again! I thank God for my Kenyan grandchildren. I'm happy to be able to spend some time with my namesake before leaving for America.

Irungu drives me to the airport. It's been a teary week saying goodbye to my Kenyan family, but nothing could prepare me for this. Our final goodbyes are very emotional. Inside, my heart is crushed; it's not a physical crush like with my heart attacks, but it's just as painful. I'm losing a son, a best friend, and a work husband. I cry rivers of tears. I watch as the doors close behind me, his forced smile burned in my retina. I thank God for modern technology so we can continue to see each other.

As I wait at the gate, ready to leave Kenya for the last time, I can't help but look back on my life and see what God has done. He took a broken child, drew her to Himself, and redeemed her, restoring her for His greater purpose. God does the impossible. He loves me in my darkness, even now (I am not a perfect person), and has the power to do the impossible in me.

"You look deep in thought," says Akinyi, the Kenyan woman who takes the seat next to me.

"Oh, yes. I'm just reflecting on my life in Kenya with Jesus."

"Tell me, how did He bring you to our Kenya?"

We are interrupted by an announcement to board the plane.

In His wisdom, God has situated Akinyi next to me. Another woman, Teyawna, is by the window. Since we have a twenty-hour flight ahead of us, I share my story.

Akinyi is puzzled. "If you went to a Catholic school, how did you not know Jesus?"

"Except for Christmas, we really never went to church as a family," I say. "There was no Bible in our house. I went to Catholic school because Aunt Ninna left us a trust fund with the stipulation that we had to go to Catholic school. That's how my parents could afford it. Even at school, it was never about a relationship with Jesus. I didn't believe anything He said. I believed that men wrote the Bible, and that if there was a God, He wouldn't have let these things that happened, happen."

"Exactly," Teyawna interjects. "How could a loving God let these things happen to you? Look at the injustices, the disparity of Blacks around the world. It's everywhere. I don't believe there's a God."

"We live in a broken world and have freedom of choice," I explain to her. "We have to live with the choices we make, and the ones others make as well. It took me a long time to understand that it's about God and not about me. All the things that happened in my life happened in His timing. His hand was always there. The ebb and flow, the valleys and ridges that I lived, are the fingerprint of God on my life. The negatives, the hardships I thought would never amount to anything, became the things I would use as a turning point. My life took shape when I came to know Him. He gave me the direction so I could use my life experiences for His glory. I just had to ask for, and accept that direction."

Akinyi smiles. "How has God maybe changed, and then given you, the desires of your heart?"

"What I was unable to accomplish in forty years without Him, I was able to accomplish in six short years with Him. He opened up the door to go to school, and my dream of working with children came to fruition when I received my degree in elementary education. It not only licensed me to teach, but allowed me to get a Kenyan work permit so I could return to my beloved Kenya and work with the children there. I'd always wanted a family, and though my dad was right that I lost mine, Jesus made me part of His family, in Kenya and in America. In this life, none of us is perfect, but my family has rallied around me, supported me, and loved me more than I'd ever hoped for. I have children, grandchildren, brothers, sisters, mothers, fathers. God is so good."

"You must be so special to Him." Akinyi sighs. "I'm nothing special. I couldn't be like that."

"Exactly, that's the whole point. Without Jesus, you can't. I couldn't either. But 1 Corinthians 1:28–29 says, *'God chose what the world considers low-class and low-life—what is considered to be nothing—to reduce what is considered to be something to nothing. So no human being can brag in God's presence.'*[13] The miracle of the whole thing is that God chooses to use people like me, people in bad shape, in deep trouble. The Bible also tells how He used people like Rahab, Ruth, Esther, and even the widow who had nothing… certainly not the typical leaders of the time. His hand has been over me my whole life—Mary Ellen's family, Dr. Santucci, Azia, in the stars and sunsets with Stephen and Bill, the reflection of Mrs. Carr in the window, and in so many other ways I just didn't see. He changed me, pushing me this way and that, using people around me, like Carrie, Dick and Gram, Damon, Colleen, Dr. Childers, and even the lady on the bus. He kept reaching out to me. He used the horrors of my life to reach out to Peter, Muchina, and the children with no shoes. I certainly wasn't your typical missionary, but I listened and followed."

Teyawna glares questioningly. "If God was with you, why didn't you see Him earlier?"

"That's the toughest question I've had for Him, bigger than what happened to me as a kid. Why didn't He reveal Himself to me sooner? I was pissed off for a long time

---

[13] CEB.

that I didn't know Him before I was forty. He was there, but I wasn't listening. It was my choice."

"Were you ever really able to forgive your father?" Teyawna asks, looking deep into my eyes.

"Yes, but it was a long time in coming. It's a process that began with that cathartic cry in the shower. I have found that my feelings about things change after I make a decision. The Spirit changed me. I decided to forgive my parents, and my feelings toward them gradually changed with that decision. I'm able to call him *my* father again, not just *the* father. I see things differently through Jesus… like a man being over me, it's more of an umbrella protecting me than a tack holding me down. Pastor J, Wachira, and James are also like that."

"You are a very happy person," Akinyi says later in the flight as we get ready to disembark. "You are running a good race."

"I am full of sheer joy, even in all the hardships I've had. As project coordinator for PACE, I've been able to do so much for Jesus: provide bread and milk for Victory School, and help build seven homes and churches in the outlying area. But the best was simply walking over to the PACE Academy with my projector, a computer, and a box full of sweets for the kids. I look forward to what He has in store for me next. God bless you both."

When the flight lands, we gather our things and go our separate ways. I pray that my story changes them, incrementally.

There is only one King, only one Man who is the perfect sacrifice for my humanness, my flawed human nature, and that is Jesus, the Lion of Judah. He has conquered over sin and death. This I know. When it gets hard, and it will, when I feel weak, unable to continue on, I have a Lion to lean on. He has a plan for me and will stand over me, protect me, guide me, and direct me for His honor and glory. He always has. He always will. He will keep me safe, and when it's time, He will bring me home to His Father… to my Father.

AFTERWORD

FOLLOWING SEVEN YEARS IN KENYA, JOANIE RETURNED TO CHICAGO FOR A SHORT time. Through an email from her sister, she discovered that her mother had passed away six months earlier. In the email, her sister talked about their mother's last moments, but the letter didn't indicate whether she ever acknowledged Joanie. To this day, Joanie prays for reconciliation with her sisters.

On her return to Chicago, Joanie worked as both a substitute teacher and the youth coordinator for Judson Church for four years, eventually moving to Storm Lake, Iowa to be closer to Jim, Heidi, and their family. In Storm Lake, Joanie has been both a substitute teacher and helped with the church's Wednesday night kids program.

Though Joanie's heart continues to beat strongly for the Lord, she still struggles with complications from her diabetes which continue to affect her physically.

Dick and Marj Gibson first met Joanie in Illinois while he was general manager of a plastics company. God called them to work full-time with several international mission organizations, causing them to move to Ohio, Virginia, Colorado, and Indiana. When they returned to Marj's home area in Iowa, Dick took on the role of paraeducator in local schools, working one on one with students with learning challenges. During that time, he observed the challenges faced by students who needed not only academic help but some skill-building and character-building. That led him to raise the funds to build and equip CrossCut, an after-school program that combines training in woodworking with mentoring for life skills. Marj has returned to her profession as a librarian and serves in a nearby school district, managing programs in six buildings from kindergarten through senior high. They are both active in programs at their local church, Faith Baptist of Danville.

Damon was awarded his Master's degree in Drug and Alcohol Rehabilitation and supported Joanie financially throughout her time in Kenya.

Janie Yarborogh lives in Chicago with her daughter Kajaria. A mere shell of her former self, Ma-J suffers from a form of dementia and no longer recognizes Joanie.

Toni lives in the Chicago area and is the area coordinator for Safe Families for Children Greater Chicago. Taking the occasional road trip together, Toni and Joanie continue to laugh uncontrollably and worship God together. Toni is a joy to be with.

Peter's grandmother rested in 2016. Peter moved to Mombasa and is working in the scrap metal industry.

Irungu is now an independent matatu driver in Nyahururu. He visited Joanie in the U.S. once and planned to visit again, although that second trip was disrupted by the COVID-19 pandemic. His family is doing well.

Wachira and Glenda continue their passionate work at PACE, helping marginalized children, developing pastors, praying with their politicians, and building up local leaders through the African Leadership Summit held each year with representatives from as many as thirteen different countries. A visionary, Wachira has mentored many future leaders.

Pastor Mugo and Faith have moved to Nakuru, Kenya to start Kingdom Destiny Ministries. God continues to heal Faith and she has been able to return to work. They continue to show God's love and forgiveness to a hurting community.

James and Heidi live in Storm Lake, Iowa with their four children. There, James is the pastor of Hope Evangelical Free Church. Joanie is not only a part of their immediate family, but of the greater church family there. I've enjoyed sailing together with Joanie and the Rolands, seeing James and the boys' vintage motorcycles collection, and been amazed by the ingenuity of the children, who have built themselves little cabins on the farm. They are such a welcoming family.

DON'T TELL

*If you can identify yourself in this story,
find someone you can trust,
and please tell.*

ABOUT THE AUTHOR

KATHY ISAAC IS AN EDUCATOR AND FAITHFUL FOLLOWER OF JESUS. IN CHILDHOOD, she became a sad statistic at the hands of a grandfatherly figure in her life. Sexual abuse stifled her desire to interact with people. God's faithfulness in healing released her.

After retiring from the communications sector where she spent most of her career in leadership and development, Kathy is focused on serving God at home and abroad.

As a follower of Jesus, she has discovered the abundance He provides to accomplish tasks. Journeying with Jesus has taken her to Kenya, where she facilitated a professional development program for teachers and was stretched beyond her own capabilities in building a well for the school. She teaches English as a Second Language (ESL) at home and has also traveled to Greece to teach English to refugees.

Her joy is in sharing how God has always demonstrated faithfulness in her life and encouraging others to amplify their lives with Jesus. She prefers the inspiration gained by unbelievably harrowing stories of truth to that of fiction, so when there's a book in her hand, it's a biography.

Her life is somewhat of a paradox; while usually a quiet-corner observer, teaching has always given her great joy. And though she likes neither chocolate or coffee, she adores Coffee Crisp.

On a beautiful sunny day, Kathy and her husband Gary can be found biking among the orchards and vineyards in her hometown of Niagara.

Stephen and Joanie, 1984.

Joanie and Azia in the yellow VW Beatle, 1985.

Joanie and Azia, 1985.

Joanie and Bill in California, 1989.

Joanie's Baptism with Richard (Dick) Gibson, 1993.

Damon, 2000.

Toni and Joanie, 2002.

Peter and the Grandmother with Joanie, 2004.

Joanie graduates Suma Cum Laude, 2006.

The Roland family.
(clockwise: James, Heidi, Maria, Peter, William, Sophia and Joanie), 2007.

Irungu loves cars, 2007.

The kid tree - PACE Ministry kids, 2008.

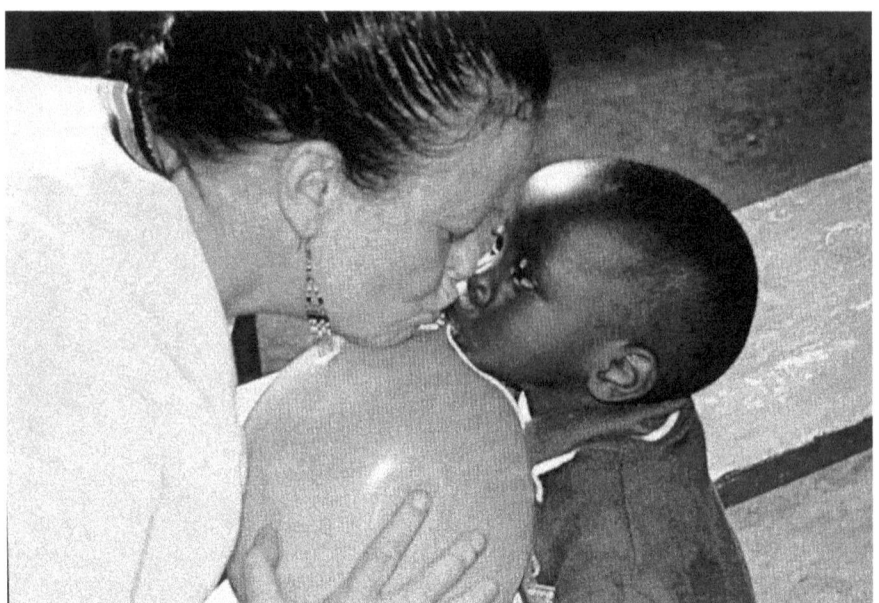
Joanie and Little Brian, 2009.

The bread and milk project that Jon started at Victory School, 2010.

Irungu's family.
(clockwise: Simon, Joangrace, Brian, and James), 2020.

www.ingramcontent.com/pod-product-compliance
Lightning Source LLC
Chambersburg PA
CBHW070643160426
43194CB00009B/1555